CW00458015

PHONE SEX

How I Made $10,000 A Month From Home

JUNE 30, 2017
AMBERLY ROTHFIELD

Copyright 2017 by Amberly Rothfield

All rights reserved. By the U.S. Copyright Act of 1976, the scanning, uploading and electronic sharing of

any part of this book without the permission of the publisher constitute illegal piracy and theft of the

author's intellectual property. If you would like to use material from the book (other than for review

purposes), prior written permission must be obtained by contacting the author at

amberly@amberlyrothfield.com

Thank you for the support of the author's rights.

This book is dedicated to Serena Cavaretti. Longtime friend and role model, though you are gone, I will always remember you. Our last conversation was your encouragement for me to release this book and go down this route. Your wise words and motivation got me through many a dark time. Gone but never forgotten.

This book is also dedicated to my father. You gave up everything for your girls and never gave up hope. You taught me independence and your strong will has helped me weather the trials of adulthood. I could not be as strong of a woman as I am if you were not as tough as you were. I miss you daily.

Table of Contents –

Forward

I first met Amberly just a year before she became Amberly. We were both active members of an online community for phone sex operators and related services, and she was this witty, curious kid, forever trying to learn how to make a successful business.

To be honest, I didn't think she'd stick around long. Most don't know when they come to phone sex thinking they'll make thousands of dollars a week from the get-go. Disillusionment sets in when the first paychecks don't seem to justify the hours put in during the first weeks, and there is always a steady supply of fresh meat coming and going.

A year or so after I first noticed her, Amberly was still active and still asking questions. We had both come to a point where we were ready to take control of our own businesses and, along with another Domme friend, we began The Mistresses Elite.

I was never disappointed to have tied my fate to charismatic, and sometimes controversial Amberly. She was and is a brilliant marketer and businesswoman with a creative mind and the rare ability to draw attention to herself and her projects. While I like to think she's benefitted from my experience and advice, I'm positive I've benefitted from hers.

In the years since Amberly first started her Fetish line, I've seen her begin other projects when a new interest caught her attention. Time and again she has turned passing hobbies into money making ventures for the time they hold her interest. I'm always impressed by the way she can take the knowledge and skills she gained as a PSO and apply them to any business.

So congratulations on having purchased her book. Read it well and take it to heart. While the specifics are geared toward a phone sex business, the skills you learn here can be applied to any mainstream business or interest you care to promote.

No, go. Read. Win the Internet.

Mistress Shayna Domina

www.shayniac.com

Introduction –

First, I want to state that this is not the best written book... I am just self publishing and from the heart. There is no big machine behind me or editors. This is just me writing down the advice I have dished out to those who have come to me for help in the phone sex industry over the years. Will there be a misspelling or two? Perhaps, but to make the money I have before, try to look at the lesson I am teaching in each section, rather than try to point out imperfections. Now, onto the book!

No job, could not afford college and no parent willing to sign so I could get financial aid. That was 18 years old for me. I was on my own since the age of 17 and in a recently crashed economy. Hunger was a feeling I felt more often than not, and I was starting down the road of homelessness. I honestly felt hopeless, despite having been an A+ student who was in all honors classes. I graduated in the top 10%, but life was looking bleak.

That is when I picked up a free classified paper and found the words "Adult Voice Actors Wanted – Make 500+ a week!". The ad went on to talk about having a phone and an internet connection. Now, this was back in 2005 when it wasn't quite as accessible for everyone to have the internet and many still even had to dial-up. Luckily at the apartment, I shared with my then-roommate (I couldn't afford my share), we did still have both of these. I figured I had nothing to lose and called the number when I got home. Within a few weeks, I was out of the little debt I had accrued and now living on my own. (The roommate situation didn't work out for more than monetary reasons).

Phone sex, while taboo, is the way MANY women (and quite a few men) pay the bills and even have a lot to put back every month. Back when I started, many of the women were millionaires, making 10,000+ a week. Yes, you read that correctly. They actually made over 200,000 a month back in the early 2000s. It honestly felt like the best-kept secret!

$10,000 A WEEK back in the day. Do not think, though, that because that was 2005 and we are well over 10 years from than that, that figure is too far off what many make now. Granted, you will NOT make that out the gate anymore BUT, it is possible to make even $2000 a week within 3 short weeks. Yes, that too is a real figure. I have taken a few hiatuses from the industry and even as close as December 2016, after a year being gone, I was able to come back and in 3 weeks make this amount.

That said, it is far from super easy. You will not be able to just flip a switch and the money rain in. You will need to be disciplined; in most cases, you will not have a boss who is coming to check in on you and your income will fluctuate. You will work longer hours at first, and much of what you do will seem to have no benefit in the beginning. Self-motivation is actually one of the hardest things to do.

Even after you get started making regular money, there will be events that cause you to have a slump in cash flow. Everything from March Madness, tax season and the cycles of customers can cause your income to not be entirely predictable from month to month. I will teach you how to prepare for those moments and ensure that you will be able to obtain the level of success that you desire.

In this book, though, I will give you the basic blueprint of how to cruise down that yellow brick road and have prosperity from home, albeit in a taboo line of work! There are more than just sexual lessons to be learned having worked in this field. You will learn how to run a business, the power of promotion, a little bit of digital graphic creation and of course become an expert in customer service. These traits make you valuable in just about any industry or company you wish to go on to build.

Chapter One – Basics

There is a distinct difference between working for a company vs. working as an independent. While I want to steer you down the road of being independent as that is where the most money is, I do understand that some will need baby steps. These basics can be used for both and if you want to skip the company step, go straight to the free chapters after.

You will need the following absolute –

1. Reliable phone (your Nokia 2007 phone that gets no signal will not be acceptable). You can use a cell phone but be sure you have a good stable connection throughout the space you will be taking calls. If you frequently drop calls, have a phone that is more than 4 to 5 models outdated or have a poor mic… you will need to upgrade. The good thing is, it is a tax write off but more about that in a later chapter.

2. Your voice (seriously, you will need to take care of your voice. Screaming at concerts, not taking proper care when you get cold and smoking cigarettes; will be the death of your business). That said, you can have a voice that is unique. Mature sounding voices are perfectly fine, but you do need to take care of your money maker!

3. Taxes – I do not know of a single company (though still possible) that puts you down as an employee. You are usually going to be an independent contractor and will owe taxes. SET THAT MONEY ASIDE PERIOD! I suggest 20 – 25%, especially if you plan to make at least 10,000 a month. The interest and penalties that the IRS will issue are NOT worth whatever you believe you need to pay now.

See there are many different ways to start and all depend on where you eventually want to go and what set up you have now. If you do not have some fancier setups with headsets and super cushy office chairs. You do not need the most up to date computer software or hardware. You do need a phone with at least a semi-decent microphone but even the cheap cell phones these days will work. Most people no longer have landlines, and most phone sex companies are finally giving up on requiring a non-voice over the internet line. I DO SUGGEST getting a corded line if you can as they are the clearest but again, if you need to bare bones this, in the beginning, you will be just fine. I actually suggest with just going with whatever you have available at first. Only invest if you believe that you can handle the work and enjoy it. Why purchase a $100 or $600 set up only to find that you do not want to continue this line of work? Few of these items will have any resell value.

All that said, if you have to use a cell phone or voice over the internet (also called VOIP), please do not be out in the middle of nowhere with no reception. Having moved a lot around the country myself, I have found myself living in a country like areas, and I can tell you... the satellite internet is very unreliable for the most part, and your customers may be upset. If you are working for yourself, you can warn your clients, and they are usually more understanding, but most companies will not be.

There are two basic options you have when entering this industry. I will go over each one briefly here and then in depth in further chapters. Most of this book will consist of information about working for yourself; as that is where you can profit the most. I do want to give a gauge though, for those who want to move a bit slower. Slower is not necessarily bad, being as many people are not educated on different fetishes or how to draw answers out of customers. Working for a company can mean learning from your mistakes while being paid. Do not look down on those who work for others vs. independent.

Company – There are so many companies, that trying to list them all here would be difficult. Some have been around for a very long time and others recently, but unlike other industries, this is not necessarily a mark against them. I would start with an establishment that has been around at least a year though. Most companies already have a setup character for you to play and a dedicated customer base. This means you are automatically tapped into a stream of clients. When you are paid per minute with no control over marketing, this is crucial. Some require you to do a bit more work to bring in your own customers and do provide training. These companies tend to pay more, while others just have a round robin technique for sending customers to you. I will go more in depth about this in the chapter about companies.

Independent – There are also so many ways to go independent as well. I am going to go from the point of assuming that you do not have your own merchant account to bill customers. (A merchant account is an account that is typically issued via a bank, which will allow you to charge your clients. The problem being here, it is excessively hard to obtain one for the phone sex industry). The workaround here is using a phone sex billing platform that usually takes a percentage. As an independent phone sex operator; you can set your own prices, hours and topics of conversation. You will be able to have your own social media profiles that you control and will be responsible for all promotion. Basically, what you create for yourself, you take home, BUT you will be working LONG hours at first.

So those are the skeleton parts of what you really need to start, but a skeleton doesn't walk around. There are still some basics that even long time vets of the industry still do not understand.

Voice – Before you put this book down, most voices are perfectly fine. I know friends who sound like smokers (some have never touched a cigarette in their life!) or had accents, yet they make money just fine! BUT you want to make sure that you do take care of your voice, it is your primary source of income after all! Try not to scream, keep throat lozenges by the pound around when you are sick, watch your carbonated drink intake and warm your voice up before you log in to take calls. No seriously, that seriously helps you when you get a 7-hour call. This is your MONEY MAKER! Yes you will get sick, yes things can happen but do your best to mitigate damage before it happens.

Voice warming is highly valuable. Not sure how? Grab a playlist of your favorite songs and sing while prepping for work. About 15 minutes before I turn my phone lines on, I am singing everything from Hello Dolly (to get my voice sweet and low) to some Mariah Carey. No, I will not be winning any Grammies anytime soon and do not look for my latest album to drop, but by stretching my voice through several different ranges, I do not strain after hours of talking. When I started in this industry, it was nothing to speak for hours, but over time, your voice box becomes not too happy with you. You do not want the largest part of your business to crash on you. Actors, talk show hosts, radio hosts and sports announcers all do the same.

Fetish education – no matter what someone is into, it is considered a fetish. Depriving yourself of this education will only hold you back with your earnings. Those who make top dollar, do not only skate their way through but frequently seek out knowledge. I highly suggest you join some kinky forums like Fetlife and start reading about fetishes that exist. You may not identify with them or are even remotely interested in them, but you need to have some familiarity with them. You may not be able to provide phone calls based on those fetishes, BUT I have drawn some unique perspective and inspiration from other fetishes for the fetishes I do cater too. It fills your confidence bank up as well, as callers ask about something and you actually know what they are referring too. All the great businesses spend massive amounts of their earnings trying to learn how their customers think. This will be paramount for you as you HAVE to connect to your callers and do so quickly.

Most I know have started out with some sort of company and worked their way to being independent. With that said, most I know also started as a beginner. If you have been in the adult industry for a while regardless of phone sex or not, you may be ready to just go independent. They are an excellent way to find out not only what works best for you but also get comfortable with talking to complete strangers about kinky topics without having any sort of traceable feedback that could lead to you. While they do pay considerably less, even in today's market, companies still can pay enough for you to be able to live entirely on your own. I will list the resources I have found along the way under the relevant sections, so you don't have to go in as blind as I did.

Taxes - Regardless of which avenue you chose from the beginning, you HAVE to pay taxes. I know I mentioned it above, but it does warrant mentioning again. So many people are not used to being 1099'd and get themselves into real trouble. If you are reading this, there is no excuse. The good thing is, the IRS is willing to work with you. I can only speak from knowledge of American tax laws, if you are in another country, please refer to a qualified tax professional. I personally use the Tax Domme, aka Lori St Kitts. (As per this writing, her Twitter does say she can prepare for other countries!). She is a fantastic accountant and tax expert who also knows well the adult industry. She will not judge you and will get you all the deductions you are entitled too. She grabbed my hand and literally walked me through the entire process when I was ready to file. Her worksheets are so simple and her response time is unbeaten. If you have trouble connecting with her, the forum www.xbiz.com has 100's of thousands of people who can point you to other adult-friendly tax professionals. My recommendation still goes to Lori though.

With that basic overview out of the way, there are a few more essentials that aren't MUSTS, but I find them to help me tremendously with my phone sex operation. I always say to model yourself off those who have done well before you, and you will get to their level faster, with fewer mistakes. Some may seem foreign or unneeded, but I do urge you to try them each for at least for 90 days and tweak as need be. You may be surprised, what once seemed dumb, actually turns out helpful!

Amberly Rothfield – How I Made $10,000 A Month as A Phone Sex Operator

- Customer Tracking – there are many ways to do this; from old school notepads to computer software. Whichever works for you! Make sure you notate things they like and don't like and even personal information so that you can show you remember/care when they call in. Ex – " Hey Ryan! How did the company basketball game go last Friday?" This helps build rapport with your clients. Being such a private business, having someone actually know you is comforting and helps your customers want to look for you rather than just random people regularly. DO Use code names though. In case someone got access to this list, you do not want to cause embarrassment to a bunch of individuals.

- Set Schedule – while you can go off the cuff if you desire, I would suggest having a set schedule, especially at first. This means your customers can know when you will be on typically. Think about this as the business that it is. How frustrating would it be to go drive up to a store only for it to be closed when you know you were there that time last week at that point? Your customers are usually active at a particular time, which will be THEIR free time. Rarely can they change their life so much that they can just call you whenever you are available! Once you have enough customers, you can potentially log on whenever you have free time but in the beginning, make a schedule and live it like a religion.

- Smile – Yup even in call center jobs I have had, you are told to smile while you talk to someone. We as humans can actually tell if you are smiling or not while on a call. When you smile, it puts the other person at ease. Trust me, you may feel strange talking to someone on the phone, but the caller does too. When I smile, I can audibly hear the caller begin to calm down and shortly after open up. The biology behind this, I will go into in the chapter on your voice, but again, there hasn't been a person I know in this industry who actually hasn't benefited from this.

- Cadence – in the chapter about your voice, I will go more in depth. Cadence is the rhythm of your speech. When we are nervous, we tend to speak quicker, and that can affect the callers breathing. Comedians that bomb in stand-up skits notoriously talk so fast that people do not get a chance to digest the information. People need an opportunity to absorb the words you say. So speak clear and slow but apparently not too slow. Make sure to take a breath before you speak and to try to speak slower. Not too slow but slow enough where you can properly pronounce each word you say. It also helps you sound sensual.

- A glass of Water – YOU NEVER know when the long calls are going to hit. I like to keep a glass of water about and sip on it anyways but for those LONG calls, nice to not have to get up and rifle for a drink. I also keep a gallon of filtered water by my desk, so I do not have to exit my room to fill my cup mid-call. Sound changes from room to room or even noise of water pouring can spoil a call in many cases. Be a girl scout and be prepared. As an extra measure, I do try to drink about 3 glasses of water on an 8-hour phone shift. It helps to increase your water intake and promotes blood circulation. Blood flow contributes to keeping your voice box lubricated. This has obvious benefits!

- Phone with a mute button – you never know what will transpire at home. Be it a knock on the door, loud noises outside, a sneezing fit or an emergency bathroom break; a phone with a mute button can feel like a lifesaver. Trust that I have had quite a few hour long calls and the call of nature didn't care that it may disrupt the flow of my call. A quick punch of a button and I can take care of what I need to while masking background noises. Another thing to be cautious about though, especially when using cell phones, is you may accidentally hit the mute button. Usually, your caller will alert you of this as they hear silence but if you just keep checking your phone from time to time, you can usually catch it if it is accidentally triggered.

- Tablet – I prefer tablets to any sort of keyboard that is noisy. I use them to look up things clients discuss. This way they do not have to describe too much/ lose that excitement factor when asking about if I provide a fetish. I also use it for character reasons. If my character is from an area, it helps to google the area in case questions are asked, etc. Do not use your tablet to play facebook games or chat with others though. If you are on a call, you are best serving your client and self by paying attention to them. Trust me, they will notice, and they will move on if they feel that you are not respecting the fact they are paying for time.

- PO Box – I would not suggest one from USPS as you have to use your real name but many mom and pop shops will allow you to receive mail for any name and are often cheaper. I use mine to receive Amazon packages from my wish list and other items that my clients will send me. It is also a tax write off. Yes, Amazon can hide your address for items off your list, BUT 3rd parties may still send a receipt with your address to your client. Be safe! If you can not afford a PO Box, only accept e-gift cards! Another note about accepting gift cards, I have heard (though no personal experience) that if you have a balance in your account that is unused and a client charges back... the company will usually deduct that balance from you. USE YOUR CODE IMMEDIATELY AND PURCHASE ITEMS. My wishlist is primarily a bookmark station so I can quickly buy items with gift cards. Also, unless the physical item purchased from my wishlist is in my hands, I do not give any services to a client. Many guys will buy things off your list and cancel them shortly after they get whatever they were hoping for. Do not fall for this scam.

- Sound replication tools – now you can go digital with this or just use household items, but you can recreate sounds (wet vagina, clicking shoe heels, etc.) during calls if you do not want to actually be doing said acts. When making spanking noises, I frequently use a silicone ball and my hand (thighs can get bruised and hurt after a while). These can be utilized for a more immersive experience. Because I do all my calls in one room, I frequently can not just put on heels and walk around the house, so a cutting board and shoes work just fine. I will go more in depth in another chapter.

- Internet connection – I know in this day in age this seems more like a DUH factor, but some who start do not have an internet connection if working for some companies. I suggest an internet connection the same as I do for a tablet. Sometimes during calls, it simply helps to hop online and look something up. My sissies LOVE having me go look at websites where they posted themselves. My CBT subs like having me go look at sex toys with them as well. You can work without an internet connection but be prepared to get some questions about why you wouldn't have an internet connection. If you are independent though, you just can't exist in this industry without some sort of access to the digital world at a moment's notice. It is also a tax write off.

- Something productive to do in the downtime – In between calls, you will have anywhere between seconds to hours. Find something you can easily put down and pick back up but is PRODUCTIVE. Sure you can watch youtube videos or run around facebook but why not have something to show for the down time? In the early days, I took to websites teaching basic HTML and then PHP. Sometimes I knit… no really I do, I LOVE fiber arts, but other times I do strength training or short burst aerobics. Make it something that will advance yourself in some sort of way, even if you went the company route. At first, I especially suggest looking up fetish erotica. Many websites are free to post to and read sexy stories on a variety of subjects. The quicker you can pick up aspects of this new world, the faster you will see your earnings rise and rise.

- Pick Me Ups – There will be calls that are just awful; calls that will shake you to your bone. It has only happened about 4 times in my career, and most were in the earlier times when I didn't know how to handle them, but it happens to everyone. I keep a playlist of songs that pick me up (thank you SIA!) and friends I can call who understand. Create outlets now to deal with calls that will bother you. Write down mantras that help get you through. Whatever you do though, try to continue working. I do not suggest logging out but rather trying to build that tough skin. The next call most likely will put you right back in the zone. Know that you are not the only one and the caller is probably just getting kicks by messing with phone sex ops. As long as I am getting paid, I am pretty ok with someone attempting to upset me.

As you begin to put together your collection of success habits and tools, you will find a confidence that will come through into your calls. Those I have mentored in the past that did not treat this as a job, frequently told me that they never got over the awkwardness of each phone call. They each called it quits after a few short months of little to no success. Those that did prepare themselves, though, they found that each week they made more and more and more and that customers were leaving rave reviews of them. Even though they still got butterflies each time the phone rang, they still felt confident that they were prepared to answer whatever came up.

I would hope that, especially if you are reading this far if you have decided to get into this line of work... that you would already be used to cursing/foul language. It never ceases to amaze me some phone sex operators who are offended by the language used during these calls. Racial slurs are frequently used (usually by someone of the ethnicity that they would like for you to make fun of) as well as sexist terms. You really need to be ready for anything and everything to come at you. It is ok to not be ok with something and take a pass (unless you are a company that doesn't allow you, make sure to do due diligence on their terms), but if you pass on every phone call... well, you are out of business. Try to pull yourself out of your comfort zone at the bit. I have grown actually intrigued by people who have different opinions or perspectives, even in the fetish world. Psychology is absolutely fascinating!

Many of the calls you will take, will also have nothing to do with sex. In fact, a good majority of the calls I receive are of a non-sexual nature. They are just people who are lonely and need someone to talk to for a variety of reasons. Sounds easy? It isn't always. Remember, they are calling you because they most likely have no one to talk to about such things (no this doesn't mean they are hermits or losers but rather can not talk about such things with others). I have callers who are extreme liberals or conservatives call me. Some are completely Pro Life or Pro Choice. They are choosing to bring up these topics, and while I do not shy away from my stance usually... if you do not know how to spin it, that will be a rather short call. The best advice I can give you in these circumstances is to ask a one-word question... "Why?" This takes the everything off of you and your opinion and allows them to explain theirs. Trust me people like to talk about themselves! Remember you are not there to change minds or argue, you are mainly there to listen.

The final bit of basics advice I can give, though, is relaxed. It will get easier to begin a conversation, and in the following chapter, I will break down how to make it even easier. The hardest part is getting those first phone calls under your wing. Once you do a few, you will wonder what you were even nervous about. Just be yourself and be careful of the pacing of your words and you will be a star!

There are also a few different ways your clients will pay, which affects how you should plan out your calls. No matter what, callers are usually billed in advance in some way, shape or form. Most companies will charge for a certain amount of time, with any extra time to disappear if unused. This means, at the end of the prepaid slot, they will need to be charged again. The other method is for you to be paid per minute no matter what. The customer will still upload a certain amount to their account, thus forcing them to have to add more if they happen to go through all in their account. With this method though, you will not be paid for any unused minutes.

How would this change your strategy for the call? The difference is only slight if you are following my methods but I want to give you ideas from all over the industry. I personally find this a bit dishonest, but many operators like to get callers off the phone before they hit their allotted time if they are prepaid for blocks of time. Reason being, they essentially are paid for the extra time that isn't spent on the phone. To me, this is not just unethical but makes no sense. While they are trying to shove a guy off the call at 25 minutes so they get a free 5 minutes from a 30 minute prepaid call; I am getting them to re-up for more time to continue our lovely conversation!

The only difference in how I approach these calls is if I know how much time I have to work within. I keep an eye on the clock a bit and before the cut off, I make sure to point out how much fun we are having and how eager I am to have more! This signals for them to add more time or for us to wrap up the call. Seriously the only difference! With systems where you get paid per minute, regardless of how much the customer has put in their account, continue until they are cut off. In most cases, you will get no warning. If you do get a warning, acknowledge it and get a feel for if the caller wants to wrap it up or go. Chances are though, if you get a warning then the customer is not ready to leave you just yet. They will add more cash to continue and off you go! If they only add on a few more minutes, do not get upset! I know so many operators who hate callers adding just a few more minutes at a time. Be grateful that they still want to talk to you vs all the other voices they could be paying to speak too!

Chapter 2 - Companies

I know above I spoke about the basics and how independents make the most. Having been with several companies, though, I know there are some benefits in starting with one first. To best serve everyone who reads this, I will cover some tips and tricks for working with companies here, but I do encourage you to create your exit strategy even before you go in. After a period of time, companies become a glass ceiling, and I want you to do more than just get by.

One of the largest drawbacks is the fact that you can be fired. While working for yourself, your paychecks are a bit less predictable, you rarely will be kicked off a platform if you are following their rules. Many companies have minimum call averages though, which can result in a contract termination. They may also have minimum hours within a week or month which may be hard to meet during certain periods. Very few companies, but worth mentioning, have strict rules on which calls you are allowed to turn down (if any) that can result in you getting in trouble if you honestly just can not take that particular type of call. All of these things and perhaps more could lead to your termination.

Another thing that is noteworthy, with 99% of the companies out there, you are an independent contractor. For those unfamiliar with this, it means that your contract can be terminated at any time and no... there are no unemployment benefits for you. In most cases, there are no benefits for you what so ever. Have a dispatcher who doesn't like you? Could be fired? New hiring managers who hate everyone named Ashley? Poof, you are gone. There doesn't need to be a rhyme or reason. NOW, provided that you are in fact performing well, companies rarely will get rid of you.

There are so many companies that it would be impossible to name them. Many also go out of business very fast, so by the time you are reading this (if I put a list), many may be gone. There are quite a few that have stood the test of time, though. My favorite place to research companies is www.adultwork.com, just put in phone actress and bam! You will find all companies looking to hire

Amberly Rothfield – How I Made $10,000 A Month as A Phone Sex Operator

talent right now. Adult Work vets the companies that go on their websites and do not let just anyone post an account. If there are complaints against a company, they will investigate and kick them off from being able to post ads if they are found to be fraudulent.

I would also Google the company to see if you can find any reviews from other phone girls out there. A word of caution about reviews though... grain of salt. Remember, few people remember to review when they love something, but everyone runs to every site they can find if they HATE something. Investigate and when you approach the company, ask them about the issues you read about. Good companies will address them, bad companies will pretend like you no longer exist.

Before we go too far, though, I do want to speak to predatory companies. There are very few of them, but they do exist, and I want to give a few red flags to watch out for:

- Forcing you to take a call for free. If someone is making you 'test' on a customer ... run. Most managers will just listen to your actual voice to decide if they like you. Companies already have a high turn over so if you are not 'good' in the beginning, they can train you. There is usually a grace period, in which your stats do not hurt you. After that, if you can not get a handle on the job, they will let you go. BUT they will not have you 'work' for free.

- Government Id isn't the first thing asked for. They are asking you to talk about adult topics, but they do not want to see your ID first? BOUNCE!

- Direct deposit is not offered, or they want you to work for more than 14 days without pay. I do not know a legit company that does not pay at least twice a week. While websites like Clips4Sale do pay once a month, they also have a track record within the adult industry. If they are a mega company that purchases tables at major adult conventions, chances are they are legit. If some small business that you can not find much on, want you to wait more than 14 days, be on alert.

- NO training provided. Even for companies that cater more to veterans, they are willing to do some training. Companies succeed if you do, remember that. Likewise, if they are unwilling to give you any training, then they are not setting you up for success. Companies should have past calls you can listen to that were 'good' and some examples of 'bad' ones. They should be willing to listen into your calls and then give you feedback afterward. They should have a resource center of links to websites to learn about more kinks or online promotion. Ditch any company that is unwilling to give you the tools you need to be successful!

When it comes to companies, there are generally two types and very few hybrids; they are trolling and non-trolling. Trolling has an entirely different meaning in this day in age, but in the phone sex world, it means that you have to go out and seek your own customers. Non-trolling companies do their own marketing and typically pay the operators significantly less due to this fact. They will send you calls as they get them and usually in a round-robin system. Many newer phone sex operators land in a non-trolling company and then move on to being independent or to a trolling company. About this book, though, going independent would be your best bet after you get some experience under your belt. As I said earlier, you can learn on another person's dime and time. No, you are not taking advantage of them in a bad way at all. All industries have companies designed for those just starting out. This is part of the reason why you would be paid less than if you went independent. Less though is not necessarily a bad thing in this case though, more on that later.

I promise to give the fully skinny in this chapter on companies but look, you bought this book because of the title. With even a fantastic company, I had to work close to 100+ hours after building my client base and STILL barely cleared 6,000 a month. Yes, that is great money but remember, I pay my taxes... Take about 25% off that off the top and then factor in all the TIME I spent working. I literally had

Amberly Rothfield – How I Made $10,000 A Month as A Phone Sex Operator

no life! Work life balance is super important if you do not wish to burn out. Burnout is one of the largest reasons why people leave the industry.

This is due to not having full control over the customer list you do eventually build up. I had no control over all the emails they received nor could create new offers/content they could buy easily. Now, I am not saying that isn't enough money, but that was also earlier in my career. As time as gone on, technology has changed, and more people have entered the field. Now I personally believe that thousands of phone sex ops can come in, but only those willing to learn can still make crazy money. Many other operators and I are living proof of this fact.

Companies are a great place to get experience, though if you have never taken calls without worrying about also generating calls. If you are not ready to learn on your own dime, they are the way to go. I would caution about staying with anyone over 3-4 months though if you desire to be serious unless it is a trolling company as they teach you how to market. If it is a non-trolling company, though, all you can learn are the different techniques of how to speak to callers and some fetish play lessons. These are highly valuable within this field, absolutely but once you have learned the basics, you are simply working a fixed rate and with little room for expansion. The higher paychecks are being independent or at least with a trolling company that can teach you about online marketing. Once you have mastered taking a few calls and feel comfortable talking to strangers, move onto a company that will not only pay you more but also teaches you the skills that will set you up for success once you go fully independent.

But why not work both as an independent and with a company? Well, most businesses are NOT ok with that and will ask you sign a non-compete (a legal document that dictates that you can not work for another company that competes with the current company and definitely can not operate for yourself in the same field). Working for two different companies will get you fired if you are caught but

Amberly Rothfield – How I Made $10,000 A Month as A Phone Sex Operator

could land you in legal hot water as worse case scenario. If you want to do this professionally, just do not risk it.

DO NOT EVEN think about stealing customers either. I do not endorse that at all, and it is rather scummy. Karma can be a bitch. The word will get back around, and you risk not only losing a revenue stream, potential friends who can help you in the industry but scoured Earth. Yes, even in this industry, your reputation does matter! People will remember that you stole customers and will be unwilling to hire you but worse, reluctant to promote you when you turn independent. You will also find that even those you did not personally burn will become leerier of you. A few bucks today can indeed cost you a truckload tomorrow.

So if you are going to contract with a company, know that few will consider you an employee. You will be regarded as an independent contractor and will be responsible for your own taxes. Make sure to set aside a chunk from each check to pay your taxes with. Being a contractor also means you will not get any sort of benefits such as medical or dental. You can easily find private health insurance, though it will be pricey. Taking care of yourself is super important when there is no paycheck or sick days, so I suggest you take the time and research the best health care plan you can afford. Lastly, there is no unemployment for losing your contract. Contractors can be let go for any reason at any time. Be sure to learn all the rules of the company you are with and make sure that you follow them to the letter.

Make sure to ask your company, especially non-trolling companies, if a customer calls in to request you if you get the call. If this is allowed, then you can indeed clean up by having calls lined up while you are on another call. Usually, the caller won't wait long times to speak with you but most, in my experience, would wait about 20 minutes before choosing another girl. Remind your guests where you can (before, middle or after) that if they enjoyed the call, they could request you next time. I say to remind them where you can because of the end of a call, is often a dial tone to your ear. Don't worry that doesn't mean you did anything wrong. Actually, it is often a sign you did everything right! Repeat customers translate to your phone will ring more often and typically much longer phone calls. I have only seen a few companies that do not allow for this. I would choose a company that does as it increases money for not only you but the company as well.

Also, make sure to ask your company about the payment structure. There are quite a few companies that have a sliding pay scale based on your call hold times. Once your hold times are high enough, you can get paid bonuses or greater per minute rates. During holidays, many companies also have pay bonuses as well. YUP! Holidays actually are important days for the phone sex industry as many people are feeling super lonely. You may consider celebrating at least some holidays, on a different day for yourself, to cash in. Ask if they also pay for referrals, as some companies will pay you if you get other girls to sign up to take calls or if you refer callers. I totally have never made business cards and sprinkled them in adult stores, me? Never. No seriously, that method actually works.

With companies, there are usually managers who will listen in on your calls. This means there are usually evaluations. Especially at first, you should expect this, but if you have low hold times, that can prompt some extra scrutiny. Do not be upset and remain humble if you are pulled aside and coached on calls. These lessons will be invaluable, and I can't tell you how many I know were let go after being deemed as un-coachable. Most companies also record all calls, so even if it isn't being listened to now, it can be later. Do not say anything you wouldn't want your dispatchers to hear. Do not try to skirt the rules, even if a caller is requesting it. That one call is not worth losing a chance at a company or burning a bridge. Remember that if a company has a rule about something not being talked about, it is probably for a good reason. The reasoning is usually due to it being illegal to talk about that on a phone line or their merchant account does not allow for those topics to be talked about. This means you become a liability and no matter how much you produce for this company, you are not worth them losing their right to process transactions.

For enterprises that offer bonuses for being on during high volume times and the like, they typically will call girls they know take calls frequently, especially during that time of day. I know I harp on keeping a schedule, but this is another incident where it can truly behoove you to do so. With my first company, I was one of the first they would call when they were slammed with callers but light on girls. I would go from making a few cents a minute to a guaranteed extra 1-4 extra dollars an hour PLUS my minutely pay. With high call volumes, that meant few minutes of down time. I could easily bank 50 dollars within that time without any extra work. If your dispatchers know you are most likely available, you will be the person they go to and offer the incentives. You can also let them know that if they ever need you, call my cell. I usually take calls on my land line, but my dispatchers always knew to call my cell if they needed me. I would tell them if I could get back home or not, but the point is, they knew I was serious about my job and they could count on me in a pinch.

Make it known how serious you are about working, out the gate with the dispatchers. Ask them when they typically have trouble having enough girls on. Now my next bit of advice is usually pretty controversial but it actually worked for myself. I let my dispatchers KNOW my weekly income goals. I was not happy until I hit 150 – 200 dollars a day. Knowing this, my dispatchers would give me tips on times to log in for the next coming days. They knew when other girls were going to be on vacation and they would have little coverage. Those times didn't always come with a bonus, but it meant more minutes on the phone for me with less down time. Your dispatchers want you to be happy and make money, you just have to give them the tools so they can assist you more.

Now with trolling companies, you have to bring your own callers to the table. Some trolling companies make it easier by having private chat rooms, mailing lists so they can post your information, company blogs that are known that can post your information, BUT the largest chunk of your cash will be coming from you/the work that you do. Again, there are a variety of rules that different companies have the control that you have, but most will provide you with a domain (website) and basic design.

Usually a WordPress based blog, you will make keyword rich blog posts with the photos the company will provide you. Now, remember, these pictures do not belong to you.Trying to use them for your own profit elsewhere without permission is not only illegal but just again... scummy. Do not burn bridges! Companies have relationships with other companies and having healthy relationships with other phone sex operators can indeed help you down the line. Only use the images however you are instructed you may. If you leave that company and know where they purchased the content, do not go behind them and buy it yourself either. Why even open the door to drama?

Trolling companies offer additional training that non-trolling companies do not. This training is unique to online marketing. Being as they only make money if you are making money, they have nothing but incentive to teach you how to go find fish, rather than bring it to you. Think about it this way, you have about 100 operators each creating an online presence. They then, direct customers to the main website for the company to process calls, that means more traffic to the main website. The company then publishes updates on each operator, which increases your exposure to other customers. The collective effort gives an instant boost to new operators but also enhances the exposure of the veterans of the site!

Another benefit of this is that you aren't as alone as non-trolling companies can be. Instead of only talking to your dispatchers, you now can talk to other operators. Most dispatchers have at one time been an operator, but there is something about speaking with those in your current shoes as well. I know talking to dispatchers, I was always on my Ps and Qs, but with my fellow operators, I could let my hair down a bit. Many trolling companies also allow for you to do multiple girl calls. Getting to know your fellow workers make this more of a possibility! Also, ask if you can collaborate with your fellow PSOs. When it comes to blogging, you can talk to each other and create fun storylines that can involve each other! In the world of social media, this also gives you someone to chat up and again, increase interest in yourself. Feel free to tweet to your newly found pso friends, tag them and promote each other. Remember that if you want to be promoted, you will have to promote others! No matter if you are independent or working for a company, getting others to support you will be extremely valuable, but the only way to get this is to foster others!

The levels of promotion that you will be expected/allowed to do varies. Make sure to ask about the full scope of what you are prohibited from doing. Trolling companies will typically have large accounts with many different promotional websites. Being as they bulk ads in bulk, they get significant discounts and thus will not need you to have an account there. While top sites were once one of the main staples to running a phone sex-based website, now having individually run forum accounts for various adult websites has become paramount. Many companies will set up the profile or they will have you do it but will demand the passwords associated with it. The same goes with any messengers used (Skype, AOL or Yahoo!), as this would be considered their property. They will want the ability to check to see if you are indeed, following the rules and not directing customers to other payment methods.

Hybrid companies offer you the ability to take phone calls and do minimal amounts of promotion. They typically have you submit articles, voice clips and may ask you to vote on some top sites from time to time. If a caller comes through and doesn't have a specific girl they wish to speak, then it goes to a round-robin system. The pay for these types of companies is somewhere in the middle between the other two kinds. I haven't seen a ton of these companies around, and most I do know of haven't worked out long term. The reason? This format just isn't really sustainable long term. Trolling means all operators and even dispatchers are out driving traffic. That hunger that the more you promote, the more you can eat really drives these companies and it shows in paychecks. Conversely, the model of one central company with a dedicated team doing the promotion being separated from operators works as well. With the separation, everyone focuses on their one task and the phone workers, of course, have a pay cut for this.

Wait though, wouldn't hybrid then work better? It seems like it would but it usually just muddies the waters. Most hybrid companies do not have adequate training for the new operators, and they tend to be disorganized. It usually ends up with everyone basically being independent and almost haphazardly collaborating together with no real organization. For example, one person may do a ton of marketing and thus driving calls. While doing all of that marketing, they will probably not be logged in to take calls, thus not making much money for the work they did to generate those calls. Another person may almost burn out on the sheer amount of calls they end up having to process. Yet another person is training the incoming operators but also not receiving new calls and thus not getting paid for them. Needless to say, there are many ways hybrids can go wrong. While a few have gotten it right, my advice, if you are new, is to steer clear until you have way more experience under your belt.

Another major tip that I kind of touched on before get in with the dispatchers/trainers. I am not saying to a brown noser but seriously make an effort to get to know them and vice versa. In the case of dispatchers, they hold whether or not you get awesome calls/bad calls in their hands. They can offer you bonuses (if available) or let you know when there is a boom in calls. Even in a round robin situation, dispatchers often have tools they can use to help or hurt you. Trainers are the same way if they are different from the dispatchers. Imagine if you are training someone you do not like. Would you give them your best tips? If some new technology comes down, would the people you dislike be the first you want to train to take advantage of this? Probably not! Also, think about promotions within the company you are working at. Dispatchers and trainers were all once in your shoes, and if you do not wish to go independent, then you will need to hose recommendations to move up.

Want to quit a company? I would say use the same advice that anyone would give you if you were to leave a typical 9 to 5 job, put in your two weeks notice. While you are an independent contractor, which means it is a lot easier for either side to terminate the contract, remember that these are businesses. Knowing how many people can take calls is pivotal to their operation and you leaving

Amberly Rothfield – How I Made $10,000 A Month as A Phone Sex Operator

them without any notice is an excellent way to burn a bridge. Yup, I am telling you NOT to burn a bridge yet again. You never know when you will need a reference or if you will want to go back to that company. Some of my best friends to this day worked many of the same companies I started out with all those years ago. The company may tell you it is ok to leave before the two weeks is up, but they may want you to honor the entire two weeks. Whatever they ask you to do, do it. Now, this is a company you have worked at for a while. If you have a company that is not paying you or training you, then yes, run like the wind!

In closing of this chapter, companies are a great place to start, but it is ok if you wish to also just stay there. The larger paychecks are in being independent though. If you are using a company to get some experience under your belt, make sure to set point (be it a date or after you have accomplished a certain number of calls) at which you will leave. Any extra time you put in with a company is just time away from starting out on your own.

Chapter 3 - New Callers

New callers cause a lot of anxiety for phone sex operators. You never know what they will want or will say. You never know how the call will go. I mentioned previously that being calm, watching how fast you speak and smiling can help tremendously in how the caller perceives you. Remember, they are calling you because they want to escape the world around them. You want to seem fun and happy (and I would hope you truly are!). They call you a phone actress or entertainer for a reason! Your job is to entertain and distract from all else that is going on.

The biggest thing I can teach you in this section is to practice your opener. Practice out loud, saying "Hello, this is Goddess Amberly!" I still do this before I turn my lines on. I practice saying it about 10 times, but early on, I would say it about 25 times or until I felt the confidence wash over me. I would practice saying it quick enough to not be boring but slow enough to ensure my beautiful and seductive tones were pronounced. Remember that everyone's style is different, but it is OK to borrow from others till you find your own. I actually listened to quite a few introductions on other services likes Niteflirt.com to hear how others did theirs. You can listen for free if you call in. I shoot for a purring sound in my voice, but again that just matches my natural style.

While others look down on this practice, I actually believe in finding some people you look up to and dissecting how they operate to create your own style. Not plagiarism but finding the actual elements and working from there to create your own style. Do not try to be exactly like someone but rather analyze WHY you like whatever they did. Break down what you are listening to/watching into elements and see how you can incorporate those aspects into your style. Despite what anyone says, we all do it! Also look outside of the phone sex or porn industry for inspiration. I often listen to interviews from my favorite actresses whom I find to have very sexy voices. Pull inspiration from all sources you can find to identify your signature style! Once you do this, you will find more confidence in yourself and thus your calls!

So why does the opener (your introduction) matter the most for new callers? Surely this could have gone into the section about your voice? I put this article here because returning guests already have an idea of what to expect. I also do not greet them the same if I know they are the ones on the other line. I like to mention that I do not recognize their voice and ask if they have spoken to me before. Sound cheesy? You will be surprised how many times I have talked to that person before. They may be using a new account or credit card, and it will slip past me! They almost always say no they haven't, to which I give a small laugh of victory because I always remember a voice. This sets the tone that while I have many regular callers, and they are indeed remembered. Is this smoke and mirrors illusion false? NOPE! It is actually factual as I do remember about 90% of all my callers. I do have many callers but again they cycle in and out, and with the help of notes/technology, my memory is easily jogged.

The method above also contributes to open up the chance to ask the caller about themselves. Remember again, everyone's favorite conversation is ABOUT THEMSELVES! It is also an easy way of finding out how you can relate to them outside of just the simple phone call. True, some just want to some dirty talk and then to leave, but many also like having a connection. When you bypass this regard, you are replaceable with any other girl they could call. Knowing your client means you can easily get into their head. It is the same reason I have the same hairdresser each time I go in to get a trim. She knows not only my head but I know about her family and aspirations. She knows about my upcoming events and is sure to ask about them. That rapport makes her familiar, so I chose to go back to her, time and time again.

That said, don't worry about trying to make a first-time caller your best friend on the first call. I like to find out where my callers live and go from there. I have personally lived all over and can connect with something in most major cities but if you haven't, just start with asking questions. Show genuine interest in where they are from and why. If they lead with talking about their fetishes, ask about the most erotic experience they have had with such. Ask how far they have gone with it or what they love the most about it. Tell them about your experiences or fantasies you have had that are similar. Connect the moment between the caller to you and show them that you are engaged in the conversation.

A word of caution though, if the caller makes it PERFECTLY APPARENT that they only want talk dirty, trying to FORCE a conversation will be a 'boner killer.' You can usually tell after attempt two of redirecting the conversation. If this is the case, go with the flow and try to knock their fantasy socks off. To turn this into a repeat situation, make sure you figure out what they want and over deliver! Do not discount these short calls! Particularly, in the beginning, they can add up swiftly. I know many operators who hate these types of calls but if you are new, take everything you can get and actually appreciate it. Even once you have an established business, these calls will come through, and it is important to remember that even if they are on the phone for two minutes, they are still customers.

If the conversation isn't headed down the fast lane of the highway, here are a few tips on how to slow pace the conversation. Now, why would you do this? Not only does it mean more billable minutes but it can also build up more ecstasy once the big moment comes for your new client. Try to pace your words at a slower rate than they are talking. People try to mimic those whom they are speaking too in cadence. This can often slow their roll and allow you to get into their head!

When a customer calls, he is usually very close to or at least have been anticipating for some time that big moment. Unless the caller actually just wants a quick call, having that erotic moment build up over time can create an incredible release. Think about it, porn is truly everywhere and free. If your caller wanted to just get off, they would just go to porn hub and have at it. They want to hear a live person and have some personalized interaction. By keeping the suspense up and upping the intensity, you can not only have more time to get into their head but also create an orgasm so well, that they will remember you the next time the... urge strikes.

Get the caller talking! I will repeat this over and over throughout the book. A person's FAVORITE topic is themselves and no matter their fetish, you will need to know more about them. This is how you get into someone's head and trust me, that is how you create amazing calls and then returning callers. Note that I continue to say to get into their heads... I am not repeating this for my health but for YOUR WEALTH!

Remember to sound super interested (actually, you should just be interested) and ask questions that do not have a yes or no answer! Why? Answering yes or no questions are as simple as one line... Phrasing a question where the subject will have to elaborate allows you to get more insight into how they think and what they desire. Will this always work? No. Sometimes, a caller will ring up and just be jerking off. They just want to get off, and well, that is what we are here for after all? You can find small tricks to increase these calls, and I will go over a few of mine in the Quicky Caller section.

New callers are the bread and butter of your business. Yup, I know that if a veteran is reading this, they are most likely SCREAMING their head off that I am wrong. In fact, I am willing to bet they have closed the book and are directed to leave a SCYTHING review about how I am an idiot. That is ok! Anyone who doesn't understand why I said that apparently has never run another business in what we call the 'vanilla' world. I can illustrate below exactly why you will need to always be very careful to convert the new 'blood' into a satisfied customer who is eager to come back (in more ways than you probably thought about!).

While loyal/returning customers help make a business stable; that influx of new blood allows you to build MORE loyal and returning customers, thus growing your business. This is more crucial in the phone sex industry than in any other business. Whereas your local grocery store knows their customers will be back within a few days/weeks; your clients may take months off at a time. This doesn't mean your returning clients aren't gold but that you should always be trying to convert new callers into repeat ones.

It is important to know why your clients may shy away from you for certain periods of time. Porn/the sex industry is viewed as taboo and wrong. After scratching their itches for a few weeks to months, many will try to quit their "vice" for a short stint only to find they need to scratch it again after a while. Can people be addicted to phone sex? Absolutely, but for the purpose of this conversation we will assume this person doesn't have an addiction. I will go over the signs of sex addiction in a further chapter.

There is nothing wrong with the above but if you put it in the perspective of someone who is solely focusing on their current customer base and not growing it… then during those periods when customers are on hiatus will be complete feminine. When you first get into the business, know that most who return to you will most likely be gone (at least for the time) in about 3 months. There is no telling when they will come back till you learn their customer pattern. It is during this period that you need to be super diligent in building up the next 'cycle' of customers as well.

All of the above is true whether you are independent or with a company. Again, most companies allow callers to connect to the operator of their choice, thereby bypassing the round robin system. When I left that first company, calls would be lined up from the time my line logged in to the time it logged out. I achieved this by ensuring that each call I got randomly, I converted into a someone who would request me first and foremost! Create demand by honing your craft and being open minded, and your business will not only be stable but grow. If your independent, this is absolutely critical that you not only understand but leverage this knowledge to help you in the future.

If you work at a company, your business will typically provide you with the customers unless you are with a trolling company. No clue what I am talking about? Visit the chapter on Companies! If you are a solo talker or with a trolling company; however, you will need to drum up your own business. While I will go depth in the chapter on marketing, I will do a basic overview here to help take away some of the fear that surrounds this subject. Most who leave the business saying that there is no money in it… typically were not marketing correctly. I know many who made crazy money when I entered, left when they had to start 'working' to be seen. They were angry at all the 'new girls' 'flooding' the industry. In reality, they just refused to learn the new methods of marketing available.

One of the most powerful things you will ever learn about finding new customers, though? Being available, no seriously this alludes so many. In the basics chapter, I covered that a set in the stone schedule is your friend. Being available at the same times honestly helps a TON! Customers know when to find you, and new potential callers have the ability to get to you. More importantly, the nature of the business is very at the moment. When someone wants to ring a phone sex operator, they usually can not and do not want to wait hours to get their kicks. It is said that someone views something at least 4 times before making a purchase. This means potential callers may need to see you 'available' multiple times before they decide to take that plunge. Callers who call during certain times but haven't called you yet, will see you and over time recognize you. This will increase the likelihood of them eventually calling you. In a world of fly by nights, it is always good to be the stable ship at sea.

Once I know I have had an enjoyable experience with a caller, I always make sure to tell them where they can find me online. Even if they mentioned knowing already, I like to remind them of my websites and social media profiles. If you work for a company, this may not be allowed/possible. If you are allowed to, make sure you capture their info so that you can reach out. I often like to tweet out and say when I will be taking calls and even make mention of phone calls I have had. I don't mention names, but it does make my callers feel very special. I also offer other wares; pictures, videos, stories, mp3s, and assignments. I have those listed for sale even when I am not available. This gives me the offline power to continuously make money but also gives my callers more to experience. I will cover this in the chapter on Offline Sales. Again, company workers, this may not be available for you.

Immediately after the call, I log as much information as I can about the caller. I try to make notes during a call but sometimes, it isn't always that easy. Making notes for guests, I have had in the past tends to be so much easier, as you already have that rapport. While it is still important to update notes, it is more important to create that file for a new customer. I spoke earlier about the binge and purge cycle of most callers, and that information is one of the first things I put down. This way I can track when they might most likely be around. For those who can contact their callers after calls, I highly suggest categorizing your callers too. What are they into? What types of things will they love to see? I create unique offers based around the fetishes I cater to each week and send out messages to all of those who fell into that category. Again, more on this in my chapter about After Call Sales.

Something to also remember is that many callers you will talk to, this will actually be their first phone call. They will have never spoken to someone else in such a way before. You have but seconds to discern why they are calling you and reassure them that their decision in doing so was smart. If they have never called someone before, they too are going to be nervous. Remember to the previous tips of course but try to also have some staple questions to ask. Taking someone out of their shell can be difficult but having some prepared questions to help draw them out can help tremendously. Here are few that I use frequently:

Amberly Rothfield – How I Made $10,000 A Month as A Phone Sex Operator

- My weekend was fantastic, guess what a pack of 4 girls and a blowtorch can do! (ok so that isn't a question, but it has a great shock value that leads to a fun story haha!).

- Oh, you are breathing awful heavy! What are you up too? (I used that more for vanilla phone calls. I do more domination, so I just alter it to ask if they are nervous of me).

- My favorite kinks are (insert 2-4 different ones), what type of things are you into?

- I do not believe I have spoken to you before. Usually, I can remember voices pretty well. (they will then inform me they haven't talked to me previously) *laughs* Oh well I am guessing you know a bit about me, why don't you tell me something about you?

- It is awful (early, late). What has you so worked up this time of day?

- Your voice is super sexy. NO seriously!?! I LOVE a nice low deep rolling sound in my ears while I rub myself! It isn't FAIR! What gets your motor going so maybe I can get you caught up to me!?!

Of course, this all depends on the kind of character you decide to portray, but they can all be tweaked slightly and still work. One of the tricks my former company trained me to do was to come up with about 4 different stories that are unique to my character. I could whip those up if the callers weren't talking too much and use it to draw them out. It is a form of method acting, and I highly suggest you do the same. In the chapter on marketing, I will go over how to use your blog for commercialization, BUT it can also act as a way to store these stories as well. Remember, we are called phone actresses for a reason. You need to be versatile but also true to your character.

Chapter 4 – Phone Tricks

Ok, this chapter is really for everyone (company operators and independent) and could fall under basics, but to me, it deserves its own section. There is a way to enhance your voice and create effects, that make the calls not only more fun for you but memorable to your clients. Anyone can just move their lips, but only a true master can create an experience. Living in Vegas, I have met many stage performers, and they too say the same thing. Remember people seek entertainment to take them away from the 'real' world and if you can create the world for your clients to retreat too, you will find that they will keep coming back over and over.

All that being said, I could honestly write a whole book on this topic and I just may! I will go over some common ones that I use and have used in calls. Knowing how to fake many types of sounds helps save your voice long-term as well. Doing countless hours of certain sounds can truly put a strain on you, so let me help you take the sting out of some of the repetitive parts of this industry. Also feel free to try out new ideas!

How To Make Realistic Sounds While On The Phone -

Wet Vagina Sounds - My first trick is to keep a glass of water about but also a sponge. The water naturally allows me to fix a dry throat from talking a lot, but the sponge is used to simulate vaginal sounds. I will admit, now that I do only domination phone calls, I have no use for this trick anymore, but at one time this trick was a life saver! In a pinch, you can grab your cheek and wiggle it. The suction action will also simulate having a wet vagina, but you will have to pause in between to make any moaning sounds. You can also chew gum in cases like this and just wiggle the gum back and forth in your mouth. The gum will help you create saliva (which helps make the wet noises) and also acts as skin in a way. Though it is one of the oldest phone hoe tricks in the book, many do dislike it and claim it adds too many calories to their diet. I would suggest sugarless, but that can be just gross. Honestly, I do not think that the calorie debate is very valid. Hit the gym, it is a tax write off after all!

High Heels Clicking – Cutting boards by the bed post? Can't lie, many a lover of mine have had raised eyebrows on this. No, I do not use them to chop late night leeks and mushrooms. Rather, I keep a pair of heels and a cutting board near (I prefer wooden, but plastic can make a real tile sound). I will often actually walk on hard surfaces, but sometimes, you just don't feel like it. That is where just lifting the shoes up and down on the board help. Alternatively, you can also keep both pairs near you and click them together in a clapping motion. This requires a sense of rhythm that I have never had, though. A headset would be needed, though, as using both hands can cause you to hold the phone with your shoulder (I find that turning my head in such a way can distort my voice and make it sound like I am breathing harder than I am). If you have a nightstand near, it can work if it is also the right material. I would be cautious of the material that the nightstand is made of. I would hate for you to break your heel or the nightstand.

Realistic Grunts and Moans – I know… BUT THAT IS SOO EASY. It can be for some, but others struggle to not sound fake. I have honestly PERFECTED this, no I am serious. Just two words! Sit ups. Yes, I am serious. Why sit ups? If you are doing them properly, they create a rhythm that is very realistic to the throws of passion. It is not only a way of staying healthy, but those grunts of determination or persistence can really come through as moans of enjoyment. When closing in on the big O moment, start doing little pulse crunches (where you stay up and push in smaller arches rather than going all the way down) or remain in the up position of the sit up. Not digging the set up the idea? Try some squats!

Your new Jen Selter ass is on its way. I even know an operator who does light samba dancing when she begins a moaning type call and slowly starts to speed up her steps. Not only will you be working off some calories but it can truly get you into the call if you do not want to actually masturbate (which very few of us will ever do).

Sucking Sounds – These can be easy enough to make with your mouth BUT after about 15 mins of simulated sucking and/or gagging? Now imagine of doing an hour or even two-hour call of doing this? Think it doesn't happen? Trust me, it does! Your mouth can begin to hurt and so can your voice. I am sure I do not have to tell you that that, is the one thing you really want to preserve. If you can record yourself doing such, that is the most ideal but only if you can replay it with the sound seeming to come from your mouth. Playing from your computer can make it appear too far away. Otherwise, the best you can do with that is a mix in a bit of your sponge trick and occasional coughing. Keep yourself from making hard coughs that go along the back of your throat that tends to do more damage. Grab a cough drop (my personal favorite are honey) and suck on it while doing all of this. They help with your throat and also help you create saliva. If the call is going super long and your throat is hurting to the point where you cannot continue to make those noises, start talking about how large the dick is and your mouth can barely take it. Remember the psychology here, they want to hear you (most likely) sucking on a penis. Your complaining will only serve to heighten this. Mix it in to break up the tone of the conversation but also save your voice.

Cracking of Whips – We do not all have a well-stocked dungeon at the ready. So what can possibly be used to make the sound of a whip cracking? Belts! Just grab a good leather belt and fold once. Catching each end, give a quick snap and voila! That is your snap, crackle and popping sound. Be very careful though, as belts can hurt if they slip and crack you. Is it after the Fourth of July? That is when I stock up on the Snap Pops. They are a firework that many children use, but they make a loud popping sound. Best yet, even if you are a city slicker you can find them in most Wal-Marts. I love to buy them in bulk after the Fourth of July or New Years. I totally do not use them for fun, nope never. I have a particular board by my desk/bed in which I toss the little bags at to make the noises. I would suggest having a place you can clean up to do so as trace amounts of smoke powder are in them and they can burn your walls. I learned this the hard way and paid my apartment complex a pretty penny when I left. A simple board that rests above a waste basket is perfect. It will pop onto the board (leaving the possible burn mark) and then drop into the trash bin.

Spanking – Still have that belt? Using a belt in the same fashion as mentioned above for the whips, can create the illusion of spanking yourself. Yes, the old thigh trick works too, but your skin can get sensitive/red/bruised. Snap the belt in the same manner but softer to simulate a strike on a body part. Alternatively, you can also place the belt on something thin and long (broomstick handle) and snap it. I know some girls who couldn't quite get a softer sound by trying to snap the belt with less force. In this case, having something in the middle can break the sound a bit. You can also use a sock with beans in it and place the belt on it, to soften the sound. Please note that if you do decide to use your skin, you use lotion. Warm the area up with smaller/softer smacks and work your way up to harder hits. Starting out without softened skin and hard hits can cause significant pain as well as bruising. You will regret this, I promise you. It is not worth testing. You will need to make noises as the smacks come down so that it appears you are doing this to yourself. There is honestly no way around this, so I do suggest being able to make cry like sounds and switch it up. A few ouches here, some begging there, whining and toss in a hit of hissing (from the stinging of that hand/whip!) as if you took a massive sting. BOOM! You have a convincing performance of being spanked into submission. **PRO TIP!** Make sure to resist a bit! Simply saying 'Yes, Master' can get the job done but showing you have a bit of a wild streak that needs to be 'punished' can not only make a much more fun call for you but often is a major turn on for the more dominant men who will be calling.

Amberly Rothfield – How I Made $10,000 A Month as A Phone Sex Operator

Crunching (crushing)– there are a few instances where crunching noises can become a part of the fantasy. Without having a bag of chips (or for my English readers, crisps) around at all times, there are a few things you can do to have realistic crunching sounds. The simulator that has become my go to is a sock for of beans. This beauty has a multitude of uses for me, but when it comes to phone sex, I can just play with it in my hand to make it sound like I am eating. If I need to make it noise like I am crushing something, just put it on my cutting board and grab a shoe! Have no dried beans? You can also use rice or even pasta noodles if they are small enough. In a pinch, you could gather up small rocks and use them as well. I would not suggest those though, at least long term. When it comes to putting that sock on my cutting board and using my shoe to simulate crushing objects, those rocks can really mess up the bottoms of your shoes/heels. Beans and rice though? They do put wear and tear on your footwear, but it will not be as harsh. Rice and beans are honestly so cheap though and if you ever need a heating pad, dropping that sock full of either into the microwave for a few seconds will become like heaven for you.

Someone in the background – this will not often be needed, but some callers want an ignored call. Before we go forward, I want to explain an ignore call. Ignore calls are where the customer wants you to just go about your regular business. During these calls, they want to hear you doing something. While phone sex ops will argue that you should do whatever you were going to do, I am in the camp that you are still performing. I like to play a track of me talking lightly in the background. I have this prerecorded as a mp3, and it is just me 'talking' on it. The caller hears my voice close to his ear but hears 'someone' speak in the background. Think the Peanut's teacher squeaking in the background. Back in the day, I would just grab another phone and dial a 'friend.' While in this day in age, I have friends in the know and willing to play along once hearing certain code words, way back when I would call the local bank's automated system. It would go on for about 15 mins before needing to be looped. These calls do not tend to last for too much time as you have little to no control over the flow of the customer. OR DO YOU? I like to treat the call like a reality tv show. I build up suspense in the beginning by alluding that something is about to happen. Perhaps I am preparing for a party, getting ready for a boyfriend to come over or beginning an 'interesting story' for a girlfriend to keep her caught up on my submissive guys. Keep their interest by building up and slowing down and building right back up again!

Sniffling (Fake Crying) – Even if you can make yourself cry on cue (I can; I was the youngest child, and this was pivotal to learn in early childhood), crying or sniffling for over 20 minutes can become irritating to your throat/voice. I have found that my cough drops have again saved my life in instances like this. They allow for me to make slurping/sucking noises that mimic sniffling sounds without actually having to cry. I do NOT suggest using cry sticks. If you do not know what they are, they are a stick used to help actors cry on cue. Kim Kardashian is rumored to use them during her ugly cry scenes on Keeping Up with the Kardashians. I caution behind these as they can be used incorrectly and cause massive pain. If the call turns out to be relatively short, you can be stuck crying for quite some time after. While we are performers, this is not Broadway. Your callers will understand that you are not going for a Grammy and it is often better that you do not try. There is really no return on investment for this type of product and the effect can be achieved for cheaper with results that do not have to last as long. Mix about a tablespoon of pepper and salt together and keep in a vial next to where you take calls. You can quickly take a small sniff (do not try to get any in your nostrils!) and tear up! Want something not so homemade? There are many types of smelling salts that can also make you tear up a bit as well and it again will not have the long-lasting effect of cry sticks.

Realistic sex – Sometimes, your caller wants to hear you just going wild. Having a squeaky bed is a great thing in this case. If your bed isn't very loud, you can move your bed off the wall a bit or back it away from the headboard. When you crawl into bed, while on the phone, you can then wiggle back and forth. This will simulate the bed rocking while in the throes of passion. Now the only reason I found this trick out, was because my bed rails needed some WD40 and instead of remedying this, I opted to leave it after a call that went well. You can also have an old office chair to bounce in (great way to work your booty muscles!). I found quite a few in buy/sell/trade groups on Facebook. I am dead serious too. That squeaking mixed with screams of pure joy can honestly add the realism that many callers are looking for. Now, not every call requires this, you have to learn to gauge this for yourself. Now you also need to consider if you have neighbors and how you may be affecting them/you. It is great to really rock a caller's world, but it is another thing to get the police called on you or a note from your landlord. I may know this from experience… I will neither confirm nor deny. If a squeaky bed or chair is out of your budget, (or you just don't want to do all that bouncing around), some squeaky dog toys can sound like a bed bouncing. Head out to Petco and test them of course, this is one where I wouldn't want to buy from Amazon and find out that it sounds like Rover is in the corner going to town but not myself!

Snapping – I know, you are thinking … Amberly, I have fingers. Well, guess what? Fingers can get awful tired if you are doing a snapping or clicking fetish call. Yes.. this is a thing, and it is way more prevalent than you think it is. Also, slave training and hypnosis calls can take hours and require tons of snaps in many cases. I have also met many people who actually can't snap, no matter how hard they try. In this case, most use tongue clicks, but that too can get tiring. As an alternative, you can record yourself doing such but playing it can be tricky (especially if you are like me and have to move around a bit) or you can put to pills in a pill bottle and shake back and forth. It doesn't sound exact but can work well in a pinch. I muffle mine a bit with a thick cloth if the call is going to be a long one. Mouse clicks can work well as well, especially if you have a mechanical mouse BUT those can be pricey. Bubble wrap can work but it is more of a popping noise and sometimes is hit or miss if the pop/snap will happen. If you do go the pill/bead/marble in a bottle route, make sure you only put in one or two max. Snapping isn't too harsh of a sound, and you do not want to shake the bottle too many times. Turning the bottle sharply once is more than enough.

Peeing – depending on the service you use, you will not be able to do this. BUT in case your service allows it, here are a few ways to accomplish when you actually do not have to pee! The old bottle of water into the toilet trick works perfectly. If you do not want to pour it yourself, you can always just have the lid hold a water bottle (watch Jennifer Lopez in the movie Enough if you wish to see an example). If you are a germaphobe, fill the bathroom sink and pour water into the plugged sink. Remember to flush even if you do the sink method though, for sound effect! (Yes, I know that is 'wasting water' but there is really no carbon footprint friendly way to achieve this, and luckily these calls are pretty few and far between). I would like to give a word of caution here though. Many phone sex operators will forego using the restroom when they are on a call. I want to warn that this can severely harm you later in life. While most services I use do not allow for potty talk, I will mute the phone if nature calls. I also have stopped diminishing my water in taking just to help me stave off the need to urinate. Mute your phone and try to be quick!

Pooping – similar to the above but of course, callers will want to have "plop" sound. I no longer offer this fetish, but back in my company days, I kept a small plastic container in my bathroom. I kept it refilled with water when I was taking calls, and on the occasion that this type of request would arise, I would just toss a small rubber duckie into the container. I would keep this bottle in my bathtub to keep splashing from causing problems with my floor. Because the tank was smaller, it would make a louder pop. Why a rubber duckie? Don't judge! No seriously, they are cheap, they work, and no one really questions a girl who has rubber duckies. Also, I am a major kid at heart. I even found one who had a whip and corset on, I fucking loved that thing. If you do not have a rubber duckie available, you can take another bottle that is smaller and fill it with water. Make small tests should be done beforehand to determine the best height to drop from to sound realistic. Too high and it will not sound like you are actually pooping.

Burping – this one is a strange one and very often hard to fake. If you do not know how to force yourself to burp, it isn't too hard, but some people just can't get it. Even if you can, long calls can cause severe irritation to your throat. The method of faking one yourself is simple enough though. It is just sucking down a gulp of air, and then it comes right back up. The problem is, like most things on this list, doing it for extended periods of time can cause pain/become harder to do. Now, this is something I have done since childhood but still can not do it for more than maybe 10 minutes in quick succession. The key here is to stall. Now when it comes to calls, I try my HARDEST not to stall but in some cases, it can not be helped. Try to tease in between using mere words. Talk about how burping makes you feel and how sexy it is to burp in someone's face… etc. Talk about foods that make you extra gassy. Ask them about how they got into the burping fetish or what turns them on most about the fetish? Remember how I continue to stress getting into your callers' head? Not only will you get more insight into the fetish but you can also save your voice box a bit here.

Drinking Alcohol – I add this one because I have honestly heard this too many times… I have had so many phone sex operators ask me about being drunk on a call or drinking with a caller. It is a very popular fetish, but so many operators actually think they HAVE to get drunk with their callers. No… again actress/actor, we are creating scenes and work within them. You can totally act drunk without being drunk. In fact, I highly suggest it. Being aware of what is going on is super important when you are directing someone who is intoxicated. Slur your words, giggle a lot, pretend you can't understand the callers but by all means do not drink. I do not suggest speaking super loud if you can avoid it, as you may miss what your client has said or even upset neighbors. I knew a phone sex operator who drank so much, she was making no money at the end of the day. How is that helping you at all? She felt the need to drink to quell her religious beliefs during her calls. If you find this is happening to you, find another line of work. I hate to be harsh, but if you need to drink/do drugs to work, then that job is not for you. (Unless your job is to taste test alcohol). You also do not want to walk away with any sort of addiction.

Remember, you are doing this job to make money. Keep a water bottle near you and pretend to swig that down and over time act more and more out of control. You can then begin to 'sober up' if the call is going longer, which can then prompt you to drink more again! The cool thing about doing drunk calls is the fact that you can pretend you do not understand the directions given and ask several times for the caller to repeat what you say. I do suggest not overusing that and also trying to work in funny things to say as you can.

Lengthening Short Calls!

Another trick, for clients who are in a hurry and just want to get to their happy ending, is to talk slowly. Regardless of the call, this is the best thing to do. I have done open mic nights and talked to quite a few professional stand-up comedians. Speaking slowly shows authority and also sets the pace of the conversation. Even if someone is shouting and screaming at you, if you are speaking slowly they will tend to slow down. Make sure to pronounce each syllable and really think out what you are going to say. As long as it isn't a long silence, silence is not a bad thing. This can cause a guy who is really going at it, to calm down and enjoy the ride more. Milking the minutes? Absolutely but trust that if a guy really wants to just get there, he will. Remember, most of these guys are not new to the game. If they can take longer, they will.

All that said, you do not want to stress each word you say or give yourself a lips/hiss at the end of every word. Many of these guys do know about these tricks, so if you are too obvious, you could take a 5-minute call and create a 30-second call. To successfully pull this technique off, focus your breathing and slow down your speech if you feel you are spilling sentences out without thinking. Take soft moments to think out what you way to say next and purr/moan a bit in between answers as a way to stall while you think. This not only sets the mood but shows you are very engaged in the conversation.

One of the last tricks I can give you and is so important is not a sound effect. It is how to get a person talking. Be they new to you or new to phone sex in general, getting someone talking is the only way to have calls that turn into repeat customers. Building rapport isn't as hard as one would believe, but it is the difference between sinking and swimming in most every business. But how do you get someone talking? It is simple!

Just ask your callers different questions that cannot be directly answered with yes or no. What did you do today? What are you up to tonight? How are you feeling this evening? What got you so worked up that you just HAD to call me? These questions break the ice, but for someone who is nervous or scared, it will not be enough. I have often had clients just try to say the bare minimum to get the question out of the way. From here you have to determine what kind of mood they are in. Are they going straight to sex talk? Then ask them to describe what actually turns them on! Are they talking more about work? This topic can be more of a red flag so tread carefully. Really any topic that can cause tension, be careful of as most people turn to entertainment to get away from what is frustrating/saddening them. Tune into what they are saying, the subtle clues will give you the idea of what to ask next. Remember that they are the customer and unlike someone ordering at their favorite restaurant, they may be scared to tell you what they REALLY want.

If they are really uptight or shy, try talking about your day… in a sexy way. Shoot for something that is pretty standard, such as you saw a hot guy and it got your pussy wet. If you're more of a Domme character, talk about how you brought a man to their knees. Use personal knowledge/stories to put out the caller. When someone calls you, it is almost like a fan situation, so making yourself seem more approachable is key. Even if you are a 'top' character, you have to be friendly enough for the other side

Amberly Rothfield – How I Made $10,000 A Month as A Phone Sex Operator

to speak. If the conversation is difficult to get off the ground, it is completely on you to find a way to jump start it. Do NOT put the responsibility on your client or you will lose them. Remember that first and foremost, you are an entertainer. Your JOB is to make the person on the other end have the experience they are envisioning... and then make it even better!

If you end up doing all the talking, usually the client will finish their business quickly. Being paid per minute, that means a decrease in your earnings. Some look down on, milking minutes but trust me, if a client is looking to be on a budget, they will be minding their minutes efficiently and make it well known they just want a quickie. I typically do more domination calls; and though I tell my submissive not to cum, time after time they still do. Sometimes after being told they are not allowed to touch themselves at all! (Don't worry, I am not delusional... I know that despite being told not too, they still do often times). There are definitely money in quickies if you want to go that route, but even those who specialize in quickies still use methods to draw out those calls.

A technique called edging also helps to draw out minutes. It is having your client jerk off at different rhythms and listening carefully to their breathing. As they get close to an orgasm, you have them slow down or stop altogether till they calm down a bit. This can lead to incredible orgasms for them (eventually), and even if they didn't request this, they would often enjoy it. It makes for a long call but a more fun session for the client. I highly suggest learning this art. It is frequently called tease and denial as well. Chances are, you will be requested to do such frequently either way as it is a very popular fetish. The more calls you do, the easier it will be to detect the breathing of your caller. If they are shying away from talking, that is a good sign that they are just getting into the physical act. This is another good reason to get them talking so that they can break that rhythum a bit too.

Ultimately though, it is all about your customer at the end of the day. Yes, extra minutes add up but your relationship with your customer should matter more. Inability to make a customer become more than a 'quickie' caller, is not mark against you at all. I still have many customers who call me for 5 minutes at a time and it will never be more than that. You get used to it and MUST still appreciate them as much as those who talk to you for hours and leave big tips.

FROM COMPANY TO INDEPENDENT PHONE SEX OPERATOR

Chapter 5 – Transitioning Too Independent Phone Sex Operating

So this book, till now, has been about general information that no matter if you are a company or on your own, you could use. If you are going to stay with a company, this is where we part ways. No ill will at all! Companies are a great place for many and I have grand relationships with many phone sex companies to this date. BUT I know if you want to be long-term successful, you will want to continue through this section and the subsequent ones. Companies are great training places, but there is a glass ceiling. For those familiar with Robert Kiyosaki's book <u>Rich Dad Poor Dad</u>, you will know that you have to learn to leverage your time. In companies, you can only make as much as you can talk on the phone. Some companies will allow you to get tips or a portion of sales of picture packs and the like but sadly, that still has a bit of a cap on it. Independent is truly where you can choose exactly how much you will make.

But AMBERLY!!! You still have the same amount of time in the day as company workers! Yes, but most businesses do not allow you to do certain things that allow you leverage your time more efficiently, effectively or even at all. I can make many mp3s to sell that can continue to sell past the day of being 'new.' I can post my content on any and all websites, which then increases sales. I can sign up to new sites like IWantClips or Clips4Sale, whereas your phone sex company would see those as competing websites (which could get you fired). Owning all social media accounts for my persona, I can post whatever I want without worry of being fired. Networking can extend my reach and collaborations become viable options for not only generating new callers but creating compelling content. You can build systems, which I will teach you, that will get new potential clients into buying loops even when you aren't around, aka spending money on you even when you are asleep or out with your family/friends. These are all things that companies just can not provide for you in most cases and even if they do, they

Amberly Rothfield – How I Made $10,000 A Month as A Phone Sex Operator

are taking a cut of it when you can do it for yourself. The initial boost in the publicity they can give you is nice, but the long term cost is not worth it if you want this to be your career.

With a company, you really only make money when you are on a call. Where I often make the majority of my money when I am sleeping or out with my friends/family. Do I still take phone calls? Absolutely, but it is not my bread and butter. In fact, my calls are often an excellent way to upsell everything else that I have to offer. Again, will cover that shortly!

For the rest of this chapter, I will be making more of a distinction between companies that give you more control (trolling) and being completely independent. The previous descriptions of companies that you read about would be called non-trolling companies. If you want to just march on into starting your own path, I suggest going to the next chapter. My reasoning behind this is to give an additional step for those who want to move on from a non-trolling company but still do not feel that striking out on their own is quite right yet. Trolling companies are not bad things and can be a good bridge if you need more time learn the ropes but are ready to leave a real dispatch firm. I know I have said it before, but it is worth mentioning again that you can use this opportunity to make mistakes on another person's dime. Any company willing to teach you how to market effectively can actually benefit you. While I will do my best to give the best resources I have available here, you are still learning on your time and dime. If you want to take baby steps, let no one shame you into doing anything different. We all have our own paths.

Trolling companies are similar to dispatch companies, but they require to do at least some promotion to generate your own calls. When I first started, I did NOT want to do any of this. I thought it would be a waste of time and would be too hard. Depending on an already established company seemed easier, but honestly, I can tell you that building your business actually is the path of least resistance. While it takes more time and effort, you can get a larger cut AND choose the type of calls you make. While some companies will have to make whatever calls come in for you, your promotional efforts can be directed towards the calls you prefer.

To illustrate this, when I first started toward going independent, I had realized that I loved cuckold calls. I began writing blog posts about the subject which then got the search engines attention for those keywords. More and more of those who called me were interested in cuckolding and seeing that I was too, would be more likely to call. More enjoyable calls led to me having more stories to write about, and more stories about that topic also brought in more clients of that type. I began doing the same thing with other calls that I enjoyed like hypnosis. You can use the exact same methodology as well. When you work at a trolling company, you can create specialties. Yes with non-trolling companies you can build up your clientele to specialties as well, but it is not as easy given that you are not doing any marketing for yourself. You have to hope the caller will be into that specialty whereas when you are with a trolling company, you can really push for those types of calls in the marketing thus increasing your chances of those type of callers wanting to talk to you!

In any business, specialty/expertise always equates to premium rates and demand. YOU NEED to focus on this. It will not be easy nor be quick but is well worth it. It took me about 3 years to find where exactly I fit best and create enough content to be considered a thought leader in my arena. Once I did though, I went from 99 cents a minute to commanding 2.99 a minute and sometimes much higher. Do I lower my rates? I sure do, but I know I can raise it at any time and still bring home the same amount of money. I literally have callers willing to wait hours just to speak to me. This is not to brag, not at all but to show you why you need to focus on a few fetishes. You do not have to be a dominant person like myself, that is just naturally what I took too. I have many friends who are more submissive by nature or switches (play either role depending on the partner). They have fetishes that are explicitly target, and while others may call in with topics that haven't be targetted, there is a core set of fetishes they can bank their callers to be interested in.

Becoming A Thought Leader in Your Fetish Sets

Before I go too far, I want you to know that you do not have to be considered a thought leader to make a living. Your goal though is to become a thought leader in whatever fetishes you decide to cater too. To prove yourself as a thought leader, you need to have bodies of works that show you are an expert on a subject matter. In the phone sex world, the first place to start is with a **blog.**

Most trolling companies will buy you a domain (also known as a website), create a simple design, give you licensed content to use on the site and give you login information to create posts. I highly suggest that you heavily research the topics you wish to speak on first. It is awful hard to sound like a qualified thought leader when you commonly misidentify the most important aspects of the kink you are talking about or use the wrong terminology habitually. You may want your first few posts to just be about your persona at any rate.

I would also not worry too much about whether or not others in your company are doing the same fetishes. Trust me, there is more than enough money out there to go around. If something legitimately interests you, then pursue it. Your personal spin on the fetish will not be the same as another and forcing yourself to go after a subject you do not care about will indeed show... and not in an optimal way. Those who are worrying about saturation are wasting time that could be spent on building their business. Everyday, someone is exiting the scene as well. Fresh blood/ Fresh spins will always be needed!

Now, Danny Iny (internet marketing guru) teaches a few things about becoming an expert in your area and if you have little to no knowledge, do not despair. What you can do is come from a place of not knowing! YUP! I am full of seeming contradictions but bear with me, I promise you that if you have no knowledge of a subject, you can still become a thought leader. You can document your journey in exploring various kinks. By showing the mistakes and mishaps, you become an expert by going through the school of hard knocks. You can also interview others who are more experienced as well. Interviewing not only gives your audience more information and the person you are interviewing more exposure, but it also will allow you to learn a lot from the giants in any space. Learn from their triumphs and their failures.

I would personally pair both of the methods to gain from the audience of the more known person. Why would someone with an audience want to speak to you? Well, anyone worth their salt will accept ANY interview. I WILL ACCEPT ANY INTERVIEW! (may mean some schedule juggling but the answer is yes). The reason is that you may know two people who have no clue who I am. I want to be in front of anyone, and everyone I can be, that is just good business. Will those two people become callers? Probably not! But maybe they have other skills I have a use for OR perhaps I can help them in some way. The only way to grow is to get more people to know about you! It doesn't matter if they will be clients or friends. Friends means more opportunities for people to think of me when they could promote me and vice versa. I am always looking for more people to collaborate with in any way that I can!

It also means more links going to my stuff. This is ideal for me as it signals to the search engines that I am more of a thought leader on that subject matter. This, in turn, will boost me search engines for those keywords. Benefits all around! Networking is another name for this method and trusts me it works! The adult industry is so large, but there are very few performers who stick around. Join forums and search out those who are willing to be interviewed. Most sites will want a link back which can pose

Amberly Rothfield – How I Made $10,000 A Month as A Phone Sex Operator

an issue if you are not independent. So you will need to speak to your company about printing it on your blog, but very few companies will turn down the interview if there is benefit back to you. I will go in-depth on this topic in the chapter on networking, YUP it deserves its OWN chapter.

Content Creation Expectations

Trolling companies usually give you your own website/profile and also have a major site that you all come together on. You will most likely have to write for their main page a few times a week. I highly suggest creating a fixed period to write out about 7 blog posts a week. This will give you about 4 update blog posts for yourself and about 3 to provide your company. Did they just ask you for just one piece? Cool, give them 3! Everyone loves an overachiever, AND if for some reason you are pressed for time, you will have a backlog. I can not tell you how crucial your backlog will be during holidays and times where you will be super busy. I have at minimum about 10 blog posts that can be used at any time in order to update my websites. Look at these posts as a bank account which you can withdraw from to keep your business going when you HAVE to take time off. I will talk more about blogging in the chapter on blogging, YES this too is so major it deserves its own section to do it justice. Honestly, I could write an entire book on that alone.

Something else that you need to nail down with your company is whether or not you make money off the sales of anything other than calls. Some companies also allow you to make money off referrals which lead to other girls joining the company or when a caller calls another girl. Make sure to meet and get close with the other girls from the company so you can refer guys to them when you are not around. Back to sales of other items though, almost all businesses own the photos/videos and actually any images you will be using to promote with. Most companies have caught on to getting extra sales by selling these photos to customers as well. At one point, it was popular to NOT pay girls for these type of sales. Now though, many savvy companies know that if you give the girls a cut, they will have the motivation to help encourage sales. Though the percents will vary, make sure that the company pays you for anything that you promote. If you are not going to get paid for it, I would not bother promoting it. I know that sounds a bit cut throat but if you want me to upsell your products, it is only fair to give me a cut! Most of these photos are royalty free, so each time the image is sold they do not have to pay an ongoing fee. This means the company loses NOTHING by giving you the incentive for selling the content or rather encouraging sales.

How do I feel about companies and selling your recorded mp3s? I am on the fence. While they can give you added sales, who owns that content once you are gone? If the company owns the content, you can not resell it or use it again. You can not record, and if you put out anything remotely similar, you are asking for lawsuits. Would you win the lawsuit? Perhaps but a headache etc.… something to consider. If you are the one who owns the content, do you get 100% of the sales? While you did record it and promote it, the company is also promoting it on their website (most likely), and they already have a network of sites to which they obtain customers to increase your sales. Be sure to get those questions answered concretely. If you are thinking "I would just keep a copy and sell it wherever I want I should leave!", Please stop reading this now… I am dead serious. I want to promote doing things legally and ethically. Would that ten-minute recording TRULY be worth going to court? The answer is no. If you choose to create content for the company, then accept it is now their property!

The other side of the above debate though, it does give your customers a better idea of what you do. Some of my clients spend YEARS buying my mp3s religiously before they call me. It is a lot easier to listen to someone talk and decide if you want to speak with them live. Many of my clients can not talk to me live frequently, due to family structure and time constraints. BUT they can listen to mp3s any time they desire. I will go more into depth about how to create offline income in later chapters, but as long as the company is willing to give you rights to your mp3s/not go after you if you make mp3s later, I say go for it if you are ok with the split they offer. Even if they maintain the rights though, this maybe the best option for your goals. Only you can decide that.

Remember that trolling companies are a transition between dispatch to being completely on your own. Some people do stop here but again, I do believe you bought this book based on the title; how I made 10,000 a month as a phone sex operator. To make the big bucks, you eventually have to shed the security blanket of having a base of customers that companies provide. You never know when these ladies and gents will need you (I still get paid to do blog posts for businesses that are short on posts) or you will need them.

When should you transition?

I can not tell you when it is best for you to strike it out on your own, as everyone is starting at different stages and has different goals. I can say to you though how I knew I was ready. I had saved up 2 months worth of expenses and felt extremely confident with every call that came through. I also had an extra 500 dollars that were to be spent on the domain, hosting and advertising. Looking back, I only needed maybe 100, and that applies modern times too. In fact, it is cheaper now to get started as you can easily use social media, which wasn't as popular back then as it is now!

I had stuck to a schedule for over three months and had a constant flow of returning customers.

Now I knew those customers were not going to come over with me, but the fact that I was able to convert clients into returning to me meant that I had honed my skills well. Online marketing and blogging were both things I was super comfortable with, though not an expert at all. The platform I was going to use for billing was not only thoroughly researched, but I also had my account set up. I had taken a few test calls (test meaning that I took calls from actuall callers to see how the platform worked) and been paid, thus proving they were legitimate. I got super familiar with all the features and rules during this time as well.

It was then I knew, I could transition and be perfectly fine. Submitting my two weeks notice, I completed the 14 days and off to the races I went. I was, fortunately, not in a non-compete at the time. Non-competes mean that you can not work in a competing industry for a certain length of time. In the phone sex world, it means you could not go to another company or start your own until that time period is over. Few companies have this clause but some do, make sure to read your contracts. This is why I was able to play around on the service I decided to use before leaving. Had I had a non-compete, I would have saved up enough to cover me for the time period of that clause (usually three months but some go up to a year!). Luckily the service was www.niteflirt.com/amberly, and it was easy enough to learn. More about that later though! I started out at a low rate and built myself up.

I bought my domain for my profile and set my web hosting. Blog posts were created, and a few offerings were posted to get those first passive income streams going. Social media profiles were also created and initial posts made. Messengers were set up so that I could easily contact customers. Within three weeks, I was banking 4x's as much as I was making previously and I never looked back.

Will it be that simple for you? It may not be. Should you follow my exact path? Absolutely not. Again, it all depends on what you are comfortable with and what options work best with you. Rather, use my path as a guide to determine if you are ready! Have you made a fully formed plan of attack?

Have you researched at least seven different options? Are pros and cons properly weighted? If you are working for a company, you have time. Do not just jump at the first opportunity but think it all through.

- Sit down and do the numbers on how much it would take for you to feel safe venturing out and then save one and half times that much! Why? Give yourself some wiggle room!

- Decide how many extra hours a day you will be working as you will not have a team working tirelessly to help promote you. Figure out what marketing methods will work best for you and how you will implement them in the most efficient way for yourself.

- Lastly, figure out what your new schedule will be an make a commitment to stick to it for three months. Three months is said to be the length of time to create a habit. Once working is a habit, it will harder to break it and getting the work done will become easier.

Chapter 6 – Starting Out Independent.

So you are going it ALONE! No one can stop you now! Fucking Kudos. I know, I have tried to keep the cursing to a minimum, but this is a book about the adult industry after all. I promise you that if you put the work in, this will be a fantastic move for you. Whether you are working part time or full time, you can earn some serious bank and have the pride that everything you have built was truly by your hands.

Sadly, none of the above comes free, but it can be made affordable. Bootstrapping is not only something I admire but something I truly believe in! I do not want to lie to you, starting out on your own can be pricey if you go for bells and whistles. In my opinion, all of that can come later and usually will be cheaper when you are indeed, ready for them. Bootstrapping typically teaches you exactly what you are best suited for and what will make you happy. Forcing yourself into the mold that someone else has out for you, can give you the feeling that this isn't right for you. That would be because it is true, it isn't actually for you... because that is how someone else is operating at this moment given the success they have built.

A good example would be me. As of this writing,

- I own over 20 websites dedicated to my persona,

- Have a customer list of over 10,000 clients with about 4,000 of those being active at any given time,

- I write about 30 blog posts a week,

- Record about 10 mp3s a weeks and take about 20 hours of phone calls a week.

That excludes my time writing articles on websites like medium, networking and spending time promoting myself on social media or my podcast appearances. (Don't forget my radio show on Tuesdays for the Kink Blast Podcast!) That would be a HUGE time investment for those not knowing how to manage their time or how to outsource effectively. If you have no clients, why would you spend the money to buy 20 websites and write over 30 blog posts? I mean maybe write that much but buying all those sites, to begin with? This a waste of time but most importantly startup CAPITAL.

The Basics – What You Will Need To Begin

Domain/Website Advice

Now I am a HUGE advocate of buying your own website but RESEARCH FIRST! Many FREE (do not pay for this) websites allow you to see recently dropped sites. What is lost site? It is a site that someone owned, worked and brought traffic too... but for some reason or another failed. It could be because the website name didn't work but it is usually because someone doesn't know how to promote. I scour these sites for premium domain names like blackmailmistress.com. As of this writing that site is pointing to my main website moneyovermen.com but once picked up free traffic for being relevant for the fetish I was promoting and of course, because I had relevant content on it. I will be relaunching it again at some point. BUT the original owner had built links to the site and when I bought it, it had some initial traffic already built up.

The point is, I got that website from a dropped site. Normally having to pay for such a domain could cost thousands but I got it for 20 bucks. So I have the prebuilt traffic already pointing to that site,

Amberly Rothfield – How I Made $10,000 A Month as A Phone Sex Operator

the Google relevance AND I get to use it to promote my wares. WIN WIN WIN WIN WIN! Google will also naturally push this website above any others competing for the keywords in the domain name. Why? Because one of the strongest indicators of a site's relevance is in the name. Moneyovermen.com? It was a famous play off of Riches Over Bitches but has no real keyword relevance. It was my first website and not well researched, so I had to try harder. Learn from my mistake. A word of caution though! Your first websites should not cost you much more than 20 dollars total or whatever the going rate for websites are when you are reading this. To check, head over to Namecheap.com (no I am not sponsored, I wish though!) and type in ANY set of words. Hit search and NameCheap will tell you whether or not the website is available, if it isn't select one of the .com suggestions. After selecting a nonpremium website, look at the price that is suggested. That should be the cheapest and standard right of .com(s) for that time. Right now, you are rocking about 20 dollars for that plus privacy protection.

Who to buy your websites from? I personally buy all of mine through GoDaddy for now but am in the process of moving over to NameCheap. Why? Namecheap is not only 'cheaper,' but they also give you free privacy protection. With GoDaddy, my websites are 20 dollars a year but to add privacy protection (a service that will hide my information from anyone searching for the owner of the website, and absolutely essential for anyone not looking to be stalked) is an additional 20 dollars per domain per year. This means $40 a year vs. $20 for a single website. To me it is a no-brainer. I do also like Namecheap's customer service much better than GoDaddy. Godaddy isn't bad to me but the Namecheap agents tend to bend over backward for me and often send me better coupons for services than Godaddy ever has. Who do I host with? Hostgator. Yes, you can also buy your domains with them as well, but the price difference is about the same. I also like not having both of the two services in one place. Call me paranoid but if something goes down, I would prefer to have my websites bought by one person and being hosted by another. Again, this is just me though. I know MANY people who have both services with the same company and have for years. They have never had an issue whatsoever but I do know of a few who have and hence why I have taken the stance I have.

Alternative To Websites & Social Media Profiles

If you do not want to own your website right off the bat, that is fine. I would still not suggest using a free hosted site though. The reason being, that free host can shut you down at any time and has no obligation to help you if there is ever an issue with your blog. They benefit from the traffic you create and sell ads on your website to compensate for the fact that you are not paying them. Yes... many of them do allow you to pay them now for services but why? If you are paying, you could still have your OWN website, and they aren't expensive. They usually will still have THEIR ads all over your site and because you are using their platform, will be bound by their terms of service. When you own the whole kit and caboodle, you will have fewer problems/rules that you will have to follow. Waking up to your website being erased because a moderator didn't like what you were selling is truly the worst feeling ever. Yes, my website has crashed before, BUT I get to back mine up whenever I want and can with one call have someone reinstall everything that was lost.

I want to add a bit more caution against free hosted websites or even paying for their standard services. Due to the nature of the content we write about, some feathers will be ruffled. All it takes is someone reporting you and the reviewer deciding that you need to be deleted. All the traffic you will have built up then, all the bookmarks your clients create, and all the links you have pointing to your homepage will be for naught. In an instant, your hours of work will disappear, and 9 times out of 10, it will not be returned. They may return a portion of your payment for that month, but that will be about it. You will have to start over and potentially lose anyone who doesn't know how else to get a hold of

Amberly Rothfield – How I Made $10,000 A Month as A Phone Sex Operator

you. It is only about $30 max to obtain a domain and basic hosting. When you own the domain and the hosting, you get little to no rules as to what will go on your website. Your hosting company will not shut you down unless you are doing something to scam people or super illegal. If there are issues with your website, the hosting company will help you fix it. You do not have to know much about website ownership or coding. I have literally been on the phone for hours with Hostgator having them walk me through basic stuff and even on holidays. Try to find a free host who is around at 3 am when your website is having issues on Thanksgiving, it isn't happening!

Instead, if you do not want to buy your own website out of the gate, you can make your social media profiles. Yes they are free, and yes they can be shut down but as long as you go with more adult-friendly sites, this probably won't happen, and they will be essential later on. Might as well take care of this chore now. My suggestions as of this writing (a new one pops up every day it seems) are:

- Twitter

- Tumblr

- Instagram

- Minds.com

No, I do not suggest SnapChat though it appears to be popular. Between the company failing to monetize to stay afloat and the fact that most of you will not be using your own photos but legally obtained content; it just doesn't seem worth the time. I also do not suggest Facebook. They are very heavy handed when it comes to anything in the adult industry. You are asking to have your account shut down, and with their rule of verifying that it is actually YOU who owns the Facebook account/using your real name, I just stay away. (I hesitate to mention this as I know some will abuse it but for those it will help... I will say this. On Facebook, if someone 'reports' you as not being the person you claim to be,

Facebook will lock your account until you send in a photo ID with your name and information. If you are using legal content, this will be a problem!). I may create a page as an author of this book, but that would be just about it. For a phone sex persona, nope! I have learned from the multiple top tier people I know who have tried, not worth it. Stay away from facebook groups as well, they are almost always shut down which can result in you having your account closed down if you are the owner.

Before you create your profiles, you will want to grab names that will help you. This is a moment where I am very much monkey see, but monkey does not do. My old twitter handle was @blackmaildomme as one of my main fetishes was blackmail. I am a Domme, and I am known for the blackmail fetish. So when people are searching for that fetish, I pop up front and center. I have since changed my handle as I started using my real photos again and am switching up my brand. Why am I allowed to do this? I am established, and my name is becoming more valuable to me than keywords. I do still have the profile @amberlyownsyou so that no one can take that BUT I do not use it, and it points to my main profile. When you are not known, no one is searching for your name, but they are searching for content they want to see. Also, once you do have a website, a twitter handle (or any other social media), sending hits to your site that are also relevant to the subjects you are targeting, also gives you a boost in the search engines. Everything should be driven out of making you more well known within your field. Grab names that will help you grow, yes you can create more profiles later or even change them.

All of that said, do NOT focus on too many social media profiles at first. DON'T DON'T DON'T! Stretching yourself too thin is not worth it. First off, you will find a lot of time wasters. So many, there is an entire chapter dedicated to them. Some more obvious than others but every avenue that you open up will invite different types. If you are opening every app in the world, managing your website, creating content and trying to take calls… you will burn out. Dominate one area (even if you are submissive! Get it? Haha?!?!) and then add another. I WOULD create a profile on each and put a link back to how people can find you on all of them. This will save the profile and direct people if they were on the app and searched you up. Just because you created the profile does not mean you have to stay on it regularly. Again focus on ONE social media account until you have regular interactions with it. I will talk more about the promotion on social media under the social media chapter.

Photos to Use aka Content

Next, you need content. If you are using your own face, done… move along, you do not need this section. If you can not use your own photos though, do not feel bad. It is a MYTH that people who use content are ashamed or ugly. Some of the hottest people I have ever known/know, use content. I in fact used content for many years as I could not legally use my face due to working for the government. Many phone sex operators use photos they legally own. Now, I absolutely demand that if you read my book, you do not steal content. Owning content means you BOUGHT IT! Yes, it can be expensive but if you do not use legal content in adult work, you can not only get sued but potentially put in jail. WHY would you risk that? How can you go to jail over jacking a photo? You are using that picture for commercial purposes (meaning you are making money off of it) and you are using it in the adult spectrum. Therefore, you need to know beyond a shadow of a doubt AND be able to PROVE that the person/people photographed are in fact over 18 and were when the photo was taken. You cannot do that when you steal a picture as you will not have access to the model's license or contract showing the date the pic was taken.

Now you can buy content that was shot by someone else, or you can shoot photos/video of a model or have a photographer due to custom content for you. The first option is the cheapest, followed by the 2nd and then the 3rd. Now I do know girls like Mistress Shayna of Shayniac.com who uses digital images or what I call Frankenmodels. She will splice legally obtained pictures together or use cartoon renderings (again legally obtained that she created or bought), but the focus of her business is mp3s and phone calls. This works very well for some but not for everyone. It also takes the time to go into these programs to create these images. If you know how to use Blender though, a program to build digital photos, do have at it though! There is a market for it but if you do not have that knowledge; trust me, there is so much more for you learn that this may not be the best use of your time! I want to make it clear that I am not discouraging this but rather maybe learn other basics of the business before and circle back around!

If you are going the pre-shot content route, my suggestion for those starting out, you can go to a fantastic website called AmazingContent.com. The prices are very affordable for the quality of the photos you will get, and I have even reached out to have them shoot custom content for me before of models. Their team is super professional, and they totally understand the adult industry from top to bottom. If you ever have a question, they are QUICK to answer it, and they run fantastic promotions often. Make sure to whitelist them on your email list, I am not kidding, or you may find they end up in your spam folder. If you are buying several sets at once, shoot them an email and see if you can get a deal.

To start, do not buy all 27 sets a model may or may not have. Do not buy all videos with matching photo sets either. I honestly would only buy one photo set, maybe two. That is enough to have a basic design for a website done and all your social media. Once you start getting calls/sales, you can invest more. Others I know in the business suggest at least 3-5 sets and to buy all a model has in case they take the sets are eventually taken down. Now I can warn that that did happen to me. I notoriously used Cate Harrington content for years (every bit was legal) and found some sets that were taken down shortly after going live on a content site. Having bought them before they were taken down meant that few others had access to them. SCORE! I also paid to have some taken down to be semi-exclusive to me

Amberly Rothfield – How I Made $10,000 A Month as A Phone Sex Operator

as well as having some shoot as exclusive content just for me. I did this all again, well after I was established with my persona. Photos and videos honestly will not ensure you will make it. I know many girls who had over 50 sets of a model and struggled to make even 500 a month. Conversely, I know some girls who have only three photos (not three sets but three actual photos) that they are allowed to use, and they bring home the serious bacon. Talent will always trump looks. This trend will show its self again in web design but more on that shortly.

A model should suit you. Not just your voice, not what your friend thinks is hot but someone you can stand to look at the face of for however long you play her. I have known quite a few phone sex ops who switched models out over time as well. You can also merge models together. I frequently used shots of a model who had a similar body type and cropped the face off for thumbnails. Again, I wouldn't stress over this too much. Most guys know you are not the girl in the photo if you do not offer webcam and FEW of those guys care that your face is not being seen. I am living proof of this. I am half black and half white, but my model only had a few similar features to myself. Why did I choose her? Her first set of photos were cheap and somewhat realistic looking. The prices matched my pocket book at the age of 19. Honestly, I have seen (in my opinion) BUSTED looking models used for phone sex, and they do WELL. I am sure there are some who do not see me as the fabulous looking myself, but clearly, there are plenty who do. Again, different strokes for different folks and I would NOT spend too much time over thinking this. Remember that if they are calling, they care more about your voice and mind than the body they are looking at. The same customers I see leaving feedback for one model will leave great feedback for someone who looks completely different and in a completely different age bracket (at least from what they are advertising on their page).

So now, you have a website (or not), social media and content... but Amberly... seriously... where is the stinking money!?! Don't you worry your pretty little head, as I am about to start talking MONEY. You need a way to bill your clients unless you have your own merchant account. That said, not all merchant accounts are equal. Adult merchant accounts are hard to come by and no you can not just use Paypal or traditional online payment gateways. The myriad of ways you would usually pay for stuff online or receive money, will not accept adult work and will shut you down. DO NOT RISK IT! Furthermore, most will give out your information in ways you especially would not want to in the adult world. I do not care that you went on Twitter and saw another girl advertising it. You are here to build a business and do not want to risk safety nor your accounts.

Yes, many places that allow adult billing charge a larger percentage but that is because of the risk incurred. There is a lot more fraud involved with the adult industry and chargebacks. When you get too many chargebacks, banks will look into your account. What is a chargeback? It is why someone gets buyers remorse and calls their bank to reverse the charge. There are MANY guys out there who do this and target new girls as they have burned all the other girls. Your new account will look like gold to them and they will try to scam you. Think you can just call the bank and tell them it is a legal charge? Being as it is a phone call which you can not record in many cases (different state laws), there is really no way to prove what the call was about or that they promised to pay you a certain amount per minute for the call. The bank will usually side with the customer. If you are billing for services you are not supposed to be, you WILL be shut down and potentially lose any money on that account. IT IS NOT WORTH IT. By losing your billing abilities, you could also have all funds frozen for an extended period of time. I knew someone who had thousands of dollars they had no access to for over 180 days. Could you have possibly thousands of dollars held up for weeks to months on end? Then you have to try to scramble to find a backup. Forget ever using that service again as well, as your name will go into company blacklists. Remember what I said about burning bridges? It is honestly best to just play by the rules.

Money Making Platforms

Niteflirt

My favorite billing platform is Niteflirt.com. They charge 30% of what you bring in (plus a connection fee if you are on a phone call or the caller listens to a recorded listing), BUT I have only once had to pay for a chargeback. If there has ever been a chargeback on my account, again I only know of one. Yes 30% is rather significant, but most other platforms charge as high as 50%, AND if you get a chargeback, you get that taken out of your check. They also have several payment options so that you get your money faster. At one point they did charge an extra percentage if you desired daily payouts but as of the date of this publication, they are not. Be sure to check with them if you are starting an account about this though. It was a rather smallish amount but it can add up for those who are really tracking their pennies (as any start up should!). Different platforms out there only pay once or max twice a month and with higher minimums. With Niteflirt, if you make more than 10 dollars (I believe unless that has changed) you get paid out. They also allow you to sell photos, videos, mp3s and just about anything digital. They do have quite a few rules though that I suggest you familiarize yourself with before you settle on them as your biller.

When you sign up to Niteflirt, you will have to enter your credit card information and have an email. PLEASE keep this email safe and monitor it often. Make sure you have every security precaution on that email because if you lose access to it and need to have your password reset/lose access to your Niteflirt account, you will not be able to get back in. Niteflirt will force you to make a new account if you can not log into the email which is in association with that account. That said, you can update and change the email to that account at any time. The best email to use for this? I would make it an email associated with the website you would have purchased earlier. You can set that email to auto-forward to any email (if you do not know how to do so, call your hosting company, and they can help you set this up).

After you have an account, you will need to scroll down and click BECOME A FLIRT. That is what Niteflirt calls us, flirts. After this, you will have to enter your tax information and banking information for payment. You will also have to create your first listing. Do not worry too much about this step just yet. Just enter some text to describe the type of character you are creating or a bit about yourself. You will be replacing this later. You also do not need to worry about having a profile photo just yet but if you purchased content/have some, feel free to enter this now.

Now there are two types of listings you can have on Niteflirt, well I guess three. The first is a LIVE listing, which is a listing to which the caller will expect to speak to you live. The second is a RECORDED listing, to which the caller will listen to a recording you have already made. To make a recorded listing, you can upload an mp3 that you have made, or you can call the Niteflirt system, and it will record for you. I prefer to record an mp3 as I can make edits rather than having to start all over again but either one works. The third type of listing is a Phone with Cam listing. Similar to the live listing, you will be expected to be there and also give your caller information on how they can see you. Unlike some other platforms, Niteflirt currently does not have a built-in cam system. You will need a service like Skype to give to your customer, so they can then view you.

Amberly Rothfield – How I Made $10,000 A Month as A Phone Sex Operator

After you have created your listings, they will go through a system called Playfair. They will check to make sure you are not breaking any rules or advertising anything that Niteflirt does not approve of. It used to be that they would approve just about any listing, so long as it met the basic rules. It would seem that Niteflirt expects at least some effort to be put into your listing now. Can this be a problem? Potentially, if you do not know about web coding. Niteflirt listings are mini web pages to which you can add HTML code too. This is where you may need to spend a bit of extra money. Either you will have to learn to do this sort of thing for yourself or pay someone. You are trying to start your business though, so you do not want to spend a few weeks learning coding right? (If you do know coding, then scoot to the next section!). This is where I would consult the Niteflirt Forums. If you go to your account section, there should be a button that says HELP. Clicking here will give you a link to the Niteflirt forums. Once there, you can find a thread which is pinned to the top where flirt services are listed. If you want to find an experienced Niteflirt listing designer I love, check out Robin Wildhart on the site. Type her name into the search bar and send her a message. Her designs are very affordable, and she loves working with new flirts.

You will need an approved listing in order to make payment mail buttons. I LOVE Niteflirt's pay to view and payment request system. No seriously, this is how I really built my business on Niteflirt. It is absolutely needed in order to build your 'off-line' presence. Pay to view is exactly what it sounds like, a customer will have to pay in order to see anything within the offering. You can load up the photos, videos, mp3 or document you wish to sell and give it an enticing description and then a price. The customer will see what you place in the preview section and then it is up to them to buy it. SO how does this make money roll in? On your listing, you can add buy now buttons! This means you can use your listing to not only advertise yourself but give offerings for when you are offline but also to help a customer who is not ready for a call yet. I have had customers who have been with me for years but never have spoken with me on the phone.

Now the payment request button is how I build my customer list! A payment request allows for the customer to download any content/see into the the non preview section before paying (if they choose to pay at all). WAIT!!! I promise there is a method to my madness! See, Niteflirt allows for customers to join your list if they meet any of the following criteria:

- They call you,

- They purchase from you,

- They click on any of your paymails,

- They message you.

So what does this mean for you? It is simple! Using a payment request button means that potential client can download something and 'try it out' before they buy it. What would you put in here? I use a mixture of videos and mp3s. Additionally, this area is an extra place to put content as the non preview area allows for more html. If someone buys a foot fetish buy now from me, then I will fill this area with other items that are foot fetish related. Trust that your customer will know what they will like and continuously serve them the same! This will mean they get into a buying loop and increase your revenue but also increase the pleasure of your clients! I do like to put in one or two items that are of another fetish as well, so that if there is any cross over that the customer can click on that offering and buy from that list as well.

So how do the clients find you? They will find you through the marketing efforts that I will outline in future chapters, but by logging in to take phone calls, you will rank within the listings of other girls. Now Niteflirt added back in the ability to feature yourself, aka pay to rank higher than other girls. Now when you go to feature, you will see a number for the amount to get to a certain position. PLEASE NOTE: that dollar amount is not the same for everyone. Many of those who are on the front page of

Amberly Rothfield – How I Made $10,000 A Month as A Phone Sex Operator

FIND WOMEN are there for free. Niteflirt ranks you based on their own algorithm and while there is much speculation on what exactly goes into that formula, they have not officially released it. All that is known in a concrete form is that it is based on how many people will click on you within 30 days (other flirts do not count against your score) and how well you convert those clicks into dollars. I can say that when I get longer calls, my LVS (Listing Value Score) seems to become more favorable.

How much should you spend to start? I would only start at $10 max. Why? There are other ways to drum up calls. There are guys who literally only seek out new accounts, and if you price yourself low enough, you will get the beginning calls that will:

- Lower your LVS to a more reasonable level to be able to bid higher,

- Give you initial clients to begin building into repeat customers,

- Start building feedback to show you are a quality flirt,

- Later allow you to raise your rate.

So what should you charge in the beginning on Niteflirt? I would suggest starting at .99 a minute. I know this will NOT be a popular opinion with many other flirts but hear me out and decide for yourself. At .99 a minute, you are making about 50 cents a minute take home. Yes, you could make 'more' per minute at some trolling companies but remember that this is just the beginning for you. Over time, you can begin to raise your rate. I would advise doing so slowly as you will have customers who will notice and resent this though.

Back to that mention of feedback though! Dr. Sue Review (also a well-known flirt on Niteflirt) recently did a podcast on this very subject. The best way to show you are worth a darn, is to have feedback. It isn't the catch 22 that many believe it to be though. Remember, there are many guys who will call you regardless of lack of feedback if you are at a low enough rate and other guys will call you just for being new. Use them to build your feedback. Now, Niteflirt has some rules about encouraging feedback... so keep this in mind. My personal favorite is to remind people when you feel the call is ending (after the caller cums or if you here the recording saying One Minute Remaining). When people do leave me feedback, I tend to make a 15-second recording (audio or video) and thank them. This shows a lot of appreciation and is typically a step above what most people will do. Feedback can be obtained another way though, not just by a review. You can get 2 points for ever 15 minutes consecutively that you are on a call. So if you have a one hour call and the caller leaves you 5-star feedback, this means you get 8 points for the call and then 2 for the 5 stars. Now you can lose points if someone gives you negative feedback! Do not worry about it too much though. Even I get bad feedback from time. You can block the person if they are abusing your feedback section. They are only allowed to leave one bad feedback. If they leave more, just send a help ticket to Niteflirt, and they will remove all but the first bad feedback.

Feedback is super important though for other reasons! Not only does it show that you are a star in your chosen fetishes but it also shows how active you are. Now, this is up for hot debate on the Niteflirt forums, as some flirts who do not have extremely high numbers in the feedback department say that their clients simply refuse to leave feedback but I have found that majority of my clients are willing with a bit of coaxing. Other flirts have hidden Niteflirt lines which the average person can not see without a direct link. There they can have tons of feedback just from calls alone. I am not here to say they are wrong or invalidate their claims. The issue here is that they are not new, whereas you are. Hidden lines are possible, just put in the title line of your new listing to not approve the listing. You will still get a link to a listing that is not approved. Yes, these are valuable down the line, BUT this does not help you when you have no public line that shows feedback. Focus on building your public presence first!

Niteflirt also has a chat function that you need to opt into! This allows for customers to send you messages for about fifty cents. Things to remember though is that you need to message back within 24 hours in order to get paid. You get paid every time you respond AFTER the customer responds. Now do not half-ass this… sending one or two-word messages will not suffice here. Clients will catch on and see that you are just milking the messages. I try to send at least a sentence or two and maybe a photo every 2-3 messages. Yes I know their chat system is not perfect, I for one would love to decide how much to charge per message but this feature is seriously the newest thing to the site as of this writing. Anyone who chooses to contact me via chat, rather than sending free messages or blowing up my skype/twitter DMs… they will get my attention. It shows they are truly interested in showing me that they are not a time waster! Sure it is just a few cents, but that money can really add up. Also, you can have multiple chats going at once! So while the payout is low PER message, it will allow you to ramp up over time, and it shows that your client has a true interest in you.

Niteflirt also created a way to connect your social media profiles to your Niteflirt page. Every time you go live for a call, post a new goodie, or log off (several other options too), Niteflirt will post to your Tumblr or Twitter account. Now, this is absolutely awesome… until you gain a decent following and then your Twitter page is nothing but automatic/repetitive posts. I may love you to death, but if you do this, I will unfollow you. It will not just be me either. No one wants to follow someone who is mainly spam posts. You can curb this by selecting the tick boxes that you want to show. For example, I once had the tribute button and a few nights later, I got about 12 tributes in very short order…. This meant SPAM on my profiles. You do not want this happening to yourself! Be selective of what will be shared and go in and customize the messages that are posting. There are some default ones there and if you want to be more unique here is your chance!

The last major part of Niteflirt is the Goodie Bag section, and IT IS THIS section that can really give you a kick start to your profile/career on Niteflirt and separates the girls from the women on the website. So at first glance, goodies and pay to view buttons seem the same. I can not tell you how untrue this is though! Goodies do not allow you to have an HTML section after the customer buys, which

Amberly Rothfield – How I Made $10,000 A Month as A Phone Sex Operator

is one of the only criticisms that I honestly have about them, well that and the name. Goodies though are searchable in their own section of the website, and it is has become a very prominent part of the website with a link at the top. You can see what others are posting, but more importantly, clients can see this. On this page, the goodies are separated by top selling of the month, week, and there is a section for NEW!!!! This is the golden area for you! Since you do not have as high of a client base as others, you will have plenty of time to create content. Make some picture packs (if you can), mp3s and written assignments (you can upload pdfs/word documents) and toss them up there! I would suggest going for quality over quantity, but the more often you can post, the more visibility you will get. This will also mean that you may make sales off those goodies! PASSIVE INCOME! Remember, that when it comes to making more money a month, you will need to rely more and more on passive income! Get that train started early and really build a solid foundation! Remember, it doesn't need to be the best at first. In fact, it is better to get started and delete/edit/improve than to wait for the 'perfect' idea to come to you. There is no perfect idea, just get out there and create. The more you do, the better you will get, and the more comfortable creating will be for you. I highly suggest you start by trying to create at least two new offerings a day.

Ok so, I am a liar. Goodies are NOT the last major aspect of Niteflirt. See, as your customer list builds, the more valuable it will be regarding sending out mass messages. Now, 'spam' has gotten a bad name over time, but in this term, it is actual monetary life blood. See this is not just SPAM but highly targeted messages that you are sending to people who have already shown interest in some way with you. When you go to 'Send Mail' You can click to add customer lists, to which everyone on that list will then receive that message. Now with the advent of Goodies, I highly suggest placing those links within your messages rather than just sending out pay to views. This means more sales of your goodies thus higher chance of ranking in the weekly/monthly results. I would also suggest NOT spamming every day. I have found that since I started, you can spam out more often than once a week (which is what the rule

Amberly Rothfield – How I Made $10,000 A Month as A Phone Sex Operator

of thumb once was), but I would not suggest more than 3 or 4 times max a week. The reason being, every time you send out messages, a certain percentage of people will block you. I know, red alert RED ALERT! Do not worry too much though. I have checked those who have blocked me before. MANY of them are accounts that have never purchased from me or had a bad run in with me (this rarely happens but has happened once or twice). I just leave it and not even bother to delete them from my list. The reasoning is simple, I do not have the time. My customer list is well over 40,000 now, and over time, you will grow so fast that you can not keep up. It is not worth it just to not see a long list of 'blocked' after you send a message.

Another reason is that your customers may temporarily block you. I know this sounds nuts, but it happens. I have had very good clients block me to help them resist the temptation to call me. Am I stroking my ego with this statement? I promise you I am not, rather just repeating what they have told me. Remember how earlier I spoke of customer buying cycles? This is just a part of it. I mention again as I have had countless girls who are struggling tell me how they block these guys right back. Well… this makes no sense. Consider the following analogy; a local pizza shack sends out coupons via snail mail, and they find out a customer threw out the coupon sheet… and then tells their employees to refuse service to that person should they ever come in. This literally makes no sense. Amberly!!!! Doesn't it not matter though?!?! That person has blocked you! Again, having been on Niteflirt for over 13 years, I can tell you, people do unblock you. Those who block people are leaving money literally on the table. I am more than happy to pick it up if you do leave it… but I suggest you do take it!

I promise this is the final note on Niteflirt and it is about blocking. I am not saying you shouldn't block someone ever but I will tell you that I rarely block. Even if someone leaves me bad feedback, I will not block them (necessarily). Unless someone is being malicious, I do not block them as many who are just trolling, they will just make a new account. To illustrate this, I actually had this one guy continuously call me and other flirts. He was very abusive verbally and clearly was trying to upset me. I watched the

Niteflirt forums as girls started talking about him (not saying names but the stuff they were saying the customer was saying was CLEARLY this guy), and they were all blocking him. He would then just go create a new name. He would leave a litany of bad feedback and this was just his thing. It was then I decided, fuck it… I am not going to spend my week (actually closer to a month) blocking constant accounts. Instead, I allowed the calls to just come in. I would pretend to never remember him and as he became belligerent, I would laugh. No not meanly but point out that it was funny (his insults). He sat there stunned. He almost seemed insulted that I would not acknowledge him. I netted about $500 out of him whereas other girls were hanging up on him within 2-3 minutes of realizing who it was. The difference? He sat on the phone trying to push my buttons and would hang up after 30 minutes of figuring out that it wasn't going to happen. Did it fizzle out? Yes but I was the victor. This is why I do not block. Think outside the box! Also do not block flirts…. Flirts will end up on your list even if you never click on their stuff. Filter them to your flirt list and do not spam them if they ask, it is not worth the fight as some girls FLIP OUT if you spend them a mass mail. I personally do not care about mass mail hits my box. Truly do not care.

Clips 4 Sale

If you are creating any kind of mp3s, I highly suggest Clips4Sale as well (and if you are doing phone sex, I HIGHLY suggest you do!). You have to make sure to go all out in pointing out that your clips are audio only though, but it is a super friendly platform. You can honestly call the CEO any time, how fucking cool is that? No, he isn't a snotty boardroom meeting type CEO, he is someone who has been in the adult industry for over 15 years and truly wants to help each person he gets in touch with being successful! He will answer your questions and is super invested in EVERY C4S store.

When you are a new studio, you are featured on the front page of their site, along with the best-selling workshops and best selling clips. Now, this seems to be based on how many new studios are opening. More studios equal you not being on that page for very long. How do you take advantage of this? My BEST advice is to make sure that you have at least twenty files, to begin with before you open the store. Yes, I did say twenty. Reason being, with that initial exposure that you will get, you will want enough content to be able to truly capitalize off the traffic and convert looky lous into clients. For this reason, you do not want to half-ass your content too. Put up the best that you can, add at least 200 word descriptions and tag with relevant tags as well as catagories. If you need to make a thumbnail that looks catchy and professional, head over to Canva.com. Make sure to make your content be within the same 2 -3 niches though. Remember, if a customer will buy one clip, chances are they will be willing to buy more if they liked that one. If the other nineteen are on subjects that have NOTHING to do with that one though… that can prove to be a problem.

Clips 4 Sale pays out only once a month, which for some is an issue. Considering you are reading a book about phone sex, and this site has no phone sex section to it though, this should not be a problem. I will be saying this soo much throughout this book but it is CRITICAL! Passive income is money you make when you are not active 'working' your business. This is the income that puts you over that 4 figure a month income bracket. DO NOT discount using sites that have no phone sex portion to their site if they can help spread your audio content!

Instead, this is one of the ways I build up passive income and for discovery reasons. No, you can not advertise competing websites on Clips4Sale, but everyone knows that customers will google search you. If someone is truly a fan, they will seek you out and more content from you. If a customer finds out that you do live phone calls (and most on Clips4Sale also know about IWantClips, VerifiedCall, Niteflirt, etc…) they will want to call you if that is something they are into. I want to touch back on the whole passive income thing though.

Amberly Rothfield – How I Made $10,000 A Month as A Phone Sex Operator

The coolest part of Clips 4 Sale is that every time you update your store, your clip appears under its category for being new. You can now set your clips to be scheduled and use THEIR Twitter to tweet out your clips. I only have one word for this... EXPOSURE!!! Clips4Sale has an amazing and they are willing to put you out front and center! Now a word of caution, if you upload and do not immediately publish but rather have it as a scheduled post, they do not give you the option of tweeting on their timeline. For this reason, I try to publish one myself per day but schedule in advance about 2-3 updates. By doing so, I get the benefit of being on their wall once or so a day, but I do not have to constantly go back to their website and set up a video every 3-4 hours. Those who do that, hats off to you but I will often forget if I do so, be late or just not do it at all. That being said, now you know you can also schedule updates!

Once you are in the back panel of the Clips4Sale site, you will notice that you upload picture packs, DVDs and even create a membership site. If you have the legal resell rights to the pictures you bought, then you can for sure set this up, HOWEVER, unless you have a source for a constant stream of photos (using yourself or you are shooting the model or have someone shooting your model for you) then you will find the money from this section dry up. Also, for customers who get upset about you not being the 'girl in the photos,' it will become very obvious over time that you are not the girl. Girls who use their own photos would constantly update this section. Having only three to even fifteen photo sets would not be enough to make this section worth it.

As for DVDs, this is more for production studios though I guess you could use it. I would be caustion against this though, being a phone sex operator. For one thing, DVD buying is on the decline as people are opting for buying more digital content, but you would have to burn your content onto a DVD and then send it via snail mail. What information goes on a postage label? An address. Sure it may not be yours, but it has to be someone you would know in case the package would ever have to be returned.

I do not personally know any solo guy or gal who is using this section of the website. If you find a way to make it useful, please send me a line! Not saying that out of sarcasm at all, I am genuinely curious.

For the membership site section, I hate to say it, but I really haven't used it too much. I once used it religiously, but other sites have cropped up that I believe work better. As much as I LOVE clips4sale, this is one area where they could really work to improve. If you decide to use this though, basically when you make an upload you can select to also place it on your membership site. For a flat fee (determined by you), your customers will get access to everything you place on the membership site. Now, remember, when you first release content, that is when you will make the most off of it (unless something goes viral later on. This means someone is able to get all your hottest/latest files will be able to do so at a discount. For many, this is a bit of a turn-off. Now, remember, I mentioned I use another service for my member site, so I am clearly not against the concept! I just do not like it on this platform. The reason some people like the idea of a membership site, in general, is because it becomes more predictable income. Once you have enough people paying that 9.99 a month to you (figurative), you can more accurately project your growth and focus more on your content.

Back to the awesome aspects of Clips4Sale though shall we? Clips4Sales gives you ALL of the statistics that you could ever need. On their front page when you log in, it shows you a graph of traffic to your page (people clicking in) and sales. This is great information just for eyeballing to make sure you are continuing to grow. Make it your goal to do a bit better in traffic tomorrow than you did yesterday. Sales is a great thing, but it is a lot easier to drive traffic than it is to try and ensure sales. If you are creating quality content, then the added traffic should convert to additional sales! More importantly, though, there is also a separate tab that even though it is pretty prominent, many creators I have talked too have NO idea about. Look for the tab at the top that says Stats! This should be bookmarked for easy reference and just become one of the main pages you hang out on when it comes to Clips4Sale outside of your upload page. This page will allow you to break down where your traffic is coming from, which means you can figure out where people are finding you. You can figure out exactly the paths people took to find you and what content they then chose to look at/buy. THIS IS A GOLD MINE! You can figure out what sites are truly converting for you and which you should ignore. You can determine what people are looking at and NOT buying (and perhaps figure out why). You can see what categories on clips4sale do the best for you and thus be able to plan out future content better. Your stats page is a page to study in depth at least once a week. Look at each breakdown and try to figure out how to use that information on how to grow.

Now your Clips4Sale clip store is like Niteflirt in that you can add to that page. You again cannot link out to a site that is not specifically set up to promote your clips4sale store only, but you can put more information here. Unlike Niteflirt, I do not find it super important to really pimp out your page here, in fact, the bigger this space is, the more chance you may not get buyers. I would suggest putting a header banner of some sort up though. You can also give a title to your page. Make sure this title has keywords in it that you want to seen for, but I would also put your stage name in there somewhere too. When setting up your page, you can also put in a description as well as keywords. Remember again that you want to focus on 2-3 fetishes or niches, to begin with. Once you have a few hundred titles live, feel free to branch out!

While we are talking about your Clips4Sale page, let us look at the featured clips option. This is where you can select the clips/mp3s that you have up that you believe really sell. Your best titles should be up here, and I suggest updating this section every couple of days. These titles are not discounted or anything but will appear above the other clips in your store. I like to place a few of my more affordable but awesome titles as they will help new viewers to decide if I am for them. The reason I like to change this out is that it gives the page a fresher looker for repeat customers. Trust me, your regulars will look to see what is new up there. Yet another reason to continue making content whenever you can!

The final tip I can give you on Clips4Sale is their messaging system. You can only message to those who have previously purchased from you before, and you can not seel their full emails for privacy reasons. This is useful though because you can put your clips in an email and send out mass emails to your audience. I would suggest doing this 2-3 times a week religiously with your latest clips included in them! Now you can not talk about anything that is against terms of service or pitches your websites that showcase other services. Do not think you can get a slick one past anyone though, there is a team that reviews each and every email mass spam before they go out. Again, do not burn bridges and follow the rules! That is not what these emails are for, they are to make it easier for your former customers to purchase from you once again and to remind them that you exist. No that is not shade but the truth. In this digital age, people come and go so fast that customers will forget you unless they are constantly reminded just how awesome you are.

I Want Clips

I would like to touch on IWantClips as they are proving to be just like Clips4Sale. You can always get a hold of their staff, and they are super invested in helping you learn the ropes and promoting you! Better yet, they are coming out with IWantPhone which makes them the cross between Clips4Sale and Niteflirt. I have tried their system, and it is pretty seamless and very user-friendly. My ONLY critic and it is minor, is that it feels like their phone system is totally separate from their clip store platform. It can be hard to navigate back to the main part of the site, but I have a feeling that will be cleared up soon.

The thing to note, their clip selling portion of their website has been around for quite a while itself, it is the phone portion that is relatively new and from what they have said on Twitter... they are continuing to expand their range of services. They allow you to sell the same things as on clips4sale, BUT they do have slightly different rules on the fetishes you can cover. Be sure to always check out the most current terms of service! Would hate for you to lose your account! If you ever have a question, their team will get back to you on whether your idea is allowed or not and relatively quickly. I have asked questions and got an answer back in less than an hour and never longer than twenty-four hours.

The way to have success on the clips side of this platform is similar to Clip4Sale and Niteflirt's goody section…. GET CONTENT OUT! The more often you put content out, the more times people will see you in the new section! Make sure to select a lane though. You do not need a clip or content in ALL categories. Try to DOMINATE one category or even up to three. Once you have a few hundred clips in one lane, feel free to add another. Look at this as building a freeway, you do not need to add a new lane until you have traffic flowing to where you will actually need that new lane. NOW if you are just trying to find what you like the most, feel free to play around a bit but try to stick to one or two places and get notoriety in those lanes.

Now, I Want Clips allows for you to create discount codes which I LOVE! This means I do not have to go in and manually edit all of my clips. This may seem like first world problems… and it is but seriously once you have 300 or 3000 files that are uploaded, it can be a PAIN to go through each and every single one and try to discount them. You then will have to UP the price back up after. Insert the meme about not having time for that! You can cancel the discount codes whenever you desire and even have them auto set to end. Whenever I am not able to produce a ton of content (like when I am traveling to conventions), I like to create a discount code and toss it out to my customers. Now I usually pre-shoot a bunch of content to ensure that I have fresh stuff constantly coming out BUT since I may not be able to take phone calls and interact with emails/messages as much I would like, I like to toss out discount codes to help boost income. Some of my guys actually look forward to me leaving…. Good thing???!?!

IWantClips also gives you options on chargebacks. You can take a larger percent home (about 5 or so more), or you can forego this in lieu of protection against chargebacks. Now we went over chargebacks earlier in part about Niteflirt so you can see where this would be useful! I personally do not mind giving up a small percent to know that EVERYTHING that hits my bank account is mine forever. Know that you can opt in or out at any time, but there are some stipulations regarding this. If you opt out, then it takes a minute or two for purchases to start reflecting this. Same with opting in, this means there is a period of time that you are still uncovered. Make sure to read the fine print. I personally have never chosen to opt out.

Like Niteflirt and unlike Clips4Sale, you can also choose how often you get paid. I LOVE THIS! With Niteflirt, you can get paid once a month or daily, and Clips4Sale allows you to only get paid once a month if you make over $50 at it's lower level (you can choose to raise that level). With IWantClips though, you can get paid daily, weekly, bi-weekly or monthly. Why is this awesome? Well not everyone does well with a daily payout. With smaller amounts, it can be way too easy to find yourself spending away your money, rather than waiting for it to amass to make your larger bill payments (such as rent or mortgage). It is truly something to get used too! The mentality that more is always coming can be both a blessing and a curse. I know for myself, I prefer to get paid every two weeks. I would love it if other platforms made this option available/ easy to use. With Niteflirt you CAN do this by suspending your payout to monthly and then the day you wish for the money to begin processing, going in and setting yourself to daily… but this is far too much for me to remember on top of all that I do.

Like Clips4Sale, IWantClips will tweet out your latest offerings each time they go live. You can also hook up your own social media networks to also allow you to do this. This is a cheap way to schedule your posts to come out on Twitter by the way! By simply creating your offerings and setting them to come out a later date, you can ensure that you will not have to worry about whether or not you have updated your social media pages in a while. I highly suggest doing this regardless if you will be around every day or not. I like to set one specific day to upload my files a week and have it set as ritual. It is a day that I typically am not shooting content, and my focus is just getting my new products on the virtual shelves. The added exposure of it going onto their timeline is just a bigger boost!

I also LOVE the IWantCLips blocking feature. With other sites, if you wish to block someone, they are blocked from everything. This is not true on IWantClips. I can block you from doing very specific things. Why would this be useful? Well if someone is sending you a BILLION messages, you can block them from sending messages but allowing them to purchase from you still. Doesn't sound useful? I promise you, it truly is. Yes, you can just ignore messages, but it can get annoying over time. With IWantClips, you can block them from calling you on their phone system or ordering custom clip orders or really anything you desire to keep that customer from doing. You can also block sections of the world as well. My only comment about this though is it doesn't always help. More and more people are using onion routers or IP spoofing programs for their security. If you are truly worried about someone finding out about you, then really think if the adult industry is for you. You may be able to keep them off your IWantClips, but other sites that are essential for you to make the big bucks on do not have this feature. Also, clips get pirated all the time or links/photos shared on forums. So while they may not be able to buy It directly from you, those same people can still see you via other means.

IWantClips also has a section called IWantCustoms, which is their custom clip portion of their website. DO not worry, you do not have to do video content for this to work for you. Customers can find your profile and what all you are willing to do and order from you. Best yet though, you get 100% of the payout for these clips! I have not seen a better payout in the entire industry! I get a lot of my customers wanting to get something specific that is just for them, and I always direct them to this portion of their site! Customers can feel safe that if you do not deliver within a certain amount of time, they will get their money back and you get to create the clip knowing the money is there. Think of it as content escrow!

Lastly, there are promotional tools for IWantClips that makes it super easy to integrate your IWantClips page with your websites. I highly suggest using the different tools they have available so that your clips are front and center of any website you build. You can also get paid for the referrals that you send to IWantClips from these tools. What is a referral? When someone signs up to IWantClips and begins buying clips (customers) or begins to sell clips (producers), then you can get paid for referring them and showing the website. At first, this may seem trivial, but I have made a pretty penny doing similar for Niteflirt. That extra 200 – 500 a month really adds up!

KinkBomb

I want to give you as many resources as I possibly can in this book, but I have not personally used kinkbomb yet as a content creator. I have to tell you though, that it has been around a while and I have not heard of ANY studios not getting paid. I would venture to say they are legit and that I am indeed fucking up in not having a studio with them. I do plan to fix this going forward. I did take the initiative to ask via Twitter DMS if they do allow for audio only content and they responded with a yes! Just make sure to label your content accordingly.

Kinkbomb allows for a split of 60/40 in payment with the higher going to you. This is pretty standard in the adult world and while some will decry this, remember that when you create a studio… they are sending their mass ton of traffic towards you. When you first sign up, unless you have a massive following, companies such as Kinkbomb are really giving you free money. Yes, I said that. FREE money. Your initial traffic will come from being on their font page, they are delivering your content and spending their resources on the hosting of your content. I do not want to hear anyone reading this book fussing about how high the percentages are. They deserve a bit of profit for helping us in carving out our places in this kinky world.

Kinkbomb works similar to Clips4Sale and IWantClips in that you get your own page which will show your clips. New studios and clips are shown on the front page so again, similar advice will be given here. Make sure you have a ton of content before you attempt to open your store. With Kinkbomb though, I would suggest a slightly different tactic. I would NOT suggest making this one of the first studios that you open. Remember, we do not want you overwhelmed or burning out. The other two stores are very popular and growing quickly. Thus I would say ENSURE you have an account with them. Once you have 100 clips, I would start your Kinkbomb store, and no I do not suggest uploading all 100 at once. Instead, I would upload the first 20 and then spread the rest of the clips out over the course of 2-3 weeks at the rate of about 5 coming out or so a day. In doing so, you will ensure that you have domination of your niches content wise while you are on the front page as being a new studio. With Kinkbomb not being quite as popular as of yet, you will find you have not as much competition and be able to rank up higher with your clips.

Kinkbomb also allows for memberships similar to that of Clips4Sale. I have not tried their options out, but in the years they have been around, I have not seen many producers using it either. I would say that when you make an account to take a look and see if it is a fit for you. More about the membership sites that I do recommend later. In future editions of this book, I do plan to give a full review of kinkbomb membership programs.

One feature I DO like about KinkBomb is that they have TOP FANS showing on the individual studios. Now some may not like this, but I know many of my fans like competition with other fans. If one fan leaves me feedback, others want to join in. I can totally see one of my top spending fans being booted from their throne, only to come raging back. This is the sort of competition that does nothing but benefits me! I would love it if other platforms integrated this feature.

In fact, upon taking a better look at the layout of this website... I may just open up my store SOONER! Seriously I love the fact that the top selling clips are off to the side, new clips are shown in a grid-like order, and you can place featured clips! The layout is very clean and easy to follow. Has a very modern feel to it which, sadly, many websites in the porn industry simply do not have!

Additional features that I am in love with include the ability for customers to favorite a store, which means they can come back to it easier and like IWantCLips, discount codes can be created. Better yet, current codes are under the promotion tab for each store. This means clients do not have to follow you on social media to get a hold of your codes. This may entice a general surfer to turn into a paying customer faster!

In general, this seems like an excellent site and yes, I know I should already have a store on it but to be able to give a good review, this would mean spending at least 3 months testing features and this book is long overdue. Make sure to follow my new blog at www.amberlyrothfield.com as I will write about my experiences on not only KinkBomb but other sites as I find them and sign up!

Verified Call

At the risk of being bashed in the head by you, I have to admit... I have not used this service either, BUT I have known about it for YEARS and know many girls who have used it/love it/swear by it. Verified Call is a website that allows you process phone calls and bill without too much hassle. They not only give you a profile page to direct potential callers too but they also give you widgets you can use for your website to indicate if you are available for a phone call or not.

The catch? Verified Call, unlike Niteflirt, has no system by which you can promote yourself. You will have to promote your phone number and pages in order to get the calls. It is a great service, but I do NOT suggest it for new girls that are just starting out. It is part of the reason I never signed up. By the time I was established enough for a service like this, I had found myself too busy with content creation and promoting my Niteflirt phone lines that the idea of starting a new account and having yet another log in was unappealing for me. I know that if Niteflirt were to disappear tomorrow, I could have the option of moving to Verified Call but again, different strokes for different folks.

That warning aside, because they do not have to host as much data for you, Verified Call has one of the highest payouts for independent phone sex operators, and unlike other phone services, they are perfectly ok with you using them to bill for just about anything. Yes, they are totally ok with phone sex. Added bonus, they have had no security breaches that I know of and never give your information out to the customer and vice versa. Now they do have a terms of service page so I would give that through read through to ensure you are not going to advertise for types of calls that they will not allow you to bill for. From what I have heard though, they are very relaxed on the type of calls they will allow.

If you are ready to start promoting yourself though, this is a great back up to have on your website. There are no real tips on how to game this system to your advantage though, really it is down your personal promotion. Find out more about that in the Basic Marketing and Social Media sections!

Many Vids

WHERE HAS THIS WEBSITE BEEN MY ENTIRE LIFE!?! No I do not mean in an I love it sense, but ever since I came out of the closet using my real photos, all I see are girls pushing this site on their social media. Manyvids is a clip platform similar to C4S, Kinkbomb, and IWantClips. The structure of this site is significantly different though. The front page is full of the different studios, rather than the top-selling clips or new studios. You have to click around to get to the actual videos. Do not let this discourage you though, most of the bigger named girls have a store here. NOW, you can not upload mp3s from what I can see... contradiction? No actually. You will have to take your audio file and affix it to a static image in

Amberly Rothfield – How I Made $10,000 A Month as A Phone Sex Operator

a video editor. There are many free video editors out there but if you want a decent one that is user-friendly and on a budget, look up AVS video editor. I have used it for years. I have upgraded to Sony Vegas and also use Adobe Aftereffects but if you are on a budget AVS is amazing and can do quite similar work without needing the technical knowledge.

Manyvids pays you 60% of the sale of your items which again is pretty typical of this industry. They also have different membership tier levels for their producers. They have a Premium tag which you can get by upgrading. Now, having no account currently, I can not verify what it takes to get this tag line, but if you can do it, I would high suggest it.

Now, why do I, knowing all the big names use ManyVids, still not have an account? Oh trust me, it is next on my to-do list! I wanted to make sure I have over 250 titles ready and compliant to roll out onto their platform. I have way over 200 files BUT, it will take me sitting down for two days straight to issue out the plan of attack I want for this website. I want to dump 30+ files into my new store and then schedule out the other 170 over the course of a month with 2-4 coming out per day. I also want to make all new thumbnails for each file. My reasoning for doing this is that it is a massive website with lots of established stars on it already. Do I believe you as a newbie would need to pull this strategy? Not at all. This site had TONS of traffic (will explain more about this below) and can really help get you those initial clients you need to begin creating great passive income. In fact, helping creators generate passive income is apart of their mission statement!

So how do I know that ManyVids has massive amounts of traffic? I will go more in-depth into how to use Twitter to your advantage later but to explain ManyVids, we need to take tap our toes into this topic now. I follow quite a few major cam girls on Twitter (notice I did not say they necessarily follow me back, haha. Not flexing on you) in order to see what websites they are on and promote. If they are on a website, then chances are I want to be on it potentially to, or at the very least investigate it. BUT WAIT AMBERLY, they are CAM girls who can use their own photos and I can't! Well, many websites do not care what images are displayed if they are A. involving consenting adults and B. you have the legal rights to place those images/videos/mp3s on there. Yes, I do follow other phone sex operators, but I really like to look outside of my tiny niche for new places to expand. Where Manyvids plays into this is that they are on almost every major creator's twitter. No, I do not mean just their new videos, but EVERY TIME THEY SELL A VIDEO/CLIP!

Unlike other platforms, every time one of the clips you uploads sells you will get an automatic tweet pop up on your feed to tell your followers that you sold another clip. Now again, if this happens too much you can seem more robotic, BUT it would seem that even those who use this site quite a bit do not have too many pop-ups. Now I would not take this as a mark that the site has no traffic, I mean why the producers would continue to upload there? With so many major producers using it, that means they are driving traffic to it simply by allowing the tweets. Do not make the mistake in beliving that many business women and men would use a useless website. Instead, this is an indication to me that you can limit how many tweets come out. Manyvids seems to be a super intelligent website and would know that no one wants to tweet out twenty times that they sold a newly uploaded clip. This to me would be a great feature for other clip platforms.

Similar to the other clip selling sites, you should not use this site to promote your other sites but use it to sell your clips. Again, trust that if a customer likes you, they will SEEK you out. If you have made your presence known on the internet, this should not be hard. I literally get people adding me on skype right and left who have not purchased my ids, and I definitely do not know them personally. I get follows on my social media profiles for the same reason. Look at this website as a way to increase your presence and give you yet another option for passive income.

Talk To Me

Talk to Me is similar to Niteflirt but has not been around quite as long. Do not let that get you down though. Many of the top girls of Niteflirt seem to have profiles over there as well. Their profile system is not as heavy on knowing HTML and thus, in my book, is a bit more new user-friendly. I would totally suggest signing up for this site along with your Niteflirt account when you are starting out.

Some striking differences though, it would seem there is a much lower cap on the rate that you can charge per minute. The max you can do on Niteflirt is $50 per minute whereas on Talk To Me is $2.99. Now I know many of you are thinking that $50 a minute is insanely high and you will never get calls but I can tell you it does happen but you are right, it isn't often. I still like the ability to be able to raise my rate to higher than $2.99 per minute though. What is more perplexing though, is the fact that they have a financial domination category on their website. For those not in the know, financial domination basically has a submissive spending a ton of money just because the dominant person wants them too. That is where the higher per minute rates come in at. It really isn't the biggest deal, but that did raise my eyebrows.

Talk To Me also allows for sexting with your customers for payment. I seriously love this feature! This really will separate the time wasters from the serious customers. If someone is serious about being a customer of yours, they will call or pay to talk to you in depth. I am not saying charge someone for every single, hello you send them, but if someone wants an in-depth conversation, they will pay you. Plain and simple.

Other interesting features is the distinction between skyping and webcamming. Skyping does not always have to be video, and many customers prefer Skype as it has such clean sound. Now, if you are available for Skyping, make sure you denote whether or not you turn your webcam. I know quite a few girls who still do not use their own photos, but they will turn on their webcam to show their feet or

Amberly Rothfield – How I Made $10,000 A Month as A Phone Sex Operator

other non-identifying parts of their body. Seriously, I had a guy who just wanted to watch me type… different strokes for different folks! Now how does this differ from their webcam section? It would seem that Talk To Me has a section and software to put your webcam feed where the customer can see it without using Skype. I have never used this service on their website, but I find it extremely intriguing. Most sites that allow you for camming on them do not allow you to promote your Skype at all. Skype being a third-party service, the company can not monitor if anything is going on or if any show is ever performed. This means a higher chance of chargeback. Talk To Me nonetheless though, allows for this.

Another cool feature is that they allow you to watch videos with your customer and pay you for it. This takes Netflix and chill to a WHOLE new level! I have had plenty of customers get on the phone and browse Porn Hub with me before but Talk To Me specifically targets this and markets it to their customers. Some would think it is strange that others would want to watch porn with a person, much less pay for it. Nope, this is very common, and I give Talk To Me major kudos for marketing it out to customers directly.

You can also create offerings to sell on Talk To Me, and much like the previous clip stores, I would suggest you do so. Remember that passive income in the goal! If your goal is to make $150 a day and you can awake every day to $50 or more dollars, then you have to take fewer and fewer phone calls. Do not get me wrong, there will always be customers who want to talk to you live, and I do not suggest walking away from taking calls altogether. It is here though that you can start to increase your rate and not rely strictly on phone calls. What happens when you want a vacation, or you get a cold/get sick? Remember this is about creating an actual business that can be expanded if you truly desire that. With that said, I would put up offerings here for sure.

Pay Per Call

This service is similar to Verified Call in that it is just meant to help you process phone calls and they do give you a few tools to help your customers know how to place a call. They give you statistics on the call, and you really are taken out of the equation other than promoting your number. I want to mention this as I know many girls do use the service successfully but for those on limited budgets, I would steer clear.

The first flaw for those just starting in the phone sex industry is the cost to start with this service. They charge a setup fee of $500 and then an ongoing fee of $50. If you are relatively unknown and have no clientele, that is a steep fee. While in just a few short months of hardcore grinding that would not seem to be too difficult to afford, in the beginning, I would not suggest it at all. Your money is initially better spent elsewhere. On Niteflirt, the bidding you could do with that $550 could easily net you a smooth $6000 or more, and you will already have a biller with a phone number.

There are a few other platforms, and while I have played with some, I always seem to go back to Niteflirt. It is just like home. Like with social media, wherever you land, I suggest that you stick with that one for at least 2 months. Feel out all of the features and then if you venture to another, do not entirely switch but rather test it out. When you are independent, it is actually incredibly wise to spread your eggs into several baskets. If one of my sites were to disappear or I was unable to use them, I could easily switch more focus onto another one without having to rebuild entirely.

If you want a billing account that goes with your website and you have more flexibility to discuss/offer what you like; I would suggest OLCI.com. His number is listed on the site, just ask for Mikey and tell him Amberly sent you. He will help you set up your site correctly to offer your phone calls as well as anything you care to sell. There are things you can and cannot talk about under his account, but I have found that he can help you offer more than the bigger platforms can't. He has been in business for over 15 years and knows all the ins and outs. What I also love about dear Mikey is that he will also help you figure out where to advertise at and even has an email list of clients to market you too. Seriously, Mikey is amazing. The only catch is, you have to build a website and begin pumping traffic into it. If you want to go independent but haven't the skills to do so yet, I would suggest going NIteflirt flirt and then figuring out the next steps after a month or two.

Some other sites that I have used and probably will be using more are ClipFoo and Rude.com. Each has a different pay structure and benefits, but they have been around for a minute. In 10 years, I have seen MANY new phone sex/cam platforms crop up, but FEW stuck around for long. A popular one was TalkSugar. They were known as the wild, wild west of phone sex as you could do anything on it for some time but as I talked about earlier, they quickly had to change their terms of service/enforce it. They bounced back but then slowly girls started complaining about getting pay, and it was all downhill from there. I also used Phone Encounters for a bit, but to me, it felt like a cheap version of Niteflirt with little to no benefits.

As you can see, there are many options and sites. I did not want to suggest just the ones I use as again, everyone has a different path. I want you to choose what will do well for you. That said though, you need to be wise and not overwhelm yourself. If you are spread too thin across many different platforms, you will see that you are not doing as well as you will have hoped. It is far better to choose maybe two different ones to get started on and familiar with and then expand from there. You surely do not want all your eggs in one basket but if you have too many baskets to keep track of, you will surely lose track of them.

Chapter 7 – Blogging

Nope, you are NOT getting away without a blog in this day in age, and WordPress is the way to go! It is simple to use and easy to understand. You can easily get just about any hosting company to install it for free (remember you are paying this company a monthly fee. Thus they should be willing to install a simple script for you for free). There are free themes you can use, again easy to install. If you need help, I highly suggest you get with DevilishTemplates.com who has a fantastic course to show you how to set it up. (Yes this a paid course and no I get to profit from you purchasing it). You can also find countless youtube videos that will walk you through it, which is your free option. I don't know about you, but I have a Ph.D. in youtube University (for things like this).

Your First Posts

Once your blog is installed and you picked a free theme (you can pay for a custom one later, or customize it yourself if you know how), get AT LEAST 10 blog posts up with AT LEAST 1000 words per post up. You also want at least one photo per post, though in this day in age I would suggest more. The image needs to be named based on a keyword, this helps the image show up in Google image search and help give you relevance in search engines (also called SEO – search engine optimization). These small boosts do add up over time in the search engines, and it is best to start it now rather than have to go back and do this all later. To change the name of an image, right click on it and then type in the name you desire. If you are doing a lot of flogging content, you may want to write female-floggger.jpg as the name. What is a JPG? Good question, I have never bothered to learn the answer to this. BUT JPG, PNG and GIF tend to be the file types that will go on your blog for images. GIFs are the images that move like a small movie clip. JPG is the most common static image type and PNG tends to be images with a transparent background. For now you really do not need PNGS unless you are doing some fancy design work in photoshop… which is not what we are covering in this chapter nor needed when you are first starting out.

So why 10 blog posts? You want content for someone to stumble upon, and you want to add it now. If you start posting too much after you get a clientele built up, people will get tired of notifications. Also, not having much on your website gives the air of you being new and not knowing what you're doing. SHSS! I know, that part is true but no one has to know it right now! The fake it till you make it adage totally comes into play here.

Now those posts need to be R E L E V A N T. I would make them all on the same topic or two and no more than three topics total to start. You will want the topics to be complimentary of each other too. If you want to attract cuckolding calls, make them all cuckolding blog posts. This again also gives you more relevance in the search engines. You also want to put something to buy if you are going to build offline sales… and if you are following my methods YOU ARE! This means you can make sales and build interest while you sleep, shop, eat and otherwise have a life. You are making a machine and this is your first cog. A real machine is built slowly, well and no shortcuts are taken. I do suggest getting a big BUY NOW button, and you can find those on most free image websites. If you don't find one you like to head over to Canva.com. I use that site frequently to make my social media graphics and graphics for my blog. They have the perfect sizing and lots of free elements you can use. They do have paid items too but you can seriously make very professional and absolutely gorgeous graphics without spending a dime.

Once you have these foundational posts, download and install the WordPress plugin for an editorial calendar. This is strictly for yourself, but it will help you plan out content. I suggest updating your blog AT LEAST 3 times a week, especially in the beginning. You can update daily, but I know many who can not keep up that pace long term, at least by themselves. An editorial calendar allows you to store ideas as they crop up, and then plan out what day the post should come out. I find that it also helps to keep me on track. Sort of like a deadline from an instructor, it is hard to log in check comments and not see that your post coming up due but still needs work. This plugin will only be shown in your admin panel, with visitors unable to see it. It lays out a calendar in which you can put post titles that you believe you will be posting. You can then click on and begin to work on them. What I really like about this, is I can see a layout of the type of content I will have coming out in the upcoming month.

Before I started using editorial calendars, I would often write about the exact same topics over and over again. I would then jump to a non-complimentary topic for a few posts and if you read my blog from beginning to end... it was just all over the place or as I like to say, a hot mess. Using an editorial calendar helped to not only streamline my website but also keep my creative process flowing. Once a week, I sit down and come out with a ton of ideas. I can then organize the ideas onto which day they should come out. When I get inspired on a call or during a chat session, I can then go to my website and leave a quick note so that I can incorporate it into my blog. This is my idea Head Quarters. My blog posts help me push my content and thus helps me decide what content is coming out. My content is what I become known for and thus attracts the type of clients I obtain. My clients then help inspire me in my future content and thus is the circle of life of content creation. This is why organizing this portion of your business is extremely important from the beginning.

Can you make this all work without the WordPress plugin? Yes, yes you can. I know many people who have an editorial calendar that is not digital. Many people work better when they can write out their ideas, rather than type everything out. If this is true of you, you can do this for sure but no matter what method you use, make sure it is something you will stick with. Alternatively, you can go the route of Savvy Sex Social. I love this site so much for the marketing tips, BUT we are not talking about that right now. The creator of this website organized her content into three categories and would post three times a week with on post on each of the categories. This is a great way to remember what you are meant to be talking about for that specific day. So, you don't need an editorial calendar then, right? Sadly, no you still need it. Even if you pick three topics and only post about that topic for that day, what if you forget that 4 weeks ago you wrote about the exact same topic on that subject? All it takes is about once a month to plan out your content, and if you use an editorial calendar, you can easily reference the previous few months and make sure you are not repeating too much content.

I want to make one more case for using an editorial calendar, and then I promise I will move on. This is again for promotional reasons! Every fetish or niche you get into will have a million sub-topics that you can talk about. If you decide to write about electro play, it could be broken up into soo many different subjects:

- Do's and Don'ts of Electro Play

- Electro Play for Beginners

- Best Toys for Advanced Electro Play

- Fun Electro Play Games for Beginners

- How I Got Into Electro Play

- Myths of Electro Play

- Funniest Electro Play Fail Stories

- Sexy Electro Play Stories

- Electro Play For Low Pain Tolerance

- First Orgasm with Electro Play

Ok, I will stop going on and on about electro play, but you can see how I easily came up with 10 ideas for posts just about this one idea. If you just try to wing it, I have found that many creators find that over time, they will sit down to write and draw a blank. They sit there for a while and then decide to do something else until they can think of inspiration. If you just take the time to plan out your content in advance though, you will find that those blocks will be easier to overcome if they even come at all. Editors for newspapers, magazines and other major publications use the same process, hell it is even why it is called an editorial calendar!

Working Efficiently

Working efficiently is working in batches. When I sit down to do blog posts, I do NOTHING but blog posts. I do not make the graphics for that post, I do not plan out the next post... I just WRITE till I have hit my goal for however many blog posts I needed to get done that day. Of course, I plan out my posts, but when I am planning, all I do is PLAN! When you are working on your blog, honestly do nothing but that. No matter what platform you use for billing, you will want a blog to showcase your knowledge in your fetishes but also it is a piece of you. Your blog is not just for talking about your latest clips but look at the greats like Ceara Lynch. A real breakout star in the online Domination/Cam/Phone Sex industry, her blog not only talks about the latest items she has for purchase but also is an intimate look at her life. I have only been blessed to chat with her briefly on the since defunct yahoo messenger (yes it still exists, but I hate it and won't go back... like many other users). Seriously, she has become a symbol in this industry and a quasi-celebrity, and I like to believe a good part of this is due to her not just using her blog as a way to push her merchandise. Make sure to mix stories about yourself/character with what you are selling. It will make getting to that 1000 word minimum seem a lot easier.

Along with efficiency, you need to have consistency. EVERY single Monday, I do my blog posts. (WARNING: On my main character site, this is no longer true since I started working on my books and radio show, BUT when phone sex was my bread and butter the following and above was ALL TRUE). I take Sunday to plan out my week in accordance to my goals and on Monday I begin the process of execution. I work my job like it is just that… a job. For 8 hours, I get blog posts done, and if I have spare time, I tackle some of the stuff I have wanted to get done that wasn't a priority. I highly suggest you do the same thing, plan out a designated date and time to get your blog posts done. Blogging, especially over time, can become tedious and something you do not wish to do. Nevertheless, though, it is essential to your marketing plan.

Even if you follow my blogs, you can see periods of inconsistency. What I can tell you during those times, my income and new customer acquisition suffered. Now usually, it means I have something else I am focusing on but trust that I do know that it will cause a dip in my income from phone sex. When I worked this full time, and it was my sole income, my blog was on point down to the minute in which the posts would come out. The reasoning behind this is simple psychology. Much like a person's favorite TV show, you want to have your blogs coming out at the same time roughly. Notifications are great, but sometimes they screw up. People I follow tend to have a pretty rigid schedule of when their content comes out. A good example is Savvy Sexy Social (yup that name came back up again!) comes out with a new youtube video 3 days a week (I do believe the host recently bumped that up recently, but for the sake of this discussion, we will talk about her old scheduel) and I know that because Amy promotes the fact she does, and it follows her name. The three S's each had a day in which the content would come out and a theme of what topics would be covered. The best way to ensure success is to follow those who have been successful before you. Find a schedule that fits you and follow it. You can post once a week (make that post fucking epic then!) or even every day. If you want to post super frequently though, start out slow and ramp up to what you believe you can do. If we look back at the example of Savvy Sexy Social, it would seem the creator (Amy) has increased her posts but it took her two years to commit to this.

Some say that making sure to have your blog posts come out on Fridays especially increases sales, as that is traditional payday. Also, have blog posts come out on the 1st and the 15th! I have heard theories of having posts come out on Thursdays because people will get their notification emails on Fridays, thus you being the first person they spend money on… I can continue on but will stop this crazy train here. There is literally no magic day or time that you can post to ensure that you get maximum eyes on your content. Those who were consistent and created quality posts are the ones who get the most conversions between new viewers to new customers. Making sure that your posts are properly marketed means more than trying to find the right day. There are so many factors that create a successful blog but trying to guess the best day before you actually have an audience is just that, guesswork.

Guest Posting

Guest posting/blogging can also help you get known in your area, and by letting others guest post on your blog, you can get free updates! Guest posting is exactly what it sounds like; you allow someone to post onto your blog and in turn, they get to put their links on their site back. I have used guest posting to collaborate and to grow my audiences on several occasions. Now you do have to have some knowledge in the area that you are going to write a post on. Throwing something together will be

Amberly Rothfield – How I Made $10,000 A Month as A Phone Sex Operator

way too obvious and will only result in you NOT getting the guest posting spot but possibly having a bridge burned. I told you… don't burn bridges. Instead, be upfront that you are newer but offer to write a blog post on something you do know about. You will be surprised by the amount sexual topics you can write about without having been in the business for a long time. Offer to write an erotic story around a popular topic for that site! Many sites will even pay you for writing the guest piece, as again you are updating their website for them. Think about it, these website owners need quality content for their site and want to have as close to daily updates as they can get. They also can not keep up with that pace plus get all the marketing they need to be done accomplished. If a daily update makes you a few hundred dollars, is it not worth it to give a link out to someone and pay them for helping you keep your site updated? This sort of deal is nothing but wins all the way around.

Still scared about approaching a website owner about doing a blog for them? A really cool fact about the adult industry, while profits are big, those working in the adult sector is truly few. Most of us who are vets LOVE helping new people as there are so few in the adult industry. BUT AMBERLY!!!?! That is creating COMPETITION! In a way, yes but a rising wind fills all sails. The more of us that there is who are actually working hard means the further the industry can go. With so many fly by nights, most blog owners will be impressed that you took the initiative to actually contact them. I know several webmasters who have worked deals with newer guest posters. Usually, the guest poster will write on an agreed upon the topic in a fictional format and then have it critiqued by the webmaster. After any tweaks that would be needed are then done, and the post goes live. Do not be afraid to tell people that you are new and do not let being new stop you from approaching people. Remember, for many website owners, you are actually HELPING them with the content. If you cannot think about what to write about, most will actually tell you what they are looking for. The worst that someone will say is no and even then, they probably will just not respond.

So why should you let others guest post on your blog? Well, the theory of reciprocity is a real thing. If you give someone good will by allowing them to blog for you, they are more likely to let you blog for them. I absolutely accept every request that is reasonable. I do not care if someone has little traffic or massive amounts that they can send to me. Networking is a super important thing, and you NEVER know who will actually take off. Helping someone today could gain you a valuable ally and friend later on down the road. It also allows you to quickly update your blog without extra effort for you! Collaborations lead to more partnerships and funnily enough if someone sees you are open to collaborating with others you will find you get more opportunities arising. I even suggest having a page on your blog so that people can contact you for just that!

I do want to touch on a reasonable request though. Certain websites of mine have certain rules on what can be posted. My Niteflirt compliant website can only discuss topics that Niteflirt deems ok and I can not link out to any of Niteflirt's competitiors. So if someone wants to write an article for that website and link to their Clips4Sale page... that is a no go. Similar if they want to talk about adult baby. If I were to post that article, I would risk my Niteflirt account at the worst and at the least having my listings suspended until I delinked the site or removed the article. Can you imagine saying YES to the article and then having to yank it? What is that smell in the air? Burning... bridges burning. I have also had people submit articles to me that were maybe 100 words long... while my articles are typically 500 at the very least. It is ultimately up to you as to what seems reasonable for you to accept but if you are submitting to others, try to get a feel for what they typically post and tailor your post to their style.

Importance of Constant Updating – Make Search Engines Love You

Why is updating your blog each time you can with quality content relevant? Google's algorithm and many other search engines take into account how often a website is updated. If you do not update frequently, search engines will believe your information could be out of date and will not put your links as high. In this age of information, having the most current information is pivotal. Whether you have others guest blog or are updating your blog, I would suggest having at least 3 blog posts done a week at a minimum.

While it is important to list things you have for sale and other ways your audience can support you; your blog posts should also be of your character/persona. Need some ideas on how to incorporate your character and add personality to your brand? Talk about birthdays, parties and even just how you chill at home. You may not believe it, but many customers WANT to know this stuff. They want to connect with a person, not just call to quickly get off. Yes, I know some DO call for a quick sexual call, but most readers/callers really want to connect with someone. Build the fantasy of your character, create a scene and a world for your customers to get swept off too and your repeat customers will continually return. Personally, I try to keep it as real as I can. While not putting any information that is too personal for you know… stalker reasons, let your amazing and authentic personality shine through. **PRO TIP – Feeling sick? This is a perfect place to also announce this!** If my voice is out, I always blog! It shows that we get sick and gives me another way to connect with my clients. Talk about the latest Netflix series you are watching or even places you dream of visiting. I actually had a reader send me a Travelocity gift card to go to New York City when I mentioned wanting to go again. Trust me, when I was writing that blog post I was NOT thinking I would get someone to pay for it! Another time I was talking about looking at trading in my car, a reader not only suggested to me on how to haggle the price of my new car but also sent me $800 towards my down payment. Wasn't the entire amount needed but it went a long way and was not expected.

Back to the point of constantly updating though! When people type into a search engine, they are entering keywords to which search engines will try to match up their request with the best sites they believe will match it. Making your website fit that criteria is a process called search engine optimization, to which we will get into in a later chapter but I do want to talk about this one aspect here, since this chapter is about blogging. Blogs became a popular way of creating a website because the software made it very simple for one to update a website without having to constantly have to go into the coding of the site and upload a new page each and every single time. When I first started, you could update your blog once or twice a month and still get crazy traffic but in 2015+, more and more people started blogs and competition has gotten fierce. With more people blogging and information coming at us faster, this means you have to keep up with the times. Information becomes more and more outdated at more rapid rates. This means you must be committed to ensure your blog will be as update to date as it can be at all times.

Commerical Blogging vs. Diaries

Remember though, this is not entirely a diary. This is a commercial website created with the intention of converting people into customers. Make sure to incorporate reminders on how to contact you, call you and buy anything you have to sell. Watch the great Youtube channels in which it is one personality/person and not a corporate run channel. You will see a trend, they all remind their viewers to subscribe to them, drop a comment, share their content and support them via different methods. You should be doing similar. Need some names? Jenna Marbles, Casey Niestat, Shawn Dawson or Trisha Paytas. You do not need to copy their formats, but you will see how they always make it clear where you can find them! Put your payment buttons there, remind customers if they can tip/tribute/donate to you.

Talk about your schedule this week and what type of calls you really love. These are called **"call to action"** moments. Creating a call to action will get your audience to do what you would desire for them too. If you do not ask, people often times won't know/remember what to do. No seriously, people can come to a phone sex website and not realize that you do want them to call. That is why BUY NOW and CALL NOW buttons are super important. Have an item that sales very well? Put a BUY NOW directing people to that article, FRONT, and CENTER!

Within each blog post, try to refer to a past blog post and link it. Why? Simple! This will make people stay on your website longer as they will click to go to that post, which is another critical Google metric. It also builds the relevancy of that page up quite a bit, which is also a Google metric for ranking your website. Linking to past content also signals to your reader that you speak on such topics often. If it is a subject of interest to them, this shows them that you are more of an authority on the subject matter. I know I personally have combed through websites after searching a topic on Google and finding they wrote tons of digestible articles on the subject. After spending 10 minutes on a site, I usually end up bookmarking it and coming back over and over, especially if they update frequently. This also allows for more of your previous BUY NOW buttons to be seen as well. There is actually a name for this phenomnia called 'blackholing'. YOU KNOW you have done this! You start on one topic and then just keep following suggested sites/topics. I find that this happens to me more often on Youtube than on any other site. I will start on a video about a new eyeshadow palette and will end up on some true crime documentary about an hour later. You can create this same effect on your blog by linking to other articles within your website or posts of friends.

Awesome Graphics For Your Blog

Your blog also needs tons of high-quality photos. How would this be defined? An image with high resolution and relatively large typically draws eyes better. 10 years ago when I started, you could use just about any photo as your blog post image... those days are gone. Now that regular cell phones have decent enough cameras on them, the bar is set higher. I know that many who read this will not be able to use images of themselves though. When purchasing photos, just try to look at the preview photos. Older photos will not have the most current aspect ratios and may seem grainy. Also, try to stay away from photos that have very dated styles too them. I know some photos I once bought clearly scream 1990s now! Dated photos mean that in 7 years or so, everyone will know that those photos are old and for some that can be a turn-off. Most guys will not care about your photos, but something that clearly breaks the fantasy will make it harder to ignore that you are not the girl in the photos. I suggest that any photo you use, have relevant text on it and some sort of style that is yours This is often called water marking. I tend to like clean lines and deeply outlined images, as an example. I will go into finding right content photos to use in another chapter, BUT I will touch on how to ensure your photos will look good here.

Canva.com (nope not getting a cent for mentioning them), is a fantastic website and for the most part free. Even if you are not photo editing savvy, you can figure out how to use this site. It seriously is nothing but drag and drop. They always update on the best image sizes for the projects you are going to create, which is pretty sweet. I have done basic to intermediate photo editing for 10 years but still, find their site to be excellent. First off, again, it is FREE! They also have legal content you can use (though they are not my primary source as you cannot reuse whatever you buy but the once) and they have premade templates that are also free and eye-catching. If you are not a branding genius, this is a great place to start. You can also save your creation so you can make minor tweaks later. This saves soo much time as you can change out the background and text and BAM have your new photo ready to download. You can save multiple templates for free as well. I have one for facebook posts, twitter and blog posts. Ads and beautiful images, I typically just make in Photoshop, but you can also do so in canva as well.

Other people swear by PicMonkey. I honestly have never used the service with any seriousness, but in the interest of providing you with the best information I can, I did check out the website. This is how it compares to Canva:

- It has a free trial, but honestly, Canva has more free elements that are… free forever. (At least as of this writing).
- While PicMonkey has quite a few more bells and whistles when it comes to editing, it doesn't seem to be too much different than Canva.
- PicMonkey also has a cap on how much storage you have for images while I have abused my Canva account regarding storage and still have room.

Could Canva change to a model with no free account? They sure could but for now, they are free, and I suggest them. Again, I am a bootstrapper at heart, why pay now if there are easy alternatives? If you decide that PicMonkey works better for you, trust me no judgment. It is a lot cheaper than buying PhotoShop or PaintShopPro for sure!

Click Bait

Click bait… this has to be addressed, and I did try to put this off as long as I can. There are definitely two schools of thoughts here; click bait is the scum of the Earth and clicks bait is necessary. Yup, that is pretty much how it goes. We have all been affected by this, and truly it is going nowhere. Everyone knows it is a cheap way to get views onto your content. Since everyone looks down upon those who do it, you would think that everyone would stop because of public pressure right? WRONG! It just means more people do it, to the point we are at now... you basically can not get away from it. Those who do not utilize it, have a much harder time to climb to the top.

The real question is WHY does click bait work? The answer is relatively simple, in that it plays with the inner workings of our mind and is purely psychological. We want to read about the tantalizing and insane things out there. We are naturally drawn to those sensational headlines over the humdrum ones and yes, even within the adult industry some things become repetitive. **This means you have to find a way to stand out with your titles in a way that is eye-catching**, which many will say is click bait. (See what I did there?). At the end of the day, you have to decide if that is something you can deal with or not. By deal with, I mean that people will talk about you on blogs/social media and not in such a positive way. Personally, if you are not adding to my pocketbook, I do not worry about it too much. Top brass in every industry are doing it, and they are focusing more on their bottom line rather than gossiping about what others are doing.

If you choose to do click bait, your titles need to have your keyword in it and within the first five words but need to be sensationalized. Now please be careful with this and make sure to follow your payment processor/companies rules. If your titles go too crazy, you are asking for your processor to come through and ban you. You also want to make sure that the content of your article is within the purview of the title. If you title an article about public sex but write an article about financial domination only... you will not only get some raised eyebrows, but you will lose trust in your customers. Would you continue going to a store advertising half-off donuts but only selling earrings? Make sure your content covers what is said in the title and the title is just a slightly exaggerated version of the content.

Amberly Rothfield – How I Made $10,000 A Month as A Phone Sex Operator

Examples you ask? Let's say I wrote a blog post about ebony dominatrix breast worship; I would title that blog post as "Black Perfect Boobs | What your COCK CAN'T Handle!". The point of the post is clearly stated but just exaggerated a little. Warnings also work well too. Any of my customers can tell you about my click bait titled emails where I warn of even opening the email. Not in a threatening way, like saying they would get a computer virus or something of that nature but saying it is too hot to handle (or something of the ilk). Challenging titles also work very well too; like the example above. Questions are the next thing on the click bait checklist but NEVER make it a simple yes or no. The reason to never put a simple yes or no is that it is that... simple. Allow the reader to have to think about their answer, which will inevitably lead to them clicking and reading. If you need examples, look up anything that went viral for Buzzfeed or Huffington Post. I am not dogging them, but they both have risen to fame for their click bait titles. While there are countless of Youtube videos that denounce both of them, they both remain relevant and known.

If you never want to use clickbait to help push your content, it is not impossible but you will have a harder time than those that do. Use titles that are relevant for sure and do include keywords. For those who look down on clickbait, remember that writing titles with keywords and placing keywords within your posts is not considered clickbait. Clickbait is written to slightly mislead and create sensationalism. Now if an article is sensational, that means the title would then not be considered clickbait. Therefore, if you can always find a way to present your content in a sensual way that delivers, you are not using clickbait. Journalists often use this tactic and have for years. Keep it super relevant and it will not be considered clickbait.

Comments!

So you have topics, you have decided your stance on click bait, you are guesting posting/having guests post, photos are on point, and your schedule is set so what else is there? Next, is gardening your comments. If a comment comes in, <u>ANSWER IT!</u> Not spam comments no, if someone is putting a link in the link field unsolicited, I almost always delete them. Do use a bit of logic with this though. If someone is making a relevant comment but also linking back (do check links though, sometimes spam bots can leave what will look like a legitimate comment), let the comment ride and message back. If someone is leaving 3 words or saying 'nothing'... delete it and move on. If they say little to nothing but put no link, do let stay that and respond appropriately. I also have a plugin called Akismet that will purge a good majority of spam comments that come by before I even see them. If someone leaves a legitimate comment though? I am ALL OVER IT! Comments are coming from someone (usually) that is a fan. Even if they are just saying hello or this is great, go in and say how are you or thanks, how are you? I try to answer comments with more questions. This leads to more conversation and more opportunities for others to hop into the conversation. This is also another great way to get people to stay on your site, as they filter through the comments.

What do you do about hate comments though? I love the Youtuber Shane Dawson and his take on 'haters' is one I have had for a long time. Haters are nothing but fans in disguise. No one spends time on anything that they actually hate or dislike. If someone is taking the time to hate on you, they care about you in some way. You cause emotions within them. More importantly though, you will never get rid of them. They will always come back and most likely will comment on everything they can find of yours. The best thing to do is engage them too. Now I do not suggest showing any sort of negative emotion back though. Never give someone who hasn't paid properly, something that they seek. Just think about the times you have responded to someone online in a negative way. (come now... it is a thing 99.9% of us are guilty of and I know I have before). Did you not get some sort of satisfaction from seeing the other person come back at you in kind? The adage, kill them with kindness, is always the way to go when it comes to business. Ignoring them rarely will see the 'troll' move along, but sometimes get them to ramp up the efforts to get seen. When the trolls see that you are unphased, they will jet!

MAILING LISTS!!!

Always try to look for ways to bring customers back! One of the top ways is to create an email list. Sean Early of https://www.delivishtemplates.com mentioned in one of his courses on marketing about a plugin by Tribulent for newsletter creating/email list. Yes, you can use companies like MailChimp, as it is free, but they are very anti-adult. This means you will have a major issue being able to keep your mailing list. Again, I believe in bootstrapping, and I am suggesting something that isn't free. It is pricey though and for some may not be affordable when they are starting out. For that, I would recommend using Feedburner. It is 3rd party, which means it could be deleted as well but for now, they do not seem to care too much about adult vs. non-adult content. (Please note, Feedburner is owned by Google now and isn't an email newsletter service per say. It can be used as one though).

Before we go too much further on though when at an Exxxotica convention, I did find out about YNOT mailing list service. While Tribulent is a one time purchase, for the most part, YNOT is an ongoing paid service and is adult friendly. They are also pricey so I would say that you will want to build your audience first before you start using their service. They are about $39 a month on their first tier which allows 2500 emails a month. To break this down, that means you can email 2500 different email accounts once a month or you can email 1450 people twice a month (so on and so forth). I believe within three months, this will be the way you will want to go for sure, but in the beginning, I would suggest Feedburner. If you are using a Wordpress blog like I suggested, you can easily take your RSS feed and connect it to Feedburner and create a feed for people to sign up for via email. Feedburner will give you code to put on your WordPress site (there are also free WordPress plugins that will do this too) and then anyone who wants to can sign up!

What do email lists even do? They allow people to subscribe to you, so that every time you create a blog post/email to them, they will get a message to their inbox. This creates more repeat business, which is the foundation of every business. That does not mean you can add people to your list. This is actually considered against the law, and while you will probably not be prosecuted, it is considered spamming. Most individuals who did not sign up but received your email will click spam on it. If multiple people do this, then their mailing services will flag your messages for spam. Once this is achieved with all the major email services, well no one is really reading what you send. It is not just best practices but also will save you the futile effort of forcing people onto your list. If you are creating quality content, you will not need to stoop to this!

I can not honestly stress how important your email list is, especially if you are independent. If one places shut down or something happens, you will have a way to communicate to your customers and move them to the track where you will need them. Now back to Feedburner, it will be based on your RSS feed. Your RSS feed can be found on your blog. Their website walks you through how to set it up pretty quickly and trust I am very pleased that they over explain things. Once your feed is set up and a widget in your sidebar so that people can sign up, every time your email notification will go out there to them. Confused about feeds and widgets? Don't worry! Youtube University I send thee! There are several websites that better explain it and show you how to achieve these things. It all depends on the blog software you have installed. If it is WordPress, Feedburner's website can walk you through it quickly as it is the most popular.

Similar to FeedBurner, Tribulent's software allows for readers to sign up, but instead of a notification going out as soon as the RSS feed updates, it will only do so if you hit the email button on the back end of your blog, after you hit send. I love this as I can put a different tempting offer if you sign up for my emails; extra racier photos, extended podcasts or more suggestive blog posts that can not be found by going to my website directly (also called hidden content). In the blogging world, this is called creating an incentive. By putting an incentive for someone to sign up, you will have a larger email list (everyone loves FREE!) and thus more of a chance to convert your audience into paying customers. Make sure the incentive is **relevant** though or you will have people signing up who will never convert into paying customers. If you are doing an IPAD giveaway, everyone will sign up regardless if they are interested in what you have to say but few will actually convert. Will that really end up being worth it?

An excellent giveaway would be an mp3 voice sample or video clip or free minutes of talk time with you. These are things your clients are looking for but make sure to state that with free minutes, they do not stack with other offers (otherwise, they could continuously sign up and get unlimited free minutes with you). One huge incentive I have found is offering free voice or video samples to my mailing list but on my blog only having links to buy. This makes those who want to hear a sample HAVE to sign up for my newsletter. I like to update the clips that I give away for free too, so that those who decide to cancel their notifications will want to resign up when I announce a new set of freebies. Note, this may make your statistics look screwy in that people may 'unsubscribe' only to resubscribe frequently.

Amberly Rothfield – How I Made $10,000 A Month as A Phone Sex Operator

Another trick is to under promise and over deliver on the incentive. If you are offering one free mp3, give 2-4, etc.… This makes the recipient surprised and in the BEST way. Think of how many times you scored something extra and how that made you feel. If you are willing to go above and beyond before even connecting with this potential customer, what will you be willing to do when they do make direct contact? Similar, when I do mp3s and the like, I like to add extra minutes onto what they paid for or take a previous mp3 that is fairly similar and add it to their order when I deliver it. Remember, no matter your character, this is a business. An excellent real-time example of this is the company LUSH cosmetics. I LIVE for their bath bombs and EVERY order I make with them, they send additional samples of other products. It was so cool getting some freebies, but they also got me addicted to their other lines because of this. Do they send me just one free sample like Ulta? Nope! I get 4-5 little samples and the more I order from them (despite being a major company) they more they seem to send to me. People get excited by surprises, use psychology to your advantage. Better yet, show them that you are paying attention to their buying habits by sending them something you know they will love.

Blog Posts – Beyond The First Posts

Yup, I hear you, I know you are upset that I am talking about blog posts again but worse, this is so far down in this chapter AFTER the first blog posts section. Again there is a method to my madness! All of the other aspects are truly more important than the continuation of your blog outside of the first few posts. How can this be? Let's dive into that!

Everyone knows that as you do something, you get better. Those foundational posts will most likely not be the most groundbreaking pieces of journalism ever or New York Times-worthy. What they will do though, is give you something to push your initial audience too. To build from there though, you

Amberly Rothfield – How I Made $10,000 A Month as A Phone Sex Operator

must have some key elements to keep your website going. Your blog will prove to be a wonderful cash cow but also a cruel Mistress. If you serve it right, you will find that your business will easily grow but if you neglect it then you will watch as you struggle to capture new customers.

Once you have learned to create images for your blog with proper watermarks, have your Feedburner/mailing lists set up and have your social media profiles hooked up; you are ready to begin churning out more blog posts! Not just any blog posts though, these will be done a bit different from your intial posts. With social media, we no longer have depend on email blasts and blog posts to update the masses but that does not mean that blog posts are useless! This means that your blog posts need to become your long form of content. On Twitter, you can only post a ton of text by taking a screenshot of it all typed out and posting as an image and trying to read long-form content on Instagram is just mind-numbingly difficult! This is where your blog will shine!

Your beginning blogs will be about 1000 words, but I honestly challenge you to write at least 1500 words for at least one blog each week. Giving way too much content? Depends on how it is delivered. By breaking up your content with subtitles, as the reader scrolls, they will catch the topics they care about and read more into it. Within each subtitle, you want to place a piece of paid content as well. Be careful though, as you do not want 15 subtopics but about 5-7 max. If you are creating content every day, this should not be an issue. Remember you can also bundle older content as well!

What you will also want to start doing differently too is to place test subtitles. If you set yourself up to really push three different fetishes, then once a week try out another one. See how it does and I would place that piece of content at the top of the post! I would even make this well known, rather than try to sneak it on your customers. Do a new fetish highlight or revisiting a fetish you haven't in a while. Remember that if a piece of content doesn't work when you try it out, it does not mean the fetish is bad or that it is necessarily a bad fetish for you. It could just mean you need to tweak it in some way! This 'new thing' feature will not only expose your audience to something new but also allow you to grow to other fetishes that you may have once believed wasn't for you.

How do you position freebies without coming off cheap? Another once a week feature that I have seen others do well is to give out free snipbits of previous releases. While many of my releases tend to be over 30 minutes, I have been known to break them up into 5 minute pieces and toss them out as freebies. NO, I do not release all pieces and especially would not do them all at once. Simply tossing out a few here and there though, it really helps for my clients to want to come back! Often times, those who never would have purchased from me before, will listen to the freebie and after the mental snack... will go on to purchase 5-10 other files. Now, when I give out the freebie, I will also list all the other previous releases that I have out which are similar. BOOM! Instant sales and all I had to do was take previous content and snip it once in Audacity. Easy Peasy!

Over time, you will need to freshen up your website. Not just for freshness sake but safety. What I like about Wordpress is that the script will tell you when the latest update for all themes, plugins, and script itself. With simple clicks, the site will update and be more secure. When it comes to freshness though, you will need to swap out photos in headers and even site layout from time to time. Now, this can cost a fortune and when you are first starting out, paying $2000 for a custom website is just not needed. While I do suggest changing out your look 2-3 times a year, you can do this for free. Wordpress has a free marketplace to which you can find without your Wordpress panel. Simple just download a free theme and usually, if there are customizable options are available, there will be a new panel on your admin sidebar that will allow you to make the changes you wish. My advice, go for a minimalist website layout, that way you will not need to change much. Instead, your blog posts will hold the eye catching content and thus a fancy header will not be needed.

Lastly, you will want to pay attention to create pages on your blog. Pages are static, where as your blog post page will be updating based on your newest blog posts. On your pages, you will want to create an about page and products page at minimum. Your about page may seem self explainitory, but for many it is not! You want to not only talk about yourself but also list what type of fetishes that you cater to and how your clients can find you. Do not skimp on this page! I would put your contact info towards the top but the page needs to be at least 2000 words!

Your product page will need to be a list of all the sexy things your customers can buy from you. If you have a store on IWantClips or Clips4Sale or the like, you can also put the code here to show your offerings from those places there. I would for sure have this page though! I know the amazing Domme Mix Trix places the code for all her stores on her website and it really helps her out quite a bit.

Other pages you may consider are an FAQ (frequently asked questions), pages that discuss use of your favored plateform (I have a page explaining Niteflirt and how customers can get their free minutes by signing up to NF!) and Deals/Specials. When it comes to deals and specials, many will thumb their nose but really... it is something all major businesses use. With yet another holiday always around the corner, there is always a reason to have a special running. Also many websites that you can use to sell on have contests going, I like to list the ones I am in the running for there and how my customers can then help me hit those goals. Feel free to use all or none of those suggestions though. If you find a page that you feel is needed, feel free to tell me! I love hearing new ideas.

Chapter 8 – SEO aka Search Engine Optimization

There are entire volumes written on this subject. As ever-changing as the internet is, by the time this goes to print, so much will have changed. Since this book is meant more for those starting out and about some of the basics that seem to never change, those are the parts I will cover here ALONG WITH how it relates to our little pond of phone sex. If you wish for a more in-depth view of search engine optimization, I would suggest joining www.xbiz.com and check out their most excellent tutorials! They are frequently updated with the latest knowledge (which, as stated earlier, is seriously changing on what seems like a monthly basis).

Why is search engine optimization super important? It is FREE traffic to your website. We have all placed a keyword into Google and came up with a site that we then clicked on. You will not only want people to come to your site from search terms but will ultimately NEED IT! This free traffic is pure and straightforward, your website's life's blood. Otherwise, you are going to have to buy traffic, which is not bootstrapping and can be super expensive. Why would you want to pay when you can simply get it for free? There are tons of search engines outside of Google, Yahoo and Bing but those are the top three. Luckily for us, they all pretty much operate similarly.

So why do I call it the little world of phone sex? In the grand scheme of the internet, phone sex is a tiny part. Being a big fish in a small pond certainly has its benefits and here is a major secret to the success I have had, most in the industry DO NOT pay attention to SEO at all. Nope, they do not even try. I have spoken too many girls, and most claim they do not have the time but have plenty of time to complain about the industry dying. I am not kidding… I have watched girls complain in group chats but not have websites or doing anything to pull traffic to them. Remember, if you are reading this book then you want success, and that means studying.

Like any industry, there are constant changes that you have to be on top of. The best way, in this case, is to follow some gurus who do nothing BUT follow the changes. Before you just follow changes though you need to learn the basics. There have been many factors that do not seem to change as they do show that a website has quality, regardless of other changes that happen around. What I will be teaching is called white hat SEO.

Black Hat SEO

Before we get into white hat though, I want to take a minute and explain black hat SEO and why I would personally stay away from it. First off, no good comes from it... period. Blackhat SEO is basically bending or flat out breaking the rules that search engines set up and 'gaming' the system. Now I am all for figuring out an algorithm and using that knowledge to your advantage, but black hat SEO often causes people to lose ranking in the long run or be banned from all search results, regardless of relevancy to the subject matter. I can also tell you, this has happened to me. They are spammy tactics, and IF they work, it is only short term.

Back when I first used my own photos, my stage name was Veronica Vain; yes another porn star has since bought the domain, but if you use the way back machine, you will see my 19-year-old self there. Back then, there were websites where webmasters could offer links to their high page ranked sites (more on that in a minute) for pay or for links to your site. This meant that your site could have no relevancy to theirs whatsoever, but you could get massive benefits from it. Sound cool? IT WAS! Till it wasn't! Google released an update and banned a bunch of sites from search engines that had a bunch of links in from many of these places. Banned means exactly what it sounds like. No matter what you typed in, Google would not pull that website up in the search. You could type in the actual full website address

Amberly Rothfield – How I Made $10,000 A Month as A Phone Sex Operator

into the search bar, nothing would populate. The only way to get to the website would be to know it's exact address and place it into the address bar of a website. Who would have thought that someone working for Google could run into the free to see the site and see who was up to being naughty? (Sarcasm, I totally should have seen this coming, but I thought this was all ok!).

Once a search engine bans you, you basically have to get rid of the website and start again. There are some underhanded practices that you can use to get your site indexed by the search engines again but again... it is black hat and can blow up in your face as well. For me, it wasn't that big of a deal as I was making a temporary exit, but if it was bread and butter website (as it was for many who also had my same fate), it could be utterly disastrous.

Instantly, my site dropped in traffic as no one could search and find me. I had become affiliated with the military by then and wasn't interested in doing cam anymore, so I just moved to using legal content anyways. I let the website go and apparently someone bought it (no hard feelings, that girl is hot!). The lesson learned though? Do it all legit, and you won't have to worry about Google spanking you! If someone tries to convince you to do something that goes against the search engine rules, disregard them. There are many scammy networks out there that will claim they will do all of your SEO for you, but they use these deceptive practices.

White Hat SEO

First, you need to understand how search engines work. Search engines send out 'spiders' that crawl your website and pick up on your keywords, frequently used words and links. They then quantify this data and figure out how to rank your site compared to others using similar keywords.

Amberly Rothfield – How I Made $10,000 A Month as A Phone Sex Operator

How do websites get found by the search engines? There are a few ways to get discovered, but the most common are; having a connection on an already recognized website, submitting your site to the search engines or waiting for the spiders to just happen to find you. Can you guess which method takes the longest to get you to discovery? YUP, the last one. I would NOT suggest that, especially if it is a website that has not been previously owned.

Now not everyone knows someone who is willing to just link to them; I know when I started out it was that way. I can tell you that if you submit your site to me (just leave a comment on www.moneyovermen.com) and you are active, I am totally willing to shout you out for that reason alone. (WARNING – if your website is under construction or spammy, no I won't… Put effort into it and follow the methods in this book though and I totally will! Also be a doll, do not just comment and say I WANT A LINK… read the blog post you are commenting on and join in the conversation or start one about the topic.). If waiting on senpai to notice you don't happen to be your thing, there are many sites called link dumps. **NOW LISTEN CLOSE**! I ONLY use these websites to help me get discovered. Search engines do not like seeing you listed on a ton of these as it can seem you are trying to game the system. I literally use a different link dump each time I create a website. Once I have a certain amount of posts, I will then go and drop my link in a link dump. You can always find a new one so I would suggest just googling one and try to find one within your topic of interest. That is often a tall order; however, well worth a look. If you do not find one that matches your exact keywords, don't worry! Just use another one that is at least within the adult industry. Link dumps are just websites that list whatever site has been most recently been submitted. You do not want too many links from 'dump' like websites though, as search engines do not like them. Their spiders do comb their sites frequently though, and thus one link on one site will get you indexed in the search engines.

Within WordPress, because I know you are using WordPress, the settings tab will allow you to place a title on your website as well as keywords. Make the title have your top 5 keywords in a real sentence. If you just 'keyword stuff' then search engines will not be too happy with you. Keyword stuffing is when you just make a nonsense sentence to get your keywords in there. I know it sounds crazy that computers actually can pick up on this now but I am editing this book with Grammarly, which does basically that! No seriously, it keeps telling me I am overusing certain words. If this simple technology can catch this, trust that these multimillion dollar search engine companies can and have been too! Don't test Google and just make a real sounding sentence. With your keyword section, put in only about 10 -15 keywords. The amount that each individual search engine will accept has fluctuated a bit over time, but 10 has been a pretty safe number. You can tweak these at any time, but I wouldn't suggest tweaking too much in a three month period. I personally revamp mine at least twice a year, but if you are new, I would check in and redo them once every quarter. Found your lane in this industry? Change them immediately to reflect that!

Since you are also using Wordpress, there is a free plugin called SEO Yoast. SOO many of the leading SEO bloggers and experts swear by this plugin and I can not tell you how simple and easy it is. It will help you keep your blog posts very search engine friendly and it will hold your hand and tell you exactly what information you need to add to every single post and page! This plugin is needed!

Another awesome plugin is that of the Google Sitemaps. This will assist spiders in documenting pages that you feel are important on your site. Once you begin to have popular content, you can direct the search engines to check those pages first and foremost, which can help you with ranking. While it is not a guaranteed way to ensure the search engines will favor that one page, it does give you a higher boost. It also helps spiders find every bit of your website. Best part of this plugin? It is free and in the wordpress databank for instant download and install.

I touched on making sure your images are named after keywords too. This is super important as it can land you some serious google image search traffic. You can also put a tag name and keywords on your images when you insert them into your blog posts. I would again make sure the keywords are relevant to your article. You can also put in descriptions as well, though I usually do not in my current blog. Reason being, I am established and have been so for years. If I were BRAND new, I totally would though. DO NOT keyword stuff though. Unless they are asking for keywords, I will make actual sentences, just as the search engines intend. You can also make various sizes for each image as well, for the different places you may post them. Make sure to mix up the keywords used for each images. This will enable you to cast a wider net and gaining you more of an ability to catch more potential customers.

Making your images have keywords in their name also helps you when you post those images to social media. This is how most search engines, as of current, look at this situation. For Google, the most used search engine, it is especially true that social media engagements (likes, comments, and shares) are highly taken into account when it comes to search results. Now Google, unlike other engines, has really cracked down on showing adult related links. Gone are the days of typing in Bambi and getting porn scenes, but rather quotes from the Disney movie. So when naming your images, make sure to name them relevant fetishes or specialties you are going for. Results from "size 7-foot fetish" will produce feet porn type links. Back to social media and your images though! If your image is named "size 7-foot fetish" and you post that image to your blog and then your social media sites, and it gets engagements then it will rank higher than that of others posting similar content. When people search for that phrase, you will get more people finding you.

Wait, why is this true though? The term is called social proof. If you are known for foot fetish content, then surely you will have fans who will like, comment and retweet (on platforms that allow for 'negative' reactions, they still count towards your social proof! All engagement is good). Your content is not really held up to all of those on the platform but all of those who are making content based on that topic you are talking about. So, if you are selecting smaller niches (like size 7-foot fetish vs. foot fetish) and gaining smaller amounts of engagement, you can still be positioned at the top of those searches. This will get those interested in said content to begin following you and engaging! As you grow, you can begin to cut into the larger audience pools and be ranked higher and higher. This is how 'overnight' successes are found. None are truly overnight, but rather they appear in larger keyword searches seemingly out of nowhere.

I want to show how quickly this can actually happen! I have personally helped many of my friends with their Instagram accounts. (Please note I will go in-depth on the different mainstream social media networks in a later chapter, this is more just an illustration of what can be done). Focusing on four keywords each, they would post daily for those four keywords. That is four posts daily. Starting with no following whatsoever, they each found they had over 200 followers within the first week. Followers though, doesn't necessarily translate into engagement though. There are many people with over a million followers but not even a 10th of those following them engage. Following my advice though, each off them had over 30% engagement on the content they put out! This means people are seeing it and each 'view' or like will mean more will see it because their content is steadily ranking higher and higher! People will find you via google searches for images, so make sure you put your best foot forward (pun intended) and name your images appropriately!

Perfecting Your Posts!

When you write your posts, make sure to use headline tags. Think of it as breaking up your post into sub-topics. If you have trouble imaging this, think back to school and creating outlines for papers. Come up with a title and then create a simple outline for the post. Follow the outline and fill in each tabbed area with sentences. BOOM! The blog post is done! If only it were that simple though. You need to work in keywords for what you are targeting into your posts! (I hate that I have to repeat this but it is super important, do not keyword stuff! If you have to force it in, you are doing it wrong).

Having your keywords spread throughout the various headline tags shows that this article is on this particular subject, thus helping it rank higher for that keyword. If your title is "Anal Play is An Ok!" then your h1 (also known as header one) tag could easily be "Why I Love Anal Sex" and then your H2 (header 2, smaller font than h1 tags) "The History of Anal Play" etc. I suggest using 3-4 head tags per post that you actually want to rank. Under each tab, you need about 2-3 paragraphs of normal paragraph text. Make sure to again, not to keyword stuff. I know I have stressed this throughout the last chapter and now again but honestly, doing so is readily detectable by the search engines and makes for sentences that seem strange. You will be repelling not only the search engines but also your audiences. Have you ever read an article that just did not seem to have natural text? No, I do not mean that it would seem the author speaks a different language as their first language but rather that someone is trying to push a certain set of terms on you? I know one industry that likes to do this is the diet/supplement industries. Their websites just seem like a text version of a sleezy car salesman. This will not invoke trust in your readers and will not grow your audience. More importantly though - **YOU CAN EVEN GET BANNED FROM SEARCH ENGINES FOR THIS**. It is considered black hat SEO.

Categories are an excellent way to group your posts together as well. Create a group for each topic you desire to talk about frequently. DO NOT stick a post in that category unless it actually talks about that issue and more than just briefly. I say this not for SEO reasons PER SAY but also because someone will read that post and be upset that it had nothing to do with what they were looking for, thus exiting your website and that itself can hurt you in search engine results. Google loves seeing that people interact and stay on your site, it must mean you are quality right? So doing anything that might make someone leave, can hurt your site's rankings. Make it enjoyable and make it relevant, then you should be golden. Google also likes to rank your category feed page. See in Wordpress, when you create a category, a link is then generated that will show ONLY those posts that have been added to that category. So then, when Google indexes that link, you have the potential of those looking for that content finding a prefiltered page of only that type of content. How awesome is that?

Tags are similar to categories, and I would totally do the same here. Make sure to tag your posts appropriately to the content you are writing about. Several plugins allow you to put links to your tags in your sidebar (if your blog has one), and I would suggest using it. It can make navigating your site so much easier and even draw attention to those tags more. Many times, even myself, website visitors are on your site for ONE thing only. If you make it easy for them to find, they will come back again. If you seem that you are not relevant for that which they searched for, they will move on to another website that satisfies them. I personally prefer the tag cloud plugins as the tags that are used more often are put in a larger font, therefore more eye-catching. Signaling to your blog readers that you write on those topics often and are more of an authority figure in that area. This isn't a must, but I personally find value in it as it seems to catch the eye better. Also, tags tend to tell everything that is in a post, not just the main topics (like categories).

To Link or Not To Link.

When considering putting links in your sidebar to other websites, think about where your website visitors will be going. Sending others traffic should have some benefit to you, and you do not want a ton of links that will take your audience off your site. Linking outside of your site is called a traffic leak. While not all leaks are bad, you do want no more than absolutely needed. As an example, I link to my Amazon wishlist on my blog. That can be considered a traffic leak as someone may go there and then not come back to my website. Most likely though, those clicking on it are going to my personal wishlist to see what I have on it, to send me a gift. I am still winning in this case! I also have links to the various things that my clients can buy, again takes them to another website but that website is selling my wares. Those are not considered bad leaks at all.

An example of a bad leak is a link that leads to someplace that doesn't necessarily help you. Why is that relevant to search engine optimization? Every site you links too is deemed more relevant to the topics you discuss. Why else would you encourage your audience to go to them? That is exactly what the search engines think. Not only do you risk losing your traffic to that link but linking too much tells search engines that maybe you aren't so important since you link to that many sources. Suffice it to say, if you are linking out to a website that you are not directly benefitting from, think of the why and if you should. I link to a few friends whom I do not mind sharing traffic with and share back with me, but I will limit the number of people who will get links to my sites. I will also link to relevant websites for resources. The keyword there is, **Relevant!**

How many links are too many? This question honestly can not be answered with generalities. Just as your links out to people signals to Google that they are another source for this type of content, you also want links to your website. You have to find a favorable balance of linking out to relevant

Amberly Rothfield – How I Made $10,000 A Month as A Phone Sex Operator

sources and also garnering links to your site. This is not a simple one for one equation. If the link benefits you, place it. It will take time for others to want to begin to link to you. Try not to stress this too much BUT keep in mind whenever you are placing a link to another website; whether or not, this benefits you. Remember, if you have to force it, you are doing it wrong.

Not all links are created equal though! There are 'follow' links and 'don't follow.' The difference is in the coding of the page, and it tells the search engine spiders whether or not you truly endorse the link. When people link to reference material to help back up their claims, they often use do follow links. This is because they want to let the search engines know that this is a natural link, placed to help you prove you're points. No, follow links tend to be links that go to ads or links paid for you to place. Yup, you read that right. People do pay for links in blog posts or on sidebars. No follow does allow for people to click and go to the link, but it tells the search engines that you do not want to be truly affiliated with that website. See, search engines are not against you placing a link that someone paid for you to do so, but they want you to disclose this so that they know that the content of that website may not be relevant to what you write about.

Follow, and no follow links are just one part of the equation though. Where links are placed also have a significant impact on your site and the sites to which you are linking too. See, in a single blog post, I am not too worried about what I am linking too (though I do follow the no follow – do follow the rules for obvious reasons). See, posts are a single page and thus the links are only found on one page. Whereas, links in your sidebar, header and footer will appear on all pages. This means every new page added to your site, will generate another link to whatever you are linking too and thus more juice for those links in the search engines. Links in my sidebar, header and footer are given extra scrutiny as to whether or not I will give them a Do Follow or No Follow attribute in the code.

Amberly Rothfield – How I Made $10,000 A Month as A Phone Sex Operator

Now that most of your on-site basic SEO has been checked off, it is time to build links to your website. If you are following me, you have done your SINGLE/ONLY ONE time link dump to get your site discovered. I will cover in depth how to use social media to build your phone sex audience in a later chapter, but for now, I will show you how to use social media for SEO purposes. Social media has been recognized by search engines to show relevancy. If people are engaging with you, you have a link to your website in your profile or people are sharing your content, chances are … you are… RELEVANT. If you are sick of that word by now, I am sorry, but it is what search engines actually care about.

I suggest making a profile on each platform that is out there, even if you do not use that platform. The reason is for branding reasons and to prevent someone trying to copy you. A friend of mine named GradeAUnderA (a massive youtuber) had someone create a profile in his name when he started getting familiar. The issue here is that he then couldn't make that profile later when he needed it to promote his wares. He had to use a name that was similar but clearly not his.

Why would someone do this? Some people will be fooled, thinking they are supporting the person they have grown to like, but instead are paying an imposter. To prevent these types of scams, make your profiles as soon as you can and write down the login information for later. I check in on my real profiles at least once a month and have links directing them to my website and stating that the profile is inactive for now. Think that is doing too much? I have a Rude.com account, and after years of being inactive, I went to check in. I had a few clips listed for sale but never got any payouts. I found out WHY! Someone had gotten into my account and turned off sale notifications and then spent all the money that came in each month! Over the years, they got thousands of dollars of free porn off my back and access to all my wares on that account. No, I did not go after Rude as it was my fault. I chalked it up to a lesson learned. (I had never been too active on that website hence why I never checked back in. I never thought that profile would get any traction).

How do you get people to share your content? Earlier, I spoke of calls to action and telling your audience what you desire them to do. Well, there is a realization you must come to when it comes to sharing adult links... few will. Most people have social media profiles so that they can interact with their friends and family. Few will be willing to share your content and show everyone what they spank off too. Now there are PLENTY of people who do 'follow' adult accounts. I put air quotes as they do not directly follow those they know of, but rather know their profiles and manually go back to the account rather than following/bookmarking. I have several of my clients who call me up and discuss something I shared on Twitter, but due to work/friends/family, they do not follow me. I find that many clients have two different profiles; one for their adult profiles and another private one. They will often retweet your stuff.

The best thing to do though is finding repost/retweeting/sharing accounts. Many people create accounts strictly to repost others content. Why? They do this so that they can build an audience, support creators they enjoy and sometimes just for kicks (or a mix thereof). These accounts are sometimes run by robots, that if you put in a particular hashtag, will find you and report whatever you put out. IF you are having trouble finding one of these reporting accounts, look for those who are established in your areas on their various social media accounts. You can usually see who spreads their content.

To walk you through how to do the above, I will use myself as an example. If you put @amberlypso into Twitter, you will see all my tweets and anyone who then tweets to me. Comb through everyone who isn't me, and when you mouse over, you will see how many followers they have. If they have RT in their profile name, they most likely are willing to retweet others. Most of these

Amberly Rothfield – How I Made $10,000 A Month as A Phone Sex Operator

accounts have thousands of followers and have no problem reposting your content. Each repost, of course, helps you increase your engagement and thus the relevancy of your work with the search engines. Do know that these accounts can disappear overnight without warning. Make sure to keep a list and constantly add to those whom you know will retweet so you can tag them! I do want to give a warning though. There is a scam going around where some RT accounts are charging to retweet you and share your content. DO NOT DO IT! I do not care if they have '1 million' followers. Many of those who charge for this service buy their followers and engagement. They are taking money from girls, pocketing a bit of it and then buying retweets and followers from bots. They also ask you for free content… another red flag. If they do not do it for free, move along. Your money is best spent elsewhere. If they were credible, they would not charge you but find sponsors. There are those who will share your stuff for free but charge to guarantee your stuff will be shared more often. This is less eyebrow-raising, but I still would not do it.

Social media posts that link back to your website also count as links to your site, just like your links out count towards that person's site. The strength of the connections depend on how well known your profile is, but it still shows that you are not a fly by night. Those who see your posts will often check your description for links as well. If you interest them, they will want to see more about you. ALWAYS put your links in your description, without exception. Not every post needs to be a link back to you, but you need that link in any pinned post you can place and in your description. Think of it as a call to action! Also with your pinned posts (if they are available), make sure to add an image or a video if you can. This helps it stand out from all other posts.

Building A Network.

How many websites do I own? I have over 20 dedicated to my main persona (Amberly). Not all the websites are about me though, some are community sites. **I would suggest that in starting out, you build JUST ONE first, that is about yourself.** Once you feel comfortable with blogging and can keep a constant schedule, don't hesitate to buy another website and start blogging on it. Commonly, there will be the main site and other sites with specific content on it. These sites are called feeder sites and only link back to the main site that you wish to have boosted the most. For example, my MoneyOverMen.com website is my main site, but I also own blackmailmistress.com. As of this writing, the website is down while having an overhaul done but it talked specifically of blackmail, one of the fetishes that I have a ton of content about. On this site, I do not take guest post submissions, and I talk about nothing but myself. Do people find me via this site? Absolutely (when I have it up), but I use it push them to my main website where they can find more than just that one aspect of what I do.

I also have several community sites where others can post their content. Of course, I give myself top billing on the website, as I pay for it and everything. Others can make posts on these pages, and if they fit the criteria listed, they get published. It gives me updates, allows them to update and in many times they will share the posts from that site, as it helps bump them to the top. They gain a link back and a mention but also link back to me frequently/mention on social media pages. Total win-win for all involved. It also allows me to network with others in my field and get to know more of the community. In some cases, someone will want to ensure they get more promotion than I usually give to a specific post and will even offer to pay me to get them more exposure. The point here being, find community websites that match what you are creating. They will be happy to promote you (for free) but also reciprocate by sharing their content as well!

You can also use free blogs like wordpress.com or LiveJournal to create feeder websites as well. I know I harped on having your own website but again, I did say create a profile on everything you can find. I promise this is not being hypocritical but creating more links to your website. These sites can serve to collect that site's traffic and send to you. Granted you need to be more active to get the most out of these websites, you do not have to run them with the same frequency as your website to get some benefit. This also generates additional links to your website as you can then link to your site from these pages.

With a few posts and an explanation of where you can be found, you will gain a link that search engines will acknowledge. This means if someone types your persona name into search engines, they can then find that profile. With a few relevant posts and hashtags/tags, you can then be found when people search for those keywords on those sites too. This means you will get a bit more discoverability. You do not have to update these sites, I can not stress that enough. If you do become successful enough though, I would suggest hiring an assistant to update such blogs. Since they are sites you do not care as much about, you do not have to be as paranoid to damage being done. Just have them update the sites about 2-3 times a week and increase from there. This will be the basis of you creating a network of websites.

Alternatively, you can also take your older posts from your main site and re-spin them for these sites. Once a month, for example, I could make a Best of Blackmail – January 2017 ROUND UP post. That post would then have a brief description of the already produced content. Thus, I am not creating content all over again but just aggregating content that I have already produced. If your site is a community site, you can do the same for others in your area. Most will appreciate your mention and will even spread the link, which of course spreads whatever material you put up that directly benefits you.

Search engine optimization is utterly integral, and as I mentioned before, the algorithm changes regularly! That doesn't mean to shrug it off, as the changes for the basics is rare and tiny. It is best to learn the basics now and practice them. I know, I have said it a lot but I will be touching on direct methods for increasing your following on social media platforms in a later chapter. My best advice is just to use common sense. If it seems like it is an overnight success technique, chances are it will not list and is not legit. Search engine optimization is more of a garden and it needs a lot of tending too at first. Once it blooms though, the fruits will be plentiful and you will find it will begin to require less maintence.

Chapter 9 – Forums and XXX Social Media Networks

Yes, we have gone over SEO and some social media, but that is not all the marketing that you can possibly do. Literally, you can spend 8 hours a day just working on marketing, and in the beginning, you should be. As time passes on, this is when many will begin to wane in their efforts to do such things. This is when I say to RAMP IT UP! When others start to get comfortable, and rest is when you will find me working over-time. There is a lot more to marketing than just social media these days. It may seem archaic, but forums and social bookmarking sites still exist. Many ignore these treasure troves and most ignore them if they do know about them at all. Allow this to motivate you!

There are plenty of other forums, and truly I couldn't possibly list them all here. On my website www.amberlyrothfield.com, I will be creating a resource page though. I will keep it somewhat updated so that the more quality places I find, I will list. If you have a suggestion, please hit me up. Google the fetishes or subjects you want to really focus heavily on and put the word forum at the end of it, see what you find. Make sure to read their terms of service though. Many websites do not want you advertising unless you official advertiser or they may not want any pay to play girlies on there at all. Sadly, many in the BDSM online scene believe that if you pay, you are not really into BDSM. Thus shunning us who get paid and those who do pay for it.

If it is ok, make sure to list your websites in your profile. Describe exactly what you are looking for as well. I like to type this out into my profile and send people back to my profile if they ask me about anything they could have gotten just by going to my profile. Simple copy and paste of a link. Do not just go into these communities and link dump though. This is an excellent way to view as a spammer and once a spammer, it is hard to lose the title. Engage with the community! I would say that ever third post you do, should be about you. Comment on other threads and not just something anyone could say but something meaningful. Add to the community, and you will find people will go look you up. You won't have to jump and shout and let others know you do phone sex.

Get at least 5 different forums that you frequent. Forums tend to shut down quickly as many do not know how to properly monetize. Having more on your list is better because if one goes down, you will have others you have a reputation on. Those who follow one forum, usually have profiles on other ones too. People seeing you all over the place, also helps you build credibility in the field as well. Really think about the psychology of it all. If you see someone running in the same circles of interest as you, they are frequently posting, and they are insightful on the subject matter… what would you think about them? Most likely that they are someone knowledgeable and worthy of knowing.

FetLife

Fetlife.com is a sex-positive BDSM based website and a pillar of the kink based community. Tried and true, I honestly believe it may have been on the internet longer than I have been a phone sex operator. It is a personal style website, where you have a profile and can find others in your area but also all over the world. There are sub-forums you can join and partake in, and each has their own rules. Be sure to read the norms of each subgroup before posting. What I love about Fetlife is that they do not care if you are pay to play person. Make sure to put it as one of the first things in your profile though. There are a lot who are looking for free hookups on the website and even with you putting that large on your profile, they will choose to 'not' read it. If they complain; however, it will be clear that THEY were in the wrong by not bothering to read your page before contacting you. To weed out those who refuse to read your profile, I suggest you do three or so bullet points talking about what you are about. When I am contacted by someone looking for my fetishes, I then direct them to type out the three bullet points on my profile. If they do not, I do not respond further. Those who do not want to talk to someone who is pay to play will just move along at this point. This process is often called screening.

Fetlife doesn't care if you post about the items you have for sale. This is awesome because many websites that allow you to post such require that you become an advertiser with them. Now, this is subject to change, but currently, it is free. I like to log in at least once a day, post blog posts there and interact with a few groups. If you find someone who is super active, friend them. Being on their friend's list means others will see you on their list and most likely add you. More friends equal more people seeing your stuff. Remember you can never have too many friends! Be friendly back though, and like/share/comment on their posts as well. Not only will it get you seen by their friends but it will make them want to interact with you more. Think of this as your kinky facebook! If you just talk to yourself and never interact, you will miss out seriously on this website. To put it in perspective, I know many girls who do well for themselves and never leave this website. The reason I would not leave all my eggs in this one basket is simply that it can go away at any time. I enjoy the security of knowing that if FetLife dropped off, I could still direct the people who knew me there to other mediums.

Now when it comes to photos, again, you need to only use legal content on this website! You must have the rights to post, but you will find that you will do better by just not showing any face whatsoever. By not showing any face, yours or models, you will get more people understanding that you do not share your photos online. On FetLife people are more accepting and understanding that you are not going to use your own photos. This does mean though, that you are basically admitting to using the content. You can in fact use photos, but many get called out for this on Fetlife if they are pretending to be the girl in the photos. If you use a face photo or just get called out in general, just cop to it. The only people who are harassed are those who lie about.

Amberly Rothfield – How I Made $10,000 A Month as A Phone Sex Operator

When you first begin on the site, I would upload a couple of photos, fill out your bio page and then find a few groups to join. You do not have to join local groups at all! Just go to the group's tab and type in a fetish keyword. Proceed to check out each and every single group and read the rules, do they mesh with you? Then join them and make an introduction post. I would not post in more than 2-4 groups a day, especially at first. Every time you make a post in the group, your profile feed will be updated. If you are making a billion intro posts a day... this could annoy your new friends. It is best to take it slow and build up naturally. If you just come on and throw out links all over the place, you will seem desperate.

You can post in many different ways on the site. You can post text updates, photos, and even video. The video will be hard for many who decide not to use their own face, but you can set audio files to a background to create a video if you are so inclined. I like to post freebies on the site so that people can get a taste of what I do. I would also suggest making text updates on your own page as well. I would not make it just like your blog posts, but a bit longer than the typical Facebook or Twitter update. A good rule of thumb would be about 250 words. A great thing to do is link afterward to your longer posts!

You used to be able to create groups of your own volition. Now they may change it in the future but as of this writing, only current existing groups will be around. If you want your own group, you will have to contact the website owners and tell them why you want to create the group. Due to people breaking rules of the site, the owners want to ensure that you will be following the rules. Now will you need a group to start? No... but after you grow enough of a following, perhaps you will want to have a one stop place where you can pin a post and put everything that is about you.

On to a newish website but a love of mine! There is a website called Medium.com. You can write articles and build a following. Microblogging I believe it is called. Currently, they still allow adult topics, but again, it is subject to change. I like to find articles there to post comments on but also post content myself. Remember, part of marketing is establishing you as a thought leader. DO NOT just copy and paste from your blog. You want original content everywhere you post. Google has long since picked up on people who copy and paste and will spank you HARD for this sin. I would even say it is one of the seven deadly sins on the internet.

Medium has been around for a little bit of time now but still doesn't have a ton of people posting. IT DOES THOUGH, have tons of people commenting/viewing. The content strategy I suggest here would not be the same as I would recommend for a blog though. Instead of a more personal diary style, I would suggest informative posts that are more educational in nature. Teach people more about the fetishes you partake in. Instead of listing specific items you have for sale, I would just link to your website in your biography. If you have educational material, then it may be appropriate to place those links. Discretion is advised in this circumstance. If you do not now much about fetish like topics yet, try to find topics about human sexuality that you do feel comfortable talking about.

Being as this is not your main site, I would only suggest posting to Medium about once a week. Make sure to visit the site a few times in a week to catch up on content and leave comments, but I would not make it a point to post there frequently. Unlike FetLife, this site is not entirely adult friendly, which means that all your effort could quickly go up in smoke if a moderator comes along and is having a bad day. Unlike say, LiveJournal or Wordpress.com, your page on Medium has a much higher chance of being discovered by others but is still not a place for anyone who works in our naughty part of the world.

It would appear though that Medium is owned by the creators of Twitter and thus I do believe that as long as Twitter is ok with adult content, so will Medium. For this reason, if you do not want to go the educational route, you may be able to get away with writing erotica. I would say this is an unusual use of the website, but that doesn't mean it couldn't work! Each profile has a place where you can find links to the author's social media pages. I would suggest that you follow those who write similar content and comment on their articles. I know you are sick of the world relevant, but it bears repeating here. Make sure the comment is about the subject matter and adds to the conversation the content is meant to start.

What I really love about Medium is their analytics section. You can see how many people read your content, where people stopped on your articles and if your article was recommended. Recommending is considered sharing for this platform, and those who follow you will be able to see your recommendations. Make sure to follow other sex articles writers!

Minds!

Another M website would be Minds.com. Born out of the frustration of Twitter soft banning people (muting) and youtube censorship (search for the Wall Street Journal vs. PewDiPie situation for more on that), Minds is a social media platform that is also allowing adult right now. They also give you points for using their platform which you can use to advertise your posts. Their claim to fame is no censorship, and having been on this website... it would seem this is really true. I won't judge but some of the content on that site even makes me raise an eyebrow from time to time, though I forecast it won't last forever. Does that mean to steer away from it? HELL NO! IT ways to get on that gravy train before it pulls out of the station but doesn't get butthurt when you see it is gone.

Truth be told, these sorts of sites are always popping up, and it is important, once you are more established and have time (a key phrase – HAVE TIME); to try to get on all that you can. Even if you pick up one person, that is one more person than you have. The death of any business is obscurity! Get known and put yourself out there. If you find you have the income but not the time, head over to fivver or Upwork and hire someone to take care of posting for you.

The best way to use Minds.com right now is to repost your content links. Pictures seem to do the best and video is hit or miss. Usually, videos do better on social media, but Minds has their image posts larger than video. Having more space on a screen means it will capture attention better and seems to be the reason why pictures do better. I suggest mixing it up either way though. You can only upload photos to their system though. Videos, mp3s, and other media will need to be hosted elsewhere and linked. For this reason, I would still have an image on the ready to upload with your description and link. This will make it more appealing the eye.

You get points for really everything you do but, the best source of points come from those that join the site through your referral link. You get a portion of points the referred accounts gain. Have a loyal following? The more your content is liked, commented on and shared; the more points you get. I believe it is still once an hour, you get a number of points as well, but by following my suggestions, you should get far more than the hourly can dish out. Of course, when you are just starting out though, take advantage of those hourly gifts as you can.

Once you have about 1,000 points (so easy to collect), I suggest you begin to 'Boost' your posts. This is Minds version of ads. You are basically getting money to advertise yourself, so long as you are active on their site. How awesome is that? You can buy points, but they are so easy to gain, I personally wouldn't. I do believe that getting as many points so easily will come to an end soon as more people use the site. It will only make sense for Minds to start slowing down free point creation in favor of being able to grow their business. Get in on this as quickly as you can!

Just as a warning though, this site tends to have people who have been kicked off other platforms. There are a ton of trolls too. Just shake it off and don't let it bother you. Remember that every comment and engagement they leave on your page means they are literally giving you money to boost your account more. If anything, I would suggest engaging with them more so that you can capitalize off of them! I wouldn't say anything malicious back though. Just calmly address them and then get back to being productive!

Free content seems to work very well on this site as well, so every time you create a preview… make sure you put it on the site and then use as many saved points as you can to boost it! Do not leave it there though, just like any other community you wish to join, you need to be engaging other people. Find like-minded people and talk to them and share their content as well. I have met several other people in the adult industry there.

They do have a messenger like functionality, but really I do dislike it, at least in its current state. I believe you have to be following the person and they must follow you back to communicate. For this reason, I would be careful to not follow just anyone. You may get spammed with messages and the site can be a bit laggy when you have a ton of messages coming in. Also be careful of people asking you to follow them back for no reason. Someone who is conversing with you in comments and then requests follow back? Ok… but someone who has never said two words to you? Tell them to kick rocks. They most likely just want to spam you with links to stuff.

Minds also have groups, much like that of FetLife. When you join one, make sure to read any pinned posts and get a feel for rules. This site is very much the wild, wild west though… so I would still

Amberly Rothfield – How I Made $10,000 A Month as A Phone Sex Operator

be careful of the content that you post. I would absolutely not use photos that show any face if you are using the content. Make it clear that you are not willing to reveal you're true identity but you are also not trying to 'fool' anyone into thinking you are the girl in the photos. Transparency on platforms like this is crucial as you do not want to risk getting people worked up to where they will want to 'out' you. Outting yourself is the best tactic when you suspect another person will!

Reddit

Another tried and true website for promotion is Reddit. Reddit has several little subforums (subreddits), much like Fetlife. Each has their own rules, so again check them out with extreme scrutiny. I say this because of the subreddits are owned by the same person. Get banned in one, you may be banned in many others. Now Reddit is a strange master but a loyal servant. People can see EVERY post you have ever made, so if you are only posting things for yourself, people will look… point it out and downvote your other posts. Unlike with other social media sites, downvoting on Reddit can actually hurt you. Your post will get pushed down in favor of the items that got upvoted. This means you will struggle to promote yourself. On this site, you want to post other people's stuff about 10 times before you post your own business again and try to comment on almost anything and everything you can. In fact, my ninja tactic is to have my links on my profile and go in and discuss relevant comments on other's threads. People on Reddit are super internet detectives, and they will go to your profile to find out more about you. Even if you haven't done/said anything that is suspicious!

Why should you especially comment on other's threads on Reddit? It makes it look like your am not purposefully attempting to just promote yourself. Seriously, this is one of the noisiest websites on the internet. People investigate the living daylights out of each other on that site. If you make any sort

Amberly Rothfield – How I Made $10,000 A Month as A Phone Sex Operator

of post that someone may disagree with, they will tear off to your profile to find something to discredit you. Someone agrees with you, they will go see what else you have commented on. Make sure your username is similar to your character name because people WILL google you. Reddit, again, can be a boom in traffic for you or a gush of hate.

Now there are thousands of subreddits out there. While it may be tempting to go to the super popular ones and drop your link then bounce… please do not do this! Seriously, do not do this. You will want to find the most relevant subreddits you can, which you can do by typing in the search bar. Once you find a few you like, make sure to read the rules. You do not want to get banned, especially before you get any benefit! To the right, you will see a number with an arrow pointing up and one pointing down. That is how you vote! The higher the number, the more people voted.

Click and see what has the most upvotes for that subreddit. Consider this your recon mission! You can see what type of things the readers of that subreddit like and then model your content after this. Note how people also respond to the content that is highly upvoted. Now for something that few people do: look at the least upvoted content as well. Now some stuff will just be new. Hence no engagements yet, disregard those posts. You can see how long ago something was posted though. Find stuff that has been around a few days but got no traction. Try to find a pattern as to why this is happening so that you can learn from it.

Frequent a subreddit? Get lots of upvotes? When those two things happen frequently, you may find that you are offered the position of moderator. While this seems like a great honor, please heed my warning… DON'T! Depending on the subreddit, this can be far too much work for little to no payout. Remember you have a business to run here. If someone tosses the role of moderator on you without getting your ok, do NOT feel obligated to have to do anything. I know it sounds bad, but seriously, when you are just starting out this is an unneeded burden. Your free time will be so precious, you will not want to have to babysit a fetish forum, even if you life BDSM as a lifestyle.

Now, I am not here to just tell you about these platforms but how to really bend them to your advantage. Remember how I spoke about the really popular subreddits? Some of these subreddits have over 400,000 active users daily, but this is not where you want to be quite yet. First, many of these subreddits are HIGHLY against personal promotion. If you post a link whatsoever to your stuff, they will ignore, delete and/or ban you. Smaller subreddits can have a few hundred people but allow you to self-promote. It is in the smaller subreddits where you can build your 'karma' aka, reddit points. These points are a badge to others that you are not a spam robot. You gain these points as people upvote your content or comments. You have two different scores when it comes to Reddit karma; comments and posts. You want these to go up, but you have to post quality content and make relevant comments.

With the small forums, there are a lot fewer rules and the point requirements that other larger subreddits have are nonexistent. The users here are more engaged, and posts are not coming in at such a rapid rate that your post will sink to the bottom. My strategy here is to make a post and private message my best and loyal customers to go in and vote for them. In these smaller forums, you can get your posts up higher and for longer periods of time, thus more people seeing them. Many people who view these subreddits are not subscribed to them but come back frequently to see updates. Those who like similar subreddits will stumble upon the one you are ranking high in, and then see you. Do not discount the smaller subreddits! In fact, here is where you can easily start making your name!

When it comes to creating your own subreddit, I will give the same advice as I would for Fetlife… not until you have several thousand customers. You have far better places to post until then. My friends at Off The Cuff podcast created their own sub group within Fet Life and it is very active but it wasn't until they had a stable following. Focus on growing your comment and post karma on reddit first and using it to build your audience before you go to create a place for your audience to go!

Dealing With Backlash

Something important to remember; any publicity is good publicity. If you are marketing yourself right, someone is going to get upset. Staying in the middle means you will not be memorable. As much as Ellen Degeneres is loved, there are those who can not stand her. How? I do not know. I mean she is stinking DORY! DOOORRRY! Still, though, there are people who are anti-Ellen. Does Ellen care though? Well, she is so sweet, I bet she does, but she knows better than to let it bother her too much (especially to allow it to show!). She knows, as well as I, that if they are talking about you, then you are relevant. The death of anyone's career comes when no one is talking about them.

If you see a hate campaign flaring up, do not fuel the fire though. Do not taunt the haters and by all means, do not use your platform to go after them! Mentioning them does to them what you want them to do to you... gives them relevance. I have had a hate mob come for me, and I actually profited from it. I did not mention it publically on my blogs or social media and just waited it out. With nothing for them to latch onto, they soon died out as they looked silly. Trust that they didn't give up easily though. Going after them is just sending your clients who have no clue what is going on, to the other side. Remember, our customers come to us to escape the drama of real life and may be turned off by this.

Those who did become aware would ask about it privately, and when I didn't outwardly bash the other side... the conclusion was simple to come too. Jealousy or childishness sparked the drama, and apparently, I was taking the high road. A few unfortunate things happened from it, and a few clients decided to make their leave, but the vast majority did stick around. I even gained quite a few new customers from it all as well. If you have a mob with pitchforks coming at you and you are lost, feel free to reach out to me. I know I wouldn't have gotten through it without some amazing shoulders in my life at the time. I did learn about the different laws governing internet harassment thanks to this and got some connections in the FBI after filing reports. You are not alone if this does happen to you. The cool thing about it? The police and FBI do not care that you are in phone sex, but they do care that someone is threatening you.

Another reason you SHOULD NOT fire back is that that fuel can create an atomic bomb in your life. My dad taught me that you should never underestimate the person you are talking too. Whatever you post publically, can be consumed by anyone and everyone. No matter who you aim the egg at, you do not know who it will land on or how they will react. Many camgirls and phone girls have lived real nightmares after seeing someone go after them and then daring them to go further. It is not weakness to ignore the drama nor are you laying down. You are protecting yourself and busying yourself with worthwhile endeavors. If someone does go too far, contact the FBI Cybercrimes division and begin documenting everything going on. My favorite thing to do when someone goes too far is to send them the link to the online form for the cyber crimes division of the FBI. That usually will shut the person down immediately.

The police and FBI can only do so much though. If the attackers are harassing you via the billers and websites, try to contact the owners of the website and tell them what is going on. In my case, I had to submit a ton of documentation proving I had the rights the content I was using and then had a few people monitoring my profiles to ensure no one was leaving feedback just to harass me. At one point, my attackers made an account that looked like mine and tried to contact everyone they could see who was buying from me. The biller stepped in and helped me out, but you can see how far someone may be willing to go. The best thing you can do is play it cool though. Yes, it was super frustrating, and yes I did cry from time to time. The best thing to do though is put on a brave face.

Major News Networks Will Link To You

Guest posting is an excellent way to market as well, and I did cover it in the blogging chapter, but there is another way of using blogs to bolster your traffic. Do searches, I suggest on Bing's search engine as it is more adult friendly, for articles on the fetishes you cover. Major publications do talk about dirty things! Once you find them, these days, there is usually a comment section. I am not kidding; the BBC, Vice and even Huffington Post have run articles about phone sex/different fetishes. What is the cool thing about these articles? You can usually slide your link in the comments (or say something to allude to how others can find you). Now again, do not be a spammer. Seriously, getting banned will be a nightmare to try to come back from if not impossible. Instead, read the article and make a relevant comment. If you can reference a previous post you made, that is awesome! (This is another reason I used Medium.com as it is an article posting forum but considered more 'legit' for linking too). If you can't, I wouldn't suggest trying to whip something together. For a major publication, I would want to make sure my article was well thought out in advance. Most of the time, your link will stay up, and I get serious traffic from this method.

You can also find journalists on Twitter. Many reporters these days have their ear to the ground and are constantly looking for another story. Search for articles along the lines of what you specialize in and see who the person who wrote the article was. In their byline, they should have listed how to get a hold of them and typically their screen name on Twitter. Leave a comment on the post and share it! No, this may not get their attention but since you are going to be asking for something from them, do for

Amberly Rothfield – How I Made $10,000 A Month as A Phone Sex Operator

them first. Asking for a favor is easy, but doing even something small for another can go a long way. Contact them and see if they are willing to do a follow up their article further or if they know another reporter willing to run the story. Why would a columnist want to pass on a story? It may be too soon for them to be able to repeat the same story. Writers frequently know other writers and sending a story to another can garner some professional currency.

Want to really ramp this up to the Amberly level? Spreadsheets will be needed. Nothing too fancy, but you do need to be able to track the following. As you contact publications and journalists, jot down the following in separate columns:

- Name

- Journalist or Publication

- Email or Twitter

- Phone Number (if available)

- First Date of Contact

- Most Recent Date of Contact

Organizing the above information allows you to keep track of the different publications you are interested in and be able to keep in contact properly. Even if I am not sending a proposal, I like to send hellos and make sure that those I am interested in get keeping a working relationship know I am thinking of them. If I have yet to have established a connection with that person, I like to send a proposal or give feedback on their most recent work. Basically, I knock until someone answers. If they tell me to go away, I gladly do so, but I will knock until I am noticed. Remember that those you are messaging receive so many messages a day. You may have an amazing story and pitched yourself perfectly, but your email may just be read at the wrong time. This is why it is important to keep knocking. The more emails you send (within reason), the more chance you will have of being recognized and remembered and thus higher chance of having your email read. This is why I like to send a message at least once a month if I do not know the person and twice a month if I do have a bit of rapport.

I can not tell you how important it is to NOT be fake though. SERIOUSLY!!! If you message a person, take the time to do your homework. READ their bios on their social media profiles, find their latest work and really show that you are not just trying to use them. With social media being so prevalent these days, it is all but TOO easy for you to be able to find this information before contacting them. I can tell you from personal experience, that those who contact me and clearly know nothing about me other than my following are ignored. While I will not block them, I do know some of my journalist friends who will.

Closing this chapter out, I want you to know there are tons more methods of marketing out there, but I do not want to send you into paralysis of analysis. These basics are a great way to begin your journey into finding new customers and building your presence. Just take it bit by bit and do not add on too much at once. As time goes on, you will find it easier and more natural to join new networks. The key is just to realize how much time you have to allocate to this and not allow yourself to become overwhelmed. Content making will always be the most important aspect of your job but marketing is a close second. Try to make sure that you are owning this task rather than it owning you. As your presense across all mediums grow, you will find that people will begin to seek you out!

Chapter 10 – Upsells

What is an upsell? Upsells are those offers you get right before you go to checkout OR right after. Once a person has shown they are a qualified buyer (items in the cart and entering information OR already purchased an item), they have also shown they are in a buying mindset. Once you make the commitment to buy something, it is a lot easier for you to be convinced to buy additional items. This is why supermarkets and most stores have little odds and ends by the cash register and put the basic items that everyone buys (bread, milk, eggs and most paper products) towards the back of the store. You will then have to pass all the stuff that is 'optional' but will catch your eye, while you are on your way to the stuff you intended. Supermarkets know that once you are in a shopping mood, you will likely buy other things if they are just presented to you. Take this concept and use it for yourself!

So how does this concept play into the phone sex industry? As I pointed out before, you will need to have multiple offerings available to generate offline sales. Being able to sell pictures, videos, mp3s and assignments will become a huge part of your business if you do this long term. Creating upsells will ensure that once someone buys once from you, that their total will most likely be MUCH higher or they will buy several items. Now that doesn't mean you can just throw ANYTHING onto a customer and create additional sales, there is definitely the best practices to this to maximize profits.

Creating Successful Upsell Offers

First off, you will need a website if you will be (or "intend to") have upsells. The reasons are the same grounds I have harped in this entire book. Now you can either use blogging software on your site

Amberly Rothfield – How I Made $10,000 A Month as A Phone Sex Operator

or use your billing platform. If you go the software route, be very careful with most payment gateways that the software will integrate with won't allow you to bill if you are in the adult industry. I would suggest going with an established adult biller and asking them what systems they integrate well with.

Since I HEAVILY use Niteflirt, I insert HTML into my after sale area (you can only do this on the pay to views, not the goodies) to redirect guys to other things I offer. The 'area' I referenced is what customers see after they purchase from Niteflirt. You can place HTML there which means you can place more items for sale. So few on this platform utilize this feature, and for me, it is pure gold! I always make the offerings RELEVANT to what they have just purchased. The reasoning is obvious, if you bought a mp3 from me about sissification… chances are you will enjoy other mp3s of that nature, assignments of the kind or feminization videos. It is the same way you and I shop. While we go in for one item, we often times will buy other complementary items. Putting two items of NO relevance together will result in fewer sales. I mentioned it previously, but LUSH cosmetics does this all the time. I have gotten hooked on so many of their products by them sending me samples after I have made a purchase and the sample is generally something that compliments that which I have already purchased!

Now here is one of my major secrets to massive sales. While people want to buy things that are similar in most cases.. this is not always true. Often times, clients will have multiple fetishes and cater to everything you feel comfortable with increases your chances of capitalizing on this. The way I have found to do this is to make about 4 – 5 offerings that are exclusively found in my sale buttons. **THE DIFFERENCE THOUGH:** I also list the different fetishes and directly below mention an offer for each fetish.

Example: Cuckolding – Click HERE to download my free introduction to being my personal cuck mp3! Usually $5.99, you can get it for free due to your previous purchase! This entices them to click on that 'freebie' and then be shown all the wares I have available for that fetish, which also has a list of other offers for different specialties at the bottom! While much of the upsell list will be on the fetish that they just purchased from or clicked to get a freebie for, I do put a list of other fetishes that I do with a link so that the reader can find more content on that subject.

Formation of the Sales Funnel

Upsells are often called sales funnels, as you are funneling your customers through a purchase cycle. Due to the structure of my sales funnel, I can take a new client from a couple of dollars to hundreds of minutes. The reason being is I start with a positively priced offering. If someone buys that offering, they usually will buy offerings for the same price or slightly higher next. Gradually increasing the price and quality of the product, the customer climbs high and higher through my funnel… eventually hitting some sort of end. That end will totally depend on you, but with me, it is usually something customized/tailored specifically to them.

A statistic to remember when it comes to making additional buttons though is that every extra click a consumer has to make cuts down the chances of your desired result by 10%. This means you do not want to make an endless loop of useless buttons and links. You want your upsell pages to look interesting, get to the point and lead to what the customer desires. Does this mean you need to hire a web designer to create several variations? Well, I do suggest doing so at a later date but to begin, you can quickly learn some basic HTML and put together 3 - 4 offerings yourself. They do NOT have to be super fancy at all. It can honestly just be a short description and buy now button. How you do so, depends on the website/billing system you are using but most have some sort of instructions. If you are using Niteflirt, just use the buy now button code they give you after you create a pay to view.

So where do you start the pricing of an upsell and begin the sales funnel for your customer? I ALWAYS…, and I do mean ALWAYS start with a **free offering**. Yes, you read that right… I did say free! Being phone sex, this is typically an introduction mp3, a discount code or free minutes. At first, my introduction mp3 was super short but now… it is close to 5 minutes. Some tell me that THAT is TOO MUCH! I am not giving away the milk while selling the cow, I promise.

When I first began giving out my introduction mp3, no one else did it. EVERYONE scoffed and laughed at me for doing such a thing. Soon though, I was ranked number one on Niteflirt for over 9 months straight! Once others caught on, I upped the duration and quality. By this time, I had a professional podcasting mic (Blue Yeti but many do prefer the Audio Technica) and better software for editing. Why keep my free offering competitive? Doing so shows the quality of my mp3s/videos and what can be expected. Why make my freebies longer than others? Well, it is just a personal choice. I personally like giving a bit more because most shy away from it and I love the shock factor from customers seeing me doing more than others do. There is a limit though, you will not find me giving away 10 minute clips…

The free offering also serves to get people onto my client list, which then allows me to send updates as the future products I create. Remember, you miss 100% the balls you do not swing at. If someone is not on your customer list, you can not market to them in the future. Building that list now is actually building your future later. Does this mean that a freebie will always convert into a paying customer today? Studies have shown no, and that is my experience too. It usually takes people about 6 times of seeing something/someone before they will buy it unless they are a returning customer. Returning customers generally take a shorter time in which they will purchase. BUT, seeing your mass messages often will make it where a new client eventually does convert; more on customer sorting later though. Freebies serve to build your list of potentials!

How do you create a customer list? It depends on the platform you are on or your biller. On Niteflirt, as soon as someone clicks on anything of yours they are on your list. On IWantClips or Clips4Sale, they must purchase from you in order to be on your customer list. If you are completely independent, then it is on you to collect emails. It all goes back to your mailing list! Remember, upsells are not just for new customers but as you create new things, you will want to put all of that through a sales funnel as well! There is a whole section in this book about mailing lists, if you haven't read it, DO SO!

What your free product also serves to do is be a basis for upselling PAID products. Remember gradual steps though. Someone going from buying into a free product may not want to go immediately into a $200 product. AMBERLY!!!!!!!!!!!!!! You just said BOUGHT a FREE product. Remember that everything has costs and someone taking their time to sign up/give you contact information is payment. They are paying you with the opportunity to market to them later. GREET this with a link to a page where you have a list of things for them to buy that matches the offering you created. They could have moved onto anyone else, but your offer stood out to them. They paid you in future passive income opportunities! This potential customer telling me what interests them and the fact that they are interested in me means that we could begin a beautiful working relationship very soon!

Did I just allude to having MULTIPLE FREE items available? YES! Absolutely. Have something for each category/fetishes you cater too. Will this take a considerable amount of time? Perhaps but isn't your business worth that? Will some customers download and then never pay you? Are some people just looking for free wank material? Yes and yes but those who do convert are INVESTED in you and believe you will show them the experience they are looking for. When I say those who will convert, do not think that it will take thousands of people downloading before you can turn a profit. Most finding you on these websites like IWantClips and Niteflirt are interested in spending money already. This increases the chances of someone downloading your content and actually becoming a paying customer.

Many thought that TV would kill radio or that free porn tube sites would kill pay sites... nope and nope. Those who are willing to pay for their porn will do so and vice versa. I do not worry about what those who will never pay will do but focus on those who will. Want to know what I have found? Most who originally came to me for free material ONLY, eventually convert into paying customers. This is true in any other industry as well. Recently, I was researching buying rental properties and found an entire audiobook on youtube. The book had so much information and presented in such a way, I wanted the physical copy! I went and bought not just ONE of the books but three others the author had written. All this to say, that samples work and you shouldn't shy away from creating them. Those that have scoffed at me for putting out freebies are often those that I see complaining about how slow business is for them.

Now, all that said DO NOT CREATE TOOO MANY free items. What I like to do is pick my top three fetishes, and work from there. I quarterly try to create an updated freebie for one category. If even numbers are a big thing for you, pick four fetishes and update one every three months. I can often use a previously recorded mp3 and chop it up a bit, thus eliminating a bunch of work for me. If you aren't keeping score, that is only 3 freebies (or four). Inside of each freebie, are links to similar products with a list showing where they can find my other freebies and their respective files. It is not an endless loop of free content, especially to start when you don't have much legally obtained content of high quality to offset it. When you see websites of unlimited free samples for every single file, check to see if they have 1000s of products. If the answer is yes, then they can afford to not only take the time to do so, but it probably helps their business. Focus on making content first but also know that this content can become promotional material later.

For each freebie offering, I have at least 10 paid products available. This gives enough variety that my customers will usually buy something additionally. Once I create more in that area, I create another free offering. Another reason to limit the number of products you mention is that of scrolling.

People are using mobile devices more and more these days. If you just make an endless scrolling experience, you are not increasing your sales but improving the thought process of the buyer. You literally have mere seconds to convert someone before they move onto something more interesting. This is especially true if the customer JUST FOUND you. Longtime clients that know and like the quality of your work will be willing to scroll through.

To illustrate this point, think of an actor or comedian that you love. Before you knew who they were, you were just browsing for something to watch right? After viewing their work, you grew to like them THEN looked up for stuff involving them. You were then more willing to dig a bit deeper and spend more time looking at their IMDB page to see what else they have done. This same idea works with new customers. You want to present your BEST stuff up front and get them hooked. Once hooked, they will be willing to comb your sites for more material.

BEST STUFF?!? I am DONE AMBERLY! How can I possibly put out my BEST stuff? … Well if you are still reading this, I shall explain. See your best stuff is never going to be your 'best stuff' forever. Unless you are a band named REM and created the song 'Losing My Religion' as your first ever song and then found yourself never able to top your first hit. As you evolve, your talent will get better. As your business grows, your equipment will get better. Your quality will improve over time so your BEST today will not be your best tomorrow. Plus when you put out your best, people wonder what more you have? It is amazing what challenges and competition can do to your product improvement. That said, do not give away everything! This is a SAMPLE! Enough to get an idea but not enough to fully satisfy. If someone wants to hit replay several times over and over to get off, well you can't stop them, but most will want to buy a longer version.

To define a freebie though, you do not want to put too much out. If you are doing free photos, no more than one per offering, period. If mp3s or audio files, I would say no more than 5 minutes. Audio files can be put on loop easily, but if you do just five minutes, it is generally hard for the average customer to get off. Even if they do though, it could make them want to get MORE from you. Videos I would make shorter. No more than say 2-3 minutes for video files as they are getting a more enhanced experience from just plain audio. It is also harder to edit video than just mp3s, and thus I would not put as much time into creating a bunch of video freebies that are on the longer side. For assignments, well that is your call. Most of my clients prefer customized assignments, so I have a bunch of basic assignments out that are free to everyone. It is once they complete the premade tasks that they are to contact me and that begins the 'payment' portion of the session.

An important thing to remember about pricing is that price is what the customer is willing to pay, not what you think it is worth. If no one is buying from you, then the value of your offerings is nothing. If someone bought something from you for twenty-five dollars though, then it makes sense to offer something a bit more expensive provided it comes with some perks. I upsell files I have not released to the public yet, blooper reels and lengthier files frequently. If there is a series, I will upsell the other 2-5 parts for a discounted price. There are literally zillions of ways to create more value for the upsell and warrant a higher price. More about defining price later in this chapter though!

Current Customer Upselling

Now upsells for people who are already customers and have been so for a long time? YUP! I do those as well. Making your customers feel special is just good business 101. Offering discounts and packages are an excellent way to generate sales and make your customer feel that they got a deal. Every year, I bundle up my previous mp3s and create mega packages for about 60% off. The content will be considered 'old' by then, but many customers who bought 1 or 2 files are now getting 25+ files for the

Amberly Rothfield – How I Made $10,000 A Month as A Phone Sex Operator

price of about 3 or 4. It is no extra skin off my back as after 90 days, most content you had produced stops selling at the rate which it did when it was new. This means that you get the most out of your content for about 3 months and then it is 'dead' content. It is this content that is excellent to be used for promotional content.

For proof of this, look no further than most porn pay websites. They post promotional material on adult tube sites, BUT pirates do too. If the content is super old, many sites do not bother with taking it down as it is just a waste of time and often times can make anyone viewing WANT to pay for the newer stuff. (By placing a watermark or mentioning the website in the video, visitors who are watching a pirated video can go find the actual source). When newer stuff is posted though (especially in full), it is taken down with a swiftness. The new full videos are the ones that actually make people want to sign up and keeping them exclusive is what makes these videos valuable. Why would anyone want to pay you if they can get that content for free elsewhere? They wouldn't! I do not want to harp on this now because you can spin piracy into being a valuable marketing tool, more on that later.

The point being, you do want to create promotional material but not out of your newer stuff (note, making a 5-20 second preview of a clip is not being counted as 'promotional' material in this instance), once you have built a library. Focus solely on building out those first 30 files first and foremost and then work from there. Once you have those 30 files, you can create promotional material, but in my honest opinion, it is best to wait till you have a few hundred files. Yes, a few hundred. If you spend your early days when the phones are not ringing making mp3s, you can easily do 2-5 a night. Even if you take two days off a week, you will have 25 files by the end of the week or at a minimum 25. This means in just 1-2 months, you will have an extensive audio library. You can mix in videos and pictures as well to create new products.

Here is where your sales funnel and upselling will collide. When you have your established cuustomers going through a new sales funnel, they will be more likely to proceed through the funnel faster. Afterall, they have an idea of your quality of content already and hopefully established rapport. So your freebie basis is established, and you now have a few upsells. That first couple of upsells need to vary in price, but no more than one or two need to hit above $50. I like to put in some pricey content because many can afford it, but even those can't afford it usually want to test your wares. Why drop 100 dollars when they do not know your quality fully yet? My goods range from 5 dollars to about 100 but most ranging between 10 – 20. Here is where many I have met differed with me, and sadly I do not see most them making the sales I have. Many believe I price myself too cheaply and am in turn being shorted. This is where my secret comes into play because my clients get into endless buying loops. They may buy a $10 file, but with the offering after, they usually send another 15, only to spend another 15 after they purchase the 2nd. Usually, this little spree ends in about 4-10 purchases and yes I do mean 10 separate purchases! If you are following my dollar amounts, it can equate to about 40 dollars to as high as 450 in one round. If they go after my more exclusive offerings, then it can turn into over $1000 in a day (and on plenty of occasions, it has!).

After purchasing any item, they are taken to another purchase page showing unique offerings that are about the same price OR higher. Very rarely will I put something that is lower in price, as they have already qualified that they are willing to pay the price they JUST did. These items are a lot more tailored to their fetish needs and therefore worth that price to them. The point is to also step people up with your offerings. Once someone decides that you are worth buying $50 of your wares, their objection to purchasing a single product for $50 will be low. Why then continue to offer them just $5 products? If they want something cheaper, they will probably go to where you list all of your public clips and purchase from there or go back to the previous step in the funnel to select something off there.

I do want to address what many have called predatory about upselling and using buying psychology against people. I used to think that using sales tactics or knowing someone cannot actually afford what they are buying is predatory. I used to turn away clients that I knew had spending addictions… only to see them go to my friends and drop thousands of dollars. That is not to say I am jealous that my friends got a big payday. No, I am very happy for them actually. What finding that out that I missed out though taught me was that, if someone has their wallet in hand then they are going to be spending. I hurt no one but myself by not capitalizing on the fact that the customer was before me and wanting to spend. I am not their mother, their counselor or accountant. It is up to your customer to know when they have to cut it off. Also, I have found many guys who act poor, actually get off on you 'abusing' them or taking from them. These tactics are used by major corporations daily, and if you want to get to that level, well you will have to take on some of their habits as well.

How do you get the three-digit upsells? It is again a progression. Out of all of your customers (unless you only cater to the elite, but do read Ceara Lynch's blog about the 'whale' type clients and how they are truly few/far between), most will not just go for a three-digit priced item unless it has INSANE value, at least upon first meeting you. By all means, create those when you can, but your average stuff just won't be. That said, do not stress it! When you get an idea that you think can pull a higher price, put it out there and begin creating a funnel for it. Will it sell a lot? Perhaps not. I have many wares for $800 or more, but they do not sell every day. They are still purchased though! Creating that opportunity allows for the possibility but I would not hedge my mortgage payment on it!

What you need to do is build content that is of better quality/value and get your customers into that funnel that delivers said content, utilizing an offer they can not refuse. Now, this could be just a massive amount of content for that price, something no one else is doing or something totally customized to them. I do custom files all the time, and for longer ones, I charge more. This is my go-to high ticket upsell and it works each time. It is something that is just for them, and they get a little more

Amberly Rothfield – How I Made $10,000 A Month as A Phone Sex Operator

control over the outcome of the file. But AMBERLY, I have seen you offer customs for cheaper. My more reasonable customs are basically someone giving me the idea they would like me to do, and if I like it, I make it and then mass send it out to others. Most individual files wouldn't work well on a mass basis as I am saying that customer's name, and my customers happily pay the extra to see their fetish being brought to fruition. It really just depends on how you personally define custom. I like to say one is giving me a custom inspiration and the other is totally customized for the customer.

Is there such thing as 4 digit upsells? I will put an end to that string of questions here. Yes, you can increase the price of your upsells to the moon if you desire. The issue will come in though, value. Short of actual prostitution, as a phone sex operator, there are limits on everything you can produce. Another distinction needs to come into play as well. While I have gotten far over 4 digit tips from phone calls or textually based chats, the sales funnel requires no attention from you. As a client progresses down this road, you are not there to manually encourage them. Proceed with that knowledge as we discuss sales funnels further. Now again, you may come up with an idea for a video,mp3, assignment or photoset that commands such a high price, but that is a truly uphill battle. All your thoughts will not be your major hits BUT think of this as a comedian. Each product is a joke, some will slay the audience and the others will make them chuckle but trying to fill an entire hour special with all hard-hitting jokes is next to impossible... even for the best comedians.

All funnels do come to an end though, so plan yours out. Psychologically, we can all tell if something was left unfinished, so I have my funnels finish with some sort of contact plan. I have my clients reach out to me for a custom file or specialized phone session. I use the last few pieces in that funnel to actually allude and talk up the benefits, so when the time comes for the final step, they are more than prepped to take it. This takes the guesswork out of selling your wares and creates the situation to make big bucks when you are offline. It also creates an incredible customer experience.

On a final note, I want you to know that when it comes to your funnels, you can be actively talking to a customer when they are going through them but the goal is to have a funnel that pushes a customer by itself. While we want your business to be a reflection of you, you do not want to have to be IN your business at all times in order to be making money. Yes, this is a phone sex based business but that passive income needs to be your goal and what is always on your mind. Your sales funnel is what will sell your content and your content will be what allows you to take breaks from your business and not worry about your bills.

Pricing – Fetching Higher Prices

Before we go much more into this chapter, I want to discuss pricing. Everyone will have a different opinion on this. Even amongst some of the top dogs in this game, some will say that this is a luxury industry and thus we all need to pay more. Others will say that those who want to charge 500 dollars for everything are leaving money on the table by the less wealthy clients (or clients less inclined to spend as much on this luxury). Pricing also comes down to how you are feeling. Sometimes I am totally digging more phone calls and will drop my rates, sometimes I want to push more content and will drop my phone rates but will make some more incentivized product offerings. All this said though, there are some basics you can follow to ensure you are not overpricing yourself or leaving money on the table.

Let's address overpricing first. Overpricing means that you are not describing that which you wish to sell in a way that the reader will see the value. How do you fix this? You will have to find a way to appeal to the reader. This can be hard though if what you are offering is not worth the price you are asking for. As an example, I knew one girl who tried to enter the phone sex industry, but she did not want to discuss many common subjects. Now I am not trying to shame her at all, but she did have some negative sexual experiences in the past that prevented her from wanting to want to talk about vanilla sex acts. She also did not want to take calls at a lower rate. She was not well known, and this was her only means of income. She struggled to sell any of her offerings and did not get many customers calling into her lines as she was well over three dollars a minute. The few who did call in often wanted to discuss topics she would refuse. As you can imagine she struggled and eventually exited the industry.

What lessons can we learn on pricing here then? The more customers you have, the more risks you can take with your pricing. We can also learn that if you only cover limited fetishes/topics, you will also have to consider your pricing as well. I know I have said you want to become a thought leader in certain subjects but that is not to say that you refuse all other subject matter or refuse to create products around them. I am known for my hypnosis fetish files, but I also have created fart fetish material. Do I have a high amount of products around farting? No, but if someone calls in and that is their kink, I am all over it. Lastly, we learn to be flexible. As business will boom and bust, you need to be able to adjust.

Let me talk about another girl who was HELLA successful when I first met her but fell off the scene over time. She simply could not adapt to the changes our biller handed down. She once commanded prices of over 5 dollars a minute, but when the shift in how we had to do business came down, she did not want to make content to sell. She wanted to depend on strictly phone calls but refused to bring down the price. Had she begun making content that could sell offline or brought down her price. Honestly, I do not know who could have ever competed with her as she had amazing psychological insight when it came to her clients. So why then did she fail? Pricing is fluid, and if you try to stay rigid, then you will lose out in the end. Even the best talent can fail if they do not listen to the market.

Amberly Rothfield – How I Made $10,000 A Month as A Phone Sex Operator

When you are starting out, you should price your phone lines no lower than 99 cents per minute. I know I said do not let anyone tell you what your price is but most billers will take a maximum of 50% of your rate. This means you are making .49 cents a minute while on the phone. Basic math will show that this means you are making 29 dollars (rounding down) an hour. Many would get geeked about this, but if you spend time in the industry, you know you will not be on the phone each and every single hour. A living wage, as of this writing, is about fifteen dollars an hour in America. At that rate with four weeks in a month on average and at the standard of forty hours a week, you are at twenty-four hundred dollars a month. This is, of course, meaning you would have to be on the phone for eight straight hours every day that you work. I know few who would want to do that. I have worked at call centers, and we got more breaks than it would take for you to break even than that.

Using those same numbers but applying it to the twenty-nine dollars an hour you will be at $4640 a month. This would not be bad living, BUT you have to pay your taxes which at 15% would bring you down to $3944. This again means you would be on the phone the ENTIRE time that you are working. For most, this would mean that you cannot qualify for any sort of government assistance but that if you are not very careful with your money, you will not be able to take a break. This is far from your earning potential, and I would not suggest staying at the 99 cents a minute rate long term. It is a great way to start and get your toes wet though as you build clientele. Raise your prices once you see that you are spending less time between calls. Once a call ends, I need about 15 minutes to unwind, get a drink and go to the bathroom. When I find that I do not have that kind of time between calls, it is time to up my rate a bit. Does this mean I will lose a client or two? I will not lie and say I never got an angry message from a client about my new prices, but this is a business.

What does your phone price have to do with your upsells and item prices? A LOT! If your normal price for your phone line is low, guess what people will expect of your other products? They will expect the same. Do not try to charge 30 cents a minute but only have 100 dollar mp3s available. Ok well, do

Amberly Rothfield – How I Made $10,000 A Month as A Phone Sex Operator

what you want to do, but I can tell you now that those two ideologies do not go well together. Price your items accordingly. Remember that something that is premade should be less than the price to talk to you live. When talking to you live, they have your undivided attention, and thus it should come at a premium. A product that can be downloaded is not only available to everyone at any time but also once purchased can be viewed/played at any time. Some have told me that because it can be played and replayed, that they want to charge more. Again, different strokes for different folks but in my experience, those who do replay my older stuff still purchase my newer stuff. I mean, I personally own every album by Coldplay and will continue to buy anything they put out. Loving the oldies will not stop the purchase of the new stuff ... but if Coldplay started charging $40 per song on Itunes, I would probably just opt to catch them on the radio.

Another thing to keep in mind is scarcity. When I used legal content for my image, I would charge a lot higher for my videos as I had few of them for my model in comparison to girls who do use their own images. When I first started, I had very few photos of my model too. That meant that my picture packages were a lot more expensive as well. Audio files though, they were a very reasonable rate because I could make new ones at any time. That which you have the least amount of, should, of course, cost more. Only you can determine what is scarce in your business model. Perhaps you will not like creating mp3s but love making assignments. Maybe you do not mind taking video of only your feet, or maybe your model is not far from you, and you can take your own photos. Just keep in mind how difficult it is to create that type of content and price it accordingly.

Speaking of difficulty, price your wares based on how much effort you place into them. There are two basic business models when it comes to this. One is to be the McDonalds, and the other is being the Apple (as in the computer). McDonald's spends and an ungodly amount of money in marketing and is on every street corner. I literally have four within walking distance of my house. Apple though, while they have the money for massive marketing campaigns now, they did not start this way. They made a

Amberly Rothfield – How I Made $10,000 A Month as A Phone Sex Operator

superior product which spread like wildfire via word of mouth. Now, let us add a dose of reality here though. Word of mouth does not have quite the same virality in the porn industry as it does in other industries. Though there are forums dedicated to certain fetishes, so many more will not go to those forums whatsoever. What this comparison does show though, you can focus on being EVERYWHERE or having superior products, and that will determine your pricing.

If you choose to put yourself in as many places as you can and is relevant, then you will have little time to create amazing quality products on the frequent. Instead, you will focus on churning out as many products as you can and then going to every place that you can and putting them out there. With your products not having the absolute best quality (notice how I am not saying poor quality...), you will most likely price them at the much more affordable rate. Lower priced items do not carry as much scrutiny as higher priced ones, and if your customer isn't absolutely blown away or there are some quality issues, they will most likely be forgiven.

On the other hand, you can just make amazing files. Going back to my one friend who understood her clients inside and out psychologically within a few minutes of talking to them; when she did try to make mp3s, she would script them out and take forever to create them. A new mp3 could take her an entire week or more. While I can truly appreciate the works of pornographic art that she created, the prices she would charge for this made it where most would never consider purchasing them. Those who did though, they were ravenous for her work! They loved that her files were longer and edited perfectly. While she did end up exiting the industry due to other reasons, her business model would be sustainable though it would be a bit too unstable for me. She had a handful of guys who were active at any given time. When one would drop off for whatever reason, this meant that a significant portion of her income just went away until she could replace him.

My personal strategy for pricing is somewhere in the middle. I do make content daily, but it is not super long and not scripted. Instead, I make about 2-3 files or bundle up stuff a day. If it is a video or mp3 then they are about 5 – 10 minutes and if it is a longer file then maybe 15 – 20. My longer files are usually custom recordings and thus that 'time' is already paid for whereas the other files I make are made for mass consumption. This means that I hope they will sell, but there is a chance they may not (never not had a file sell at all before though). When I have an idea that is 'golden,' I do take extra time to create it and put a lot of effort into it, but trying to sit and only produce perfect pieces of art is not my focus. Those pieces that I do create, I promote the living daylights out of them and showcase them across my networking channels. What I especially like about this strategy is that I get a lot more content out and thus more exposure on the platforms I publish on. I also get more customers (at least at first) than those that hyper-focus on quality. If one of my customers decides to exit the scene or take a hiatus, I do not notice as much (at least in the pocketbook). That added exposure also increases my chances of finding the higher spending clients. With thousands of studio accounts uploading daily, the more content I can get up, the louder I will be in my space.

In conclusion, pricing is ultimately up to you in the end but if you want to be wise about it, follow what the market tells you. If when you post, you never get sales or very few then lower the price. Do not let someone shame you about your choice in pricing unless they are someone who is actually putting money in your pocket. If you find that your items sell too easily, you may want to raise prices as well. The market is the best judge as to what your prices should be and the best way to find out what suits you, is to pick a business model and then do some testing. Everyone has their own formula and it is your job to find out what works best for you!

Look at any major clothing retailer website and try to see a common trend for moving product. I have yet to have found a seller of any sort who doesn't have a clearance section. I get daily emails from many of my favorite retailers that tell me about the massive sales they are having. Ever seen those ads that say you get free luggage set with the purchase of $150 worth of items? Learn from the big box and physical retailers! Digital content creators, rarely think about their creations as being on clearance because we do not need to delete anything to make room for more items… or do we?

Your website display area is considered your store shelves for this analogy. Once you have thousands of wares available, you will not be able to display them all reasonably. When you have thousands available, you will also have quite a few that are older and undoubtedly not selling as frequently. This is where content packages come in, and they are PERFECT for your sales funnel. While I touched on this earlier, I want to go in depth to this now as there are many in the industry that scoffs at this very thought.

I honestly go through once a month, much like brick and mortar retailers, and determine what is selling and what isn't. Many of the platforms you are on, will allow you to view these statistics but I also like to keep my own personal spreadsheets to track sales of items over the months. I try to find out why this has occurred. Sometimes, it just wasn't my best work, or it was something that didn't suit me well. Other times, it was a poorly worded description or bad pricing. If this is the case, I try to make tweaks and sometimes will re-release. If selected for this process, I make sure to note why and when it was re-released. I check back in after a month, and if it sold well, then I will package up the item with similar stuff. If it didn't, I chuck it out! I will not risk having sub-par products available that may turn off a potential long-term client. I call this my monthly purge. Look to Jenna Marbles on this one, sometimes what we find to be genius and awesome, the market just isn't ready for. Ms. Marbles had said several times that videos that she found to be hilarious just did not work out when she presented it to her audience. This is no indictment of your talent and does not let having to purge an item get you down. Take it as a learning lesson for what your audience expects/likes from you.

After purging, I go back over what once sold well but has slowed due to newer items coming out. Typically these are files that are all over at least 60 days, but if there is a TON of content fitting this criterion, I will further limit it to content that is over 90 days old. I will then package up this content that is of similar topics and prices. I shoot for at least 10 or so, then total up the collective price. The next step really just depends on how I am feeling, how the previous items sold and type of content that was created. Essentially though, this is where you decide on the price of the new package. I suggest at least making it 20% less though, the reason being that it takes no effort for you to deliver the items to the customer. They just select BUY NOW, and then they have it. Remember that these products are no longer selling at the rate they once did, but this discounted package can now allow you to obtain any missed sales.

Another tactic that often goes with content packages is to put a time duration on the item. I believe this is a great tool when you are trying to push for sales, and again, major retailers do it all the time. The catch is, you have to stick to your guns. If it is ever shown that you will give the same price after the sale 'ends,' then your offers will not carry much weight. You also want to watch having too many sales going, especially if you have not established yourself quite yet. You want to really know your customer base to decide on pricing and then what type of sales will work best for them.

Ever think that you could take marketing advice from the Disney corporation for an adult business? I sure have! I have some files that sold REALLY well, but if you want them… you have to wait until certain periods of the year for them to come out! What does this have to do with Walt Disney? The movies many of us have grown up with cannot be just purchased whenever you want them. Certain times of the year, the videos are released. This marketing tactic is a just pure genius! If they videos were available at any time, then the price would potentially go down over time. Instead, the videos can sell for the same prices as their newer counterparts as people run to buy them before the cut off time. People will put aside other purchases in favor of the 'vaulted favorites.' Know that if you ever use this for your products, you must commit to keeping those items 'vaulted' or the next time you try to use this process, it will not work as well.

In closing this chapter, quality is important, but you also need quantity as well. Yes, you want an extensive library, BUT if you just have pure garbage, your customers will not return. When the phones aren't ringing, you should be planning and creating content. Once you have pages of content, consider repackaging it into deals, but the biggest take away from this chapter should be …

ONCE YOU HAVE 30 PRODUCTS, CREATE SALES FUNNELS FOR YOUR CUSTOMERS and of course learn from your customers/the market.

Chapter 11 – Social Media

If you are screaming internally (or even externally) that I am JUST now addressing this, it is because it is NOT a basic; though it is needed. Many phone sex operators are successful and do not use social media. Also, building out your social media space before you build out a place to send people is a bit of putting the cart before the horse! To this point, you needed to create the website to drive traffic too. Grabbing a social media profile and trying to build is about as smart as building your house and then thinking to try to place a foundation. Without products you can't sell offline, building your social media profile means you would have nothing to sell if you are not actively taking calls. Without a website, your client has nothing to bookmark to come back to see your latest blog posts. Without a sales funnel, you can not maximize their experience or your profits.

There is a reason I am walking you through these steps in this way. I want you to be successful and efficient and for those beginning customers to have a way to find you again and continue to help you grow your business!

While there will always be a new social media apps popping up, I am going to go with some tried and true rules to help you get the best start. Remember that no easy street or yellow brick road exists to growing an audience, and it will take time. Try to steer clear of perceived shortcuts and remember the bootstrapping ways! You will find that social media is a kind mistress if you are ethical and put out great content!

Now I mentioned Canva.com earlier, for making graphics. There is always a new social media platform and always updates to existing ones. This means that ideal or optimized image sizes are ALWAYS changing. I use canva.com not because I can not photoshop but that their templates are amazing and they keep current on the optimum size for the images I need to use. They also have a ton of free graphics you can use to pair with your own content, and it really makes your images pop. You can also gauge what social media websites are of interest or are at least popular by the suggested image sizes they give you. Example : They have a section for Facebook, Twitter and Instagram (other sites as well but too many to get into in this moment). This tells me that those are social media websites worth looking into!

You need to have the best-sized images for whatever platform you are posting on. Having images too big or small can distort the images. This can make them hard to read or just unappealing to the eye. With so many websites out there, you need to stand out. What I also like about Canva is you can create a brandable profile. You can make all your images look similar so that if someone sees that style, they will think of you. Reflect on the board game that shows you labels without words on them. Most people can still tell what the brand is, even if the letters are not on there. You want to create the

Amberly Rothfield – How I Made $10,000 A Month as A Phone Sex Operator

same feel by having the same elements to your graphical design. If someone looks at an image, they should be able to tell that you are most likely the one who created it!

Every post you do on any sort of social media platform needs to have a photo or preferably a video. Anyone can make a text post at any time, but few can create truly captivating photo images or entertaining videos. Well, I guess anyone still could, but most will not take the time and effort. Simply not being lazy can take someone without talent further than someone with talent. Video right now is really a big deal, and no you do not need a video of your model or yourself. You can honestly just set your voice to images and create a slideshow. Look up GradeAUnderA as an example of setting your sound to image clips. On youtube, though he isn't as active as he once was, he has gained over 3 million subscribers and did not show his face till he had well over his first million subscribers.

Scheduling is a major part of social media marketing, posting whenever you think too... that is for someone with a profile that has a lot of engagement and customers already. When you are starting out, you want to target your hashtags, keywords and times. You want to post as regularly to your social media accounts as you do for your blog! The only way to achieve this is to use a social media scheduling app or program. Now there are hundreds of them, and new ones are popping up every single day. There is no one size fits all when it comes to social media updates, it really depends on the social media platform you are focusing on, your budget and what features you are looking for.

Hootesuite is freemium. What is freemium? It means they have a free account, but the better features are paid. In my opinion, it is more than enough to get you started. No matter how tempting it is, remember that all of those 10 DOLLARS A MONTH programs can quickly add up. HootSuite allows you to schedule posts on multiple platforms in advance. This means you can post when you are asleep. Why would this be important? Well, MANY of my customers are in other countries, so I take into account

Amberly Rothfield – How I Made $10,000 A Month as A Phone Sex Operator

their schedules. It also helps me see how much of my material is my stuff and how much is other people I am promoting. You read that right, I support other people. If I want to be helped, I need to help others. It is funny how if you do for others first, they will be more willing to do for you later. This is basic networking and considering we work from home, it is easy for us to do so with really no excuses as to why we don't.

Buffer is another freemium program that is frequently used. I personally use Buffer. I use the browser app so that whenever I find something interesting to share, I can "bank" the link so I can compose a message later. Their free version is honestly VERY generous and also allows you to load up multiple accounts at once. No, you can not have as many items banked for free/scheduled as you can with Hootesuite, but I can schedule a couple of days in advance. Now I HATE saving links to my bookmark bar or elsewhere, so this app is a lifesaver as I can just keep it and look later. I also LOVE their emails telling me that I need to bank more information etc. You can re-Buffer old links you have posted (links to your past products!), and they give you stats on how your content is being shared, liked and consumed.

Similar to the above, there is TweetDeck. This is also a freemium program that allows you to schedule your posts and is mainly for Twitter. Their backend is not quite as busy as Hootesuite and I know those who are not super tech savvy love it for that reason. I have used it from time to time and even seen people pair all three free programs to help prolong their need to upgrade and pay for the services. This to me is a bit too much work. I would get confused as to what I have posted where and then I would have a social media page that posts the exact same thing about 5 times. If you can make it work for you, no shade do your thing! I would just advise against it if you are as prone to forgetting smaller details as I can be. I like to keep it simple where I can.

Now for the mack daddy of social media schedulers. This program I have used off and on, but I highly suggest it if you can afford it. The only reason I ditched it but will be going back is due to my schedule. I personally did not have the time to update it as I should. Meet Edgar. I know, silly name but fantastic product! You can categorize posts you would like to repost and then say how frequently you would like to see that type of content posted. You get a calendar to which you can say what times to post your information. Their price is 50 dollars a month with no cheaper options. This is NOT a starting out scheduler. Even if you have the money, till you have the following, I would not suggest this. I personally am very flakey at messaging people back on Twitter based on what I have going on at home and if you use this plateform.. you will have A LOT of individuals finding/messaging you.

Each of these scheduling programs have their pluses and drawbacks but the main drawbacks is that few can allow you to post on several different platforms. Namely Instagram! I believe that only Hootesuite really allows you to post to it using a true prepopulated schedule. Buffer will set a reminder for you but to me that is quite useless. Instagram is a great place for those in the adult industry and thus I have searched high and low for a stable company to allow me to schedule on it without having to have subscriptions to twenty different services. Again, even if you are making great money.. you need to pay attention to your bottom line and making sure your spending is not out of hand or needless. My suggestion is to pick only one scheduling service and then if they do not allow you to connect to one or two services, then to do them manually rather than have a bunch of services you are paying for and using.

Following to Follower Ratio

Following to Follower ratio... Here is a topic of major controversy. I will give both sides as fairly as I can. I personally am solidly in the middle, I do not believe it matters which method you choose. There are merits to both sides, but I have seen plenty of people succeed in each school of thought. The only things you really need to be prepared for is that people from the other schools of thought will judge you and I have seen some epic fall outs publically about this subject matter. Just ignore them and do your thing, as you will be perfectly fine.

So the first camp believes that if you have a higher following to follower ratio, you are a nobody and not worth talking too. (meaning if you are following as many people or sometimes more than are following you). Is this true though? I can personally tell you that I have tried this method, plenty of people follow me back, and once engaged they usually engage back with me. NOW this will mean your feeds will be CLOGGED with people. I personally cannot stand that, BUT most social media platforms allow you to create lists. I go to those private lists, which typically have very few people on it and use that to filter out the noise. Even though I am not using this method for growth as much anymore, I still use my lists. For more about how I like to use lists, check out the section on Twitter, where I will go more indepth into this topic.

Those who use this method frequently purge people who do not follow them back after a period of time of time. This helps to keep the following ratio down some. This creates a problem that could put your account at risk. Social media sites have grown savvy to this method as it is used by many spammers. I am NOT accusing you of being a spammer if you use this method but the fact is, many who have used it in the past were/are. Due to this, social media websites have decided to shut down accounts that do this OR force them to verify they are a human. Now the later is not very bad, I have had to do so in the past. I just give a phone number and BOOM, everything is all good. There are those who totally lost access to their account though. Even a website called Tweepi, which helped people do this process of following and unfollowing quickly, has stopped their tool that helps you mass unfollow those who aren't following you. They did this because Twitter asked them too. Think about the

Amberly Rothfield – How I Made $10,000 A Month as A Phone Sex Operator

implications there. I also want to mention now that Tweepi has a freemium model, if you are looking into using this method to grow on Twitter. I totally suggest checking them out and can personally endorese their service.

Also, ask yourself, are these people ACTUALLY my fans and will share/read my content? Chances are no... they won't. Most who will follow you back are doing so just to get their numbers up as well. This means little to no extra exposure if you can get any at all. If you are following 10,000 accounts, your feed will be updating so fast that you will not be able to keep up with everyone. This is the reason that these accounts actually cannot engage with your posts, they simply won't see them. These accounts also spit out a ton of content throughout the day, which further clogs up your main feed. Consider that the page may be run by a robot as well, which means even fewer engagement opportunities.

All of that said, I actually have one of my best friends to this date by using this method. I followed her and she noticed. She saw that I follow a ton of people and figured that I was just following people but she saw my content and bookmarked me. A few days later, she was checking out her lists of sites she bookedmarked for later and found me interesting enough to tweet me back. We began talking and now she works with me on several projects. Yes, social media should be intended to find more customers than friends but I am illustrating that this method can help you. People will notice that you are following them and thus get curious to check you out. When you are building a brand, your goal should be to get everyone possible to know who you are. This is why many who are starting out, chose this method.

If someone looks down on your following ratio, ignore them. Seriously, if someone has time to critize you, then they are not focusing on what they should be doing themselves. No two business models (even if similar) are ever run the same. Do remember though, that if it isn't working out for you,

Amberly Rothfield – How I Made $10,000 A Month as A Phone Sex Operator

that you can always change it up. I suggest experimenting to see what actually works best for you but keep your eyes open. This all goes back to listening to your customers/the market.

Organic Growth Methods

Now for team organic growth! If you are on this team, you are not following people just to get follows back but wanting to engage with whoever you support and focus on creating an experience out of your social media platform. This means you will have to follow people still, but at a slower rate. You will want to dig a deep well instead of spreading yourself out. Again, this isn't a bad way of going about spreading your influence. Your tactics will for sure be different, BUT the growth will be more explosive once you get moving vs. having more numbers from the onset.

Start with exactly, no more and NO less, 10 people to follow. Not just anyone, but someone who caters to the fetishes that you want to get known for. I would say pick five fetishes; so that would be two people per fetish. Turn your fetish into a hashtag and do a quick search to see those who talk about the subject. Do not make the grave mistake of judging them by their follower number. Look to see how many retweets they have, how many likes they have. I next take their handle and do a search on it to see the people who are talking to them. Do they have a couple of people actively engaging with them? If so, they are an excellent candidate for someone to participate frequently with. Please make sure this person is still active. If the tweets you are seeing are from two months ago and when you click on their account, they tweet once a month or haven't tweeted since the ones you found… move along. I am not saying you can not get to know that person, if they are even still in the industry, but clearly this this platform that you are using is not one that they use frequently. You want to find active people who are also talking about topics to which you are working on building a presense in.

Amberly Rothfield – How I Made $10,000 A Month as A Phone Sex Operator

I call this tribe selection. We all have our own tribe, regardless if we choose to recognize this or not. Those in your tribe, are those who will promote you and you promote in return. Even just liking someone's status is a way of showing support, though you will want to also share their content as well! While you want to be careful of whom you trust to a degree, do not snub your nose at those who are smaller than you now. I have seen so many people who started out small and grow so quickly that their audience makes mine look non-existent. Due to harboring a relationship when they had just started, we are still friends to this day, and they constantly give me shout outs. I in turn, regularly mention them as well. Build your tribe by talking to people casually and showing them love. Don't suck up or be fake, just simply read their message and respond like you would if you two were alone in a room chit chatting.

Now that said, remember that phone sex is a small world and even the adult world, in general, is relatively small compared to other industries. Someone having just a few thousand followers can be considered a thought leader in their area. Also, remember that networking isn't always about finding the largest people in a field. Some of the major opportunities I have gotten came from people who weren't 'famous' in any field. Instead, they were just fans of the subjects I was looking into and knew who to push me towards. If someone is having people pay attention to them, then they are someone who can probably point me in the direction I need to go. An amazing lady who truly embodies this is that of Sofia Rose. She is a BBW porn model and has over 200,000 followers on Twitter. You would be hard-pressed to make me think she has purchased these followers too, as she had broken size barriers and been in many mainstream porn websites. When I met her at an Exxxotica convention, she sat and talked to me as an equal despite me being quite insignificantly smaller than her. Sofia knows that even people who do not have crazy high numbers on social media platforms matter. If you are willing to be real and talk to her, she is willing to help you and bring you into her tribe. We need more people like this in all industries! Be like Sofia, pay attention to everyone!

Make sure that you also GIVE BACK! If you want to be put on my block list in short order, ask me for something BEFORE you do for me. Seriously, this happens daily! Messages often pop up for me out of nowhere and demand advice. No hello... nothing indicating they know anything about me other than seeing my following count. Share someone's content, publically comment on their content, write a blog post about them and point them to it. Doing this shows you are someone who pays attention to them so they will WANT to pay attention to you. Want an example? Tweet me and say I READ YOUR BOOK! That shows me that you actually follow me and will instantly give you my attention (and appreciation). Ok maybe not instant, I do sleep from time to time. Those that get ignored though, they just demand that I follow them or retweet something and they have never even said hello and sometimes aren't even following me. Would you ask a stranger for something?

Once you have that attention though, do not STOP there. If you are just using a person for a shout out and not developing at least a professional relationship... it will be obvious. Remember that people talk. I have had several people message me about people like this when they start coming my way. Blacklists may be illegal, but they do exist, and you do not want to be on one. Instead, make sure you are at least touching base throughout the week a few times. To ensure that I am still promoting those who I wish to keep a professional relationship with, I like to preload my social media schedulers with their content as well. Trust me, no one cares if the engagement is automatic! They care that you still want to connect with them and it keeps you at the forefront of their mind as well. This also makes others want to share my content. Do not worry about competition! Seriously, look at the girls who have 100k+ followers and get nominations for awards. Often times they are sharing each others stuff though they are all going for the same award. Successful people like to promote other people! If you spend your time worrying about promoting someone and if they are getting more out of it than you are, you have missed the point of networking!

About every two posts you put out there should be other people's content. Again, this is basic networking and creating a value offering situation for you. Not only will your fans enjoy seeing content that isn't just you saying BUY NOW, but many fans like seeing the other people you discover. I have found so many of my clients have contacted me after seeing someone I mentioned to discuss how awesome they are. You are not boosting competition but helping keep healthy relationships within an industry. The owner of Wonder Bread does not hate the owner of Nature's Own, as competition signals a healthy industry. If there was no one to compete against, then it may be that there isn't enough demand for that industry. Trust me though, there is MORE than enough demand in this industry!

I want to touch on the slow growth method. It can be almost disheartening at first. It may seem you are getting nowhere at first BUT once shown that you give genuine interest into everyone who messages and you actually pay attention to those you seek out; the growth will come. It takes the time to not seem like a fly by night, remember that we see it every day. It also takes quite a bit of time to show that you aren't just trying to use someone. I get people frequently who comment or share my content once or twice, and once I share something from their feed, they disappear and onto the next person. If you are focusing on cultivating relationships and helping others out, they will get back to you if they are a decent person. I am a lot quicker to getting back to those who comment to me on social media than most I know in the industry as I am not as jaded. (Jaded not being a bad thing, they have their reasons). I hate harping on the fact that you have to give it time and be genuwine but if you saw the amount of messages I get a day, from people who are upset that they do not get the attention they feel they deserve… Do not focus on what others are doing back for you, but rather focus on those who do engage you back.

So those are the both sides. Adding a ton of people will result in you getting more follows but the follows are fickle. Adding only those you are interested in and networking on a real level is slow growth but it is more real growth. You can do a combination of the two and do the first doesn't mean you can't get 'real' growth later. Many will take you seriously for having larger numbers but those who do any sort of investigation, may view you as more of a spammer and not pay as much attention to you. Either way, you do choose, make sure whatever you put out there is interesting and relevant. Then, whoever discovers you will want to follow you regardless of your follower/following ratio. While you are deciding which route to go, look at fetish famous photographer Dirk Hooper. I love him to death and he does follow a BUNCH of people back, compared to his followers. Yet, he is famous, successful and Twitter verified! Just some food for thought.

Trolls and Keyboard Warriors

Everything till now has been sunshine and blossoms, but I want to touch on the dark side of social media. Keyboard warriors exist and think they are honestly not hurting anyone when they pull trollish antics. If anyone sends you anything that makes you feel uncomfortable, DO NOT ENGAGE. I can not repeat that enough. Most people that are trolling are doing so for attention, but there are a few who go entirely too far. If someone is threatening to post your personal/private information, contact the authorities. The FBI has a special task force for cyber crimes. Even if they are unable to do anything just yet, start the paper trail and report it.

As a story of caution, I had an ex-client begin to message ANYONE I would publically mention. It got so bad that I stopped actually talking to everyone publically or promoting others for some time to try and halt the behavior. This client wanted my attention but was unwilling/unable to pay for it. When I did

Amberly Rothfield – How I Made $10,000 A Month as A Phone Sex Operator

what I normally do and ignored him, he began making more accounts and more accounts to contact me. I would block each one without responding but that amplified his behavior. No worries, I have dealt with this too and read the book The Gift of Fear. Now, I won't block the new accounts but just hide them so I couldn't see their messages, but they never saw if I saw them. (Blocking indicates that you did see the message). After a few days, he took to contacting anyone he saw me approach. This is where his cyberstalking began.

The book The Gift of Fear outlines how stalkers think/work. They ultimately want attention so whenever you give them attention, that tells them the 'price' to get your attention. They are willing to hold out longer and pay a higher 'price, ' but they will give up. If you cave, that just shows them they have to try a bit harder then last time aka the price of attention was just raised. Back to the situation where he was contacting others, it became virtually impossible to ignore as he paid people to send his messages to me. Apparently, I was dealing with someone super sick and desperate. Yes, you read that right, he would PAY others but not me. Please note that at this time, I no longer would even accept his payment for a session but what drove me to ignore him was his refusal to pay. He simply wanted my attention for free and on his terms. Meanwhile, I just wanted him to go away.

The reason I tell you about this cautionary tale is that you will encounter these people. There is only one thing you can honestly do. I had to tell absolutely everyone about what was going on. Not only did it make them stop talking to him but they also check in on me constantly to make sure I am ok. The best thing to do is to keep attention on these cyberstalkers minimal but do tell those around you so they can help you handle the situation. The more people know, the more protected you will be. Create a plan now on how you will deal with internet stalking behaviors as they usually begin on social media first. When telling those around you though, I would do so privately so that your stalker is not getting more attention.

Turning them into the social media service will often render you little to no result. I have sent a slew of accounts in for sending threatening messages and very few times was there any intervention. Sometimes even being told that a death threat is was perfectly ok... thanks, Facebook. I am not saying not to turn them in but do not bank on anything actually happening. Try to just ignore as best you can as very few will do anything outside of just harass you online. You have better things to do than to argue with them or inform them what they are doing is wrong. Trust me, they usually know and probably are getting off on you mentioning it. Turn it into the platform by reporting it and if it is a threat of any sort, then file a cyber report with the FBI. That is all you need to do! If you get scared or delete your accounts, just remember that they then are happy and win.

A great tool in these cases happens to be Google itself! If someone starts setting off alarm bells, I quickly google their handle. Many other phone sex operators will blog about 'time wasters,' in fact quite a few dommes have walls of shame. The idea is that guys have to pay to be taken off. If their name appears anywhere, I will grain of salt it but will proceed forth carefully. If they actually make me think something is afoot, I will do my best to throw cold water on our conversation. Raising your price sharply often does the trick. With that said though, one person's trash is another person's treasure. Some of my good clients have been found to be on the 'walls of shame' of other dommes, and even those that have had bad run-ins with me are great clients for some of my good friends. If someone is causing you alarm and they show up on a wall of shame, remember grain of salt. If what that person put them on that list is matching some of the behaviors they are exhibiting to you then proceed with caustion.

If things really go too far, you can contact the FBI Cyber Crimes Division. You have to go online and fill out their form. I highly suggest taking screenshots of everything that has transpired and uploading them to the complaint along with a detailed recollection of dates/times that events occurred.

Should something else happen, you can again submit another claim. Documentation will be critical in cases such as this. While I have had nothing that required the FBI to step in, I had made complaints before and had agents call me back. They were friendly and through. Do not be afraid to reach out, no matter how minor the issue. They are skilled at recognizing if something will escalate or not. Listen to your instincts.

What is the difference between a keyboard warrior and a troll? Trolls are just doing what they are doing for shits and giggles. They just want to mess with you. Keyboard warriors are upset about something, and they are out to teach you a lesson. Being in the porn industry and especially if you cater to more taboo topics, you will find PLENTY of keyboard warriors. They usually just leave spam-like comments on your blogs or publically message you on social media. They may call in their hate mob of 'friends' to do the same, but I usually find it is the same person... with a handful of accounts. With free services like HootSuite, you can monitor several social media accounts in ONE place. This makes it easy for someone to make you feel that more people disapprove than actually does.

Dealing with keyboard warriors is similar to trolls but they can tend to have more staying power than the average troll. They are actually upset by something that you have done. I once had a wife of a client come after me. Her blog is actually still up to this day on a free blog website. It took about two months for her to give up but with no attention coming from me and gaining no traction in gaining haters of me... she packed up and moved on to better things. She never made a threat about me but just did moral grandstanding and trying to convince others to take a stand against the evil that is Amberly! She reported a few public messages I made, but none were ever taken down. She called my website host and asked them if I am breaking any rules, in hopes that I was. They contacted me and nope, I wasn't. Just ignore them and watch as they run out of energy. It is actually quite funny!

Fake it till you make it? That is the common reasoning from those I have spoken too who admitted to me that they bought followers. No, I will not name names… because it is no one's business. I will openly admit that I have purchased followers myself before as part of a test. What were my findings? It ultimately was never worth it! Sure, a few people were impressed at first to see how many followers I had but they were actually few and far between.

Wait so.. Having 100,000 followers can somehow be unimpressive? It absolutely can be unimpressive! First off, there is a website called SocialBlade, which was created to give statistics on how accounts across Instagram, Twitter, Youtube, Twitch and I believe now Daily Motion grow. You can see daily stats, weekly stats and monthly stats on any account that is in the database. If someone has over 5,000 followers across those sites and are not in the database, chances are they bought the follows. You can see large spikes in followers, which can indicate purchasing followers or some massive publicity. To check that, just type that account name into Google and set the filter to the day before and the day after, if some news pops up then boom there ya go!

Furthermore, anyone who has a true online presence will tell you, it is not the followers that matter but the views/engagements. I love using personal examples as this shows you how these types of things play out in real life. I had a girl begin messaging me on Twitter one day, and she had over 1 million followers. Strangely though, she was not verified by Twitter but being in the porn industry, I can understand why she may not be. I was truly impressed that she would take the time to private message me in the first place and we had a lovely conversation. That was until I went to her profile and began to do some basic research into her. I had never heard of her, but there are so many of us in the adult industry, that it is possible for this to happen.

Amberly Rothfield – How I Made $10,000 A Month as A Phone Sex Operator

Once I started digging though, I realized… when she would tweet out, no one liked/commented/retweeted compared to the number of followers she had. With a million followers, I would figure at least 5k likes on a photo of her surely, right? She was barely getting 10 likes per sexy photo, which is about what I was getting at the time. She also was only following about 100 people, so it was not a case of her following a bunch of people who were then just ignoring her after following her back. It really was bizarre. When I followed her links to her platforms, I found she did not have much in the way of feedback or activity going on. Her Social Blade showed that she had random spikes in followers and also spikes in purges. It was clear at the end of the day that she bought her followers. No, I never let on that I knew and continued to be friendly with her and even share her content. Why would I be mean to her? She did nothing to me!

Another reason why buying followers just did not seem to work for me though is one of the reasons I touched on above. Purges. Social media platforms will get rid of spam/robot accounts every so often. This means that if you bought 1000 followers, then in 2-4 months you will see about 600 of them just delete overnight if not all 1000. It is so obvious when your numbers are on such a huge rollercoaster all the time. That said though, companies that sell followers have gotten smarter. They also allow their bots to follow genuine people as well. This makes it where the robot accounts do not just become a list of people who purchase followers. There used to be a time you could go to a known robot account and check the list of everyone they follow and immediately know who was buying followers. Those days are gone though. This means that even if you never buy a follower, you may still get robot follows that will be purged. The difference being, you will not lose 600 followers but maybe about 50 or so when the purges happen.

Amberly Rothfield – How I Made $10,000 A Month as A Phone Sex Operator

Why do those who I know continue to buy followers and engagement? Some do believe that faking it until you make it is truly important in the eyes of their clients. I cannot attest to whether or not that actually matters. I have friends who have a few hundred followers, and they do just fine. Truly I think it all depends on what makes you feel better. I can not lie and say that having more followers doesn't help you in getting more attention, but it is not the end all be all. I do not have as many followers as most, but by engaging others, I have seen amazing growth.

At the end of the day, it is totally up to you if you want to go this route, but do know it is very against terms of service if you do. You are risking your account when you purchase such services. Honestly, I do feel your money could be better spent elsewhere and by the time you do have the money to do this, you will not need too.

Twitter

I love Twitter. No seriously, of all social media platforms, this is my favorite. Yup, I am admitting to a bias on this one. Twitter, I have found, is super easy for those just starting out. The best part is that it is super adult friendly. You can literally put completely nude photos up, and not worry about them being taken down! Its basis is for short replies, and open-ended conversations. While you can create a private account, on Twitter, I honestly do not see the point. Some use special accounts that are closed off so that they sell access to exclusive content. You may want to use that eventually but for now… this is about spreading the awesomeness that is you.

To get your Twitter game in check, you will want to start by creating a content release schedule. You will want to figure out how often you desire to update. At first, the more frequent, the better but again, my favorite word of relevancy really matters here. I suggest no more than every 4 hours. I

Amberly Rothfield – How I Made $10,000 A Month as A Phone Sex Operator

touched earlier in this chapter on free Twitter schedulers you can use. Simply sign up and once a week, fill in the upcoming days with your content. This makes it set and forget! That is not to say that you can not post on your own aside from that. These posts are simply just for self-promotion and ensuring that you push the content of those whom you wish to network with. With all that we have going on in the day, it is nice to know you did not miss getting the information out that you intended!

Next, you will want to pay special attention to what grabs the most attention on Twitter. I will give this first bit of advice to anyone using their own photos. Live streaming! Twitter, Instagram, Google, and Facebook are trying to compete with Twitch as king of the live streaming world. Once relegated to cam girls, people now live to stream their lives! Twitter has a separate app called Periscope which integrates with Twitter. If you are live, Twitter will promote you to more people than you have following you, simply to get eyes to stay on their platform. One of my favorite things to do is to hop on Periscope when I take a bath and show off my legs. Seriously has gained me quite a few followers. You do not have to live stream for an extremely long time at all. It can be just a few minutes, which you can then say hello and say a few things about your day and promote what you have coming up. About to start taking calls? Hop on your live stream and tell everyone! Word of caution though, you can not be nude on their live streaming network. Why? I have no clue, I just report to you the rules. Once your show is over, it is saved on your Periscope for I believe two weeks at least. I am not sure because I have heard some say that they do get deleted but none of mine have been unless I have myself deleted them. Anyways back on the track shall we? Grab the link to your previous cast and share it on your social media. This will help you gain followers on Periscope and get you more people watching when you go live!

A very close second to live streaming is, video! Something that has become super popular is to take a single image and place in a video editor (most computers have basic video editing software that will allow for this) and then just make it a few seconds long. I have some reservations for this as it comes off as gaming the system a bit too hard in my book and I can see platforms cracking down on this in the future. What you can also do though, is to make quick voice samples and set the image to something you have the legal rights too. Similar to how Twitter will promote the living daylights out of you if you are live streaming, Twitter puts additional promotion behind **VIDEOS UPLOADED TO ITS PLATFORM!** Amberly… why did you put extra emphasis on this? If you upload to say youtube and place the link on Twitter, you are taking people potentially off Twitter. Twitter also wants more videos on their site. Rather than fight, accept the extra promotion and follow the simple rules. It is like getting free advertising dollars from Twitter.

If live streaming and video are beyond your current capabilities, do not feel bad. Honestly, do not stress it too much because photos work very well too. Photos do not have to be just for yourself either. Many people reupload funny memes that they find; especially ones that they think will be shared. While I wouldn't ONLY do this, I have used it as filler to break up my feed from being strictly just photos of me. I am very arrogant at times, but even I do not want an entire feed just of myself. I do suggest that majority of any photos you upload though, be of content you have rights too. Since photos get a ton of views, I would also suggest posting a link to something you are promoting with every picture post you place. Yes, I did catch that I said 'majority of the photos you upload though, be of content you have rights too.' If you are uploading a picture of Thumper the rabbit from the Bambi movie, and his eyes are bugged out and then add the caption "When you get a random tribute from a customer," then you are transforming the work, which is considered Fair Use. No, do not use this type of stuff on your billing platforms but on social media profiles, you can usually get away with it. For this reason, though, I would try to keep this to a minimum.

The last type of post you can make are just sure textual posts. Even I get lazy and will do just text posts, but I highly do not suggest them as your primary way of interacting on Twitter. In people's feed, the text posts just do not stand out as well and often are glossed over. You will see you get little to no engagement with these sorts of messages. Make them the last resort or just one-off quips. I would not schedule such posts at all. I use text posts to respond to people but even then I will often use one of the prepopulated gifts that Twitter has uploaded.

Hashtags are the next on our list to tackle! Hashtags are a great way to see what is going on in a current conversation and to assess if such a conversation is even worth having. If I look up a hashtag in the search bar and find that the last post to it was a few months ago, I may still use it, but I will research a more active hashtag first. Remember, you only have a limited space to say your message on Twitter, gumming it up with irrelevant hashtags does you no good. That said, if the hashtag is just too perfect like say #cuckold (though that is for sure a popular one), I would still use that hashtag at least twice a week. That way, if someone does search that hashtag, they can indeed find you and you will most likely be at the top of that hashtag! Remember to keep it all relevant though! Bet you thought I was done with that word right? Nope!

What makes a good hashtag? A good hashtag on Twitter is one that has at least 2000 or so people using it and at least has someone in the last 2-3 days using it. In a bit of irony, really popular hashtags can actually be bad. Due to the sheer amount of people using it, you may not get discovered as easily for the hashtag. Hashtags are often sorted first by how popular the post was (likes, comments, and shares) and then by most recent. If a lot of people are using a hashtag and most are more popular than yours, your post will swiftly be buried before anyone gets a chance to see it. This is why, when you are small, I say go for small to medium hashtags where you can sit at the top for a while. **PRO TIP – also use smaller hashtags once you have built up some posts. You can sit on top of those little hashtags for MONTHS and get follows from people who love that niche content.**

Amberly Rothfield – How I Made $10,000 A Month as A Phone Sex Operator

Select about twenty different hashtags that you want to focus on. I suggest even writing them down. You will want to make sure that you make posts just for those hashtags throughout the week. I also suggest bookmarking that hashtag feed so you can find other relevant people to follow. This is how I do the majority of my own personal networking. Clearly, these are the people who make up my community, and thus I need to get to know them. The people who are prominent in the hashtags I am now following will also point me to other relevant hashtags I may never have thought about. Look at the other hashtags these people are frequently using. This can be an easy clue of other overlapping circles that you may want to run in!

On Twitter, you will find people who have accounts that they solely use for retweeting others. They frequently follow a ton of people to get a ton of follows back. If you tweet at them or use certain hashtags, they will retweet you. I could go into the variety of reasons some people create these accounts, but really that has no bearing on what you are trying to achieve by using these... services, yes we will call them services. I know what you are thinking now though, how do you find these accounts?

Honestly, I found many of these accounts by finding people I wanted to add to my tribe. I would go to research them and input their Twitter handle into the search bar. I began to notice accounts with RT (retweet) in their bio and usually a few hashtags that they follow in their bio as well. When looking that their feed, I saw that they did nothing but retweet others! I started tagging them in my tweets or using the hashtags they were following. Instantly, I was getting more retweets and engagements with my posts.

Now these retweet accounts, because they do follow a ton of people, do not often have a ton of engagement on their reposts. It may gain you a few followers, but many will unfollow if you do not follow them back. Worry not though! You are not engaging these retweet accounts to gain a ton more followers but rather to get them to retweet your posts. This adds more engagement and will bump you

206

up in the hashtag rankings of your posts. I know I went into retweet accounts in a previous portion of this book but did not get into using them for hashtags, as that wasn't relevant to that section. I would still NOT pay for any of their services as they usually do not have followers who are not other girls or bots. Are you using them? Well yes, but arguably that is what they want to do. The ones who do not require payment are more than happy to help spread your posts as a way to encourage you to post more sexy content. You wouldn't want to disappoint!

What I especially love about Twitter though…. THEIR STATISTICS PAGE! When it comes to running your business, nothing should be loved as much as having hardened statistics. Statistics tell you if you are growing or shrinking. Twitter breaks down absolutely everything about your account, for free! The type of information that it gives you typically is something someone would have to pay for, but they hand it to you. It tells you about your growth in followers, impressions (how many times people saw your content), retweets, likes, comments and even who your top followers are. You can see what of your content performed the best and what content other people tagged you in that performed the best.

The main thing I pay attention to though is the fact that you can compare yourself to the previous months. This is pivotal when you are planning your content and really focusing on growth. Being able to identify if any new tactics are working will only serve to show you where your brand direction should go and really tells you what the market expects out of you. Try to find common themes in what types of posts are performing the best and figure out how you can create more of that. Success is truly a science and Twitter is literally giving you the key to figuring out what elements you need for your formula.

So, time to put your tin foil hat on but don't worry, you do not need to screw it on too tight. I feel I can not tell you about Twitter without talking about some of it's more controversial aspects… The biggest one being that of 'shadow banning.' I will admit, I believed I was in fact shadow banned at one point. When I would give people my twitter handle, they would put it in their search bar but never were able to find me. I flipped the FUCK out. I started down the internet rabbit hole of searching out why this could be. I stumbled upon the conspiracy theory that Twitter bans certain accounts, without actually banning them. The idea was originally that Twitter did not want to ban 12 accounts of one troll, but rather to make it where no one could ever see their messages. This would satisfy the trolls need to spew vile rubbish and keep them from creating yet another account.

Then why would I be shadowbanned then? I do not tend to hop in the middle of 'shitposting,' and I am not known as a spammer or scammer. It turned out, within my settings, I selected to have my profile 'hidden' by marking myself as an adult account. I suggest you do this as well! If you are discovered to be posting content that is not family friendly, but you do not age gate yourself, you could lose your account or actually become shadow banned! If you age gate yourself, only those who are directly looking for you or stumble upon you when you enter conversations (replying to others or hashtag conversations). This means they can still find your profile by going to twitter.com/amberlypso (as an example) or if they search for your handle under the people tab. This is to help protect children from stumbling upon material that they should not be accessing. Yes, it does make it harder for us in the adult industry to get seen by those seeking us out but if it helps children stay away from adult material, I am all for it! This just means we need to try a bit harder and I have no problem putting in that effort! If you are truly shadowbanned, no one will ever be able to find you, and if you are just age-gated, well it just means you will have to work a tinge harder to get seen. That does not mean it can't be done. In fact, it makes me happy to know it is harder. Harder means fewer people will persist and thus more money on the other side for those of us who do!

To be successful in any social medium, you have to understand the culture of each platform. On Twitter, one of the more popular things is to tag people each day of the week (especially in the adult

Amberly Rothfield – How I Made $10,000 A Month as A Phone Sex Operator

industry) in the daily tag. Now there are different variations each day, so I will not list them all here, but one of the more popular ones is the #FF tag. This stands for Follow Friday. By placing this tag in your tweet and then adding as many people as you can, you are signaling all the people that you truly value. Most who are tagged in these types of posts will like and retweet (and you should reciprocate). Another common thing is to follow those to which others have tagged you with. It is the perfect excuse to get to know other people who run in your similar circle. Take this a step further and engage those who you are tagged with. Respond back and do not only say thank you but start a conversation. If another person does the same, JUMP in on that chit-chat. The more engagement you get on your profiles, the more the platform will begin to push your content. Social media sites only do well if they have people who are super active. The more active you are, the more the algorithm will push your content. Get out there and get talking!

I would like to talk about the Direct Messaging aka Dm on Twitter. I highly suggest having your direct messaging settings set to where anyone can message you. Many will argue with me on this, but even some MAJOR youtube creators have open DMs, and their life is not over. By default, Twitter will only allow for those that you follow and follow you back to message you. Now on my personal Facebook, that is how it should be, and I like it. I am not trying to promote my personal facebook though, so on my public and business Twitter... I allow anyone and everyone to message me! If you need to contact me, I want all points to be open. You never know who will be messaging you or the opportunities that can come your way.

Now what you need to know about opening your direct messages up.. well it is a lot so buckle yourself in. First off, yes... you will be getting a ton of unsolicited dick pictures. You will awaken to dicks of every shape and size. Many guys will see that MESSAGE button and believe that you indeed want to get a photo of their dick. If this sounds like something you can not tolerate, just exit this book now and perhaps find another industry. Not trying to be mean but this job is not for you. The good thing though,

Amberly Rothfield – How I Made $10,000 A Month as A Phone Sex Operator

Twitter will sort your messages between 'requests' and your inbox. Inbox is anyone you have messaged/replied too or those who also follow you back. Messages that go to your inbox will be from friends and people that you admire but that "request" section will be where your fans will be able to send you messages. What I do love about Twitter, I can view the entire message without the sender knowing until I click accept. This is how I screen messages for those that I will respond too and those which I will ignore. If the messages warrant a response, I will message them back. WARNING: do not allow those messaging you to be a time vampire though. I will often times say hello and if they want an in-depth conversation, I will drop a link to one of my billing platforms. This will weed out people very quickly.

What about the messages you will get from people 'not worth' messaging back? I still do, just not right away. I always go through my request messages and get to those I feel deserve my immediate response but when you assume things about people, you will leave money on the table. Pick up what others leave behind! Once a week, I send a message to those who sent requests to me and see how things will go. Often times, my original instincts were right but about 20% of the time, I do convert someone who seemed like a freebie seeker or troll into a customer. Be cautious though, do not spend more than a few minutes (collectively) on these accounts. Do not sit there sending additional photos without payment. If you private message me and ask for a photo, I will send you a link to my Twitter media feed. If someone sends me a photo of their dick, I will pretend they sent me nothing. I will ask if they have read my profile or checked out my website. If they show signs of being willing to have an actual conversation, they can get a few more minutes. If someone is just pushing their agenda though, just nope the hell out. No need to be rude or block, just stop answering them.

Twitter is truly one of the best places to begin when you want to build your presence. Just remember that it is a lot like watching the snowfall. When you first look out, all you can see are a few flurries in the air, but an hour later you will see a small layer. Next time you peak out your window, there will be a few inches, and before you know it, there will be a thick layer of snow out. Each made of the tiny little flurries you saw before. It takes time, but it builds and then will continue to build upon itself! Be sure to tweet and let me know you read my book, I will gladly engage in a conversation and cheer you on!

Instagram

My ONLY complaint about Instagram for those in the adult industry is that you cannot show nudity, and that to me is not that big of an issue. Instagram is fairly easy to gain a following on if you really try at it and is a great way to start anyone's career if they are serious about it. Another difference with Instagram is that you can not schedule posts (Hootesuite may allow out too now) like you can with other platforms and any links you apply to a post will not be clickable. You can only place a link on your profile page. This can suck, but I have found that I get plenty of people who click through from my profile. The way to view Instagram posting is more of that of being a photo/video blog. You can not do text posts without some sort of media (photo or video) to go with it. Ok, I just realized I lied… I really hate the fact that you can't break up your paragraphs whatsoever on the Instagram. If you go on a rant, it is just a wall of text.

Another thing that is super different about Instagram versus other social media giants is that you can do little to nothing on the web version of the site. You need to be logged into the application to post images. To understand this, you have to know the original intent of the site (which can help you get ahead of others later!). Instagram's founders envisioned people snapping photos and video clips and uploading automatically/instantly. They hoped to have a platform that is more organic and not overly photoshopped. Is that how it is used now? Of course not. You can see watermarks all over the place and edited clips. Now if you do edit your pieces, no you will not lose your account. I see people spouting that myth a lot. It is not against the rules, but clearly, there are barriers to try and keep this from happening. This is part of the reason that you can't schedule your posts using most social media scheduling sites. Instagram literally will go after services that find a way around their system.

So how does knowing this information help you? Where there are barriers, you should see opportunity. I know many girls who quit on Instagram because they find it too hard to upload the photos they want to, especially when they are not using pictures of themselves. Here is the secret to being able to do this on your computer. You can either download a free program called Blue Stacks which is a mobile phone immolator (the program acts like an android device, but it is on your computer). You can also email the photos to yourself, download them and then upload as you need too. Now this will require that you have some memory space on your device. Getting a memory card can be very affordable these days vs. when I first started.

If you do have a bit of money or you will be upgrading your phone soon, I would suggest getting an extra phone. This phone is not meant to be in a phone plan. Thus you will not occur any charge other than the purchase of the phone. All this phone needs to be able to do is access the internet. As you edit photos and have them ready, you can upload them to a cloud (Google Drive or any cloud service you like) and then post to Instagram from there. I personally have two phones for this purpose. My favorite phone is not good for taking photos, but I LOVE it. My old phone though was a Samsung Galaxy 6, and the photos were amazing. I just couldn't part with it, but I did not want to keep an extra phone that had no use. I decided to use it for just uploading images to Instagram! This frees up space on my phone that does accept calls, AND when I am recording (voice or video) I do not get calls that will break up my workflow!

Back to more tips on how to make Instagram work for you though eh?! Instagram uses hashtags just like Twitter does. Now, when you look at Instagram hashtags though, there are two separate sections. One is MOST popular, and the other is MOST recent. To get listed in most popular, you will need to have the most likes, views, and comments on items tagged with that hashtag of all time, whereas most recent is exactly what it sounds like. Just like with Twitter, I would suggest going after smaller hashtags to start. Trying to break into the #bigboobs hashtag could be extremely hard when you have little to no following. You can still use the larger tags but make sure to make the majority of your tags to be smaller ones. My ratio is about 5 tags with 3 being smaller, one being medium and one being a very competitive (but relevant) tag. As you gain traction in the lower two tags, the engagement they bring in will push you higher for the larger ones.

So what makes up a small, medium and large tag on Instagram? Well, there is a lot of conflict on this subject but here are my basic rules of thumb. First, you base the size of the hashtag off of the engagement to get into the number one slot. If the first piece of content under the most popular area has under 50 likes and comments, it is a small category. Now, this is WONDERFUL for you. Seriously, this is where you can post content and know you will sit at most popular for a while. Small tags are still searched by people, and as they see your pieces, they will like them and thus get you more engagement. If you have other tags on that image or video, then the engagements that you will gain from being high in the smaller tags will make those medium and high competition tags easier for you rank in.

As a personal example, I placed about 6-7 tags on one photo once. Most of my tags were smaller, and while at the time my Instagram was brand new for that account, I found I got over 3000 likes/views within my first hour of posting a photo. This was due to getting ranked high for a smaller tag but getting enough engagement that it pushed me to the 4-5 spot in most popular for a much larger hashtag. This gained me more and more likes/views and then the ONE major tag I listed… I found myself in the third spot of most popular for over two weeks. Use those small ponds to help you become a big

Amberly Rothfield – How I Made $10,000 A Month as A Phone Sex Operator

fish in the ocean. These smaller tags are overlooked by girls who want to be 'InstaFamous'. Many focus on just posting a TON of content in the larger tags. Usually, unless super lucky, they burn out before finding success.

Now how do you use Instagram if you are not using photos of yourself? With Instagram, you can always do captioned photos, but you will still need some sort of substance in the background. Honestly, if I were using content again, I would take photos and not show faces. Going to the mall? Snap some photos of sexy outfits in Victoria Secret. Same skin ton as your model? Take some sexy foot and shoe photos. Heading to a sex shop? Take some suggestive photos of some sex toys that your customers may want to imagine you using. There are ways you can create a photo blog (aka Instagram) without ever showing your face. A good thing to remember is that if you take the photo in public, you are allowed to use it however you see fit. That said though, given this is the adult industry, I would still blur or crop out faces. In my opinion, it isn't fair to possibly connect someone to an adult page when they did not consent to it. Be careful as well to ensure there are no minors in the photo. Try to make the subject of the image to be something sexy but not having other people in the shot.

Instagram stories, we can thank SnapChat for this. With Instagram stories, you can record videos that will stay up and your followers will get notifications of. Again, you do not have to show your face at all. This does require recording via their software though. For this, be creative. Perhaps decorate a section of your wall with your character's name and website and then just talk from behind the camera. You can also just show your legs and feet. Think outside of the box and try to make a new story every 1-2 days. I do not see many people using this feature but those who are have experienced better growth on the platform. Here is a major secret that truly applies to any and ALL websites where you can grow an audience on... when new features are rolled out, the platform will promote all who are actually using them. Instagram stories are still fairly new to the site, and thus, they are giving an advantage to those who are using them. Try to find a way to incorporate this feature into your content promotion strategy!

Instagram also allows for the posting of the video, but their system for promoting said videos is a bit different than other social media sites. On Youtube, someone has to click on a video for the view to be counted. It would seem that on Instagram and now Facebook, that if the video appears in your feed... it will be 'played' and thus gets a view. Regardless of the sound is used or not, you will get a view which on Instagram counts as a like! What this equates to is that video content ranks better than photo content, by algorithm sake alone! Even if you are not using your own photos, it just makes sense to try and create some sort of video content. Even if it is a static image that is then set as a silent movie. Use this rather than just an image! Instagram wants to encourage people to use more video than images to compete with other social media sites. They are actually pushing video content and giving you free advertisement! Take advantage of this and use it to your advantage!

Make sure that you are following people on Instagram, just like you would on any other social media site! I can not tell you how many girls come to me about trying to market, but they follow no one. Use those hashtags that you studied earlier to figure out who you will want to follow. Now Instagram does not have a list system like Twitter does so you can not filter people about. This will make it hard to keep up with key people if you are following a ton of people. This is where my engaging technique differs from the engaging technique I use on Twitter. Instead of really not caring who I follow, I am more selective on Instagram. If I were to follow just about everyone I came across, it would be difficult to see the important updates of those that I truly do want interact with on a frequent occasion, if not impossible. You do not want those whom you are networking to think you are just using them (nor should you just use them), but it can be hard to keep up with them if you can't see their updates due to your feed being flooded. Don't worry, I have a foolproof plan to allow you to continue having amazing engagement with your network.

Instead of following everyone, I suggest just commenting on EVERYONE's posts. Ok, within reason and relevancy but yes, I do suggest trying to make as many comments and likes as you can.

Amberly Rothfield – How I Made $10,000 A Month as A Phone Sex Operator

When you are doing your hashtag research, really look at the top posts and make a comment. Engage the person who posted that content and try to ask a question. Questions beg for answers and answers mean that the person who has that top piece of content will engage back with you. When you are just starting out, try to make at least 25 comments a day to new people. If someone comments back, then comment back to them as quick as you can and try to also work in another question. Keep that conversation going by whatever means necessary and really try to get to know this person. If someone engages with me at least three times, I tend to start shouting them out and resharing their stuff. Watch as others begin to do the same for you!

Now Twitter has recently allowed for users to allow for anyone to send them messages and even Facebook is now allowing for filtered messages based on if you are friends with a person but, Instagram has always had this feature. If you are not following the person, the message will be filtered, but one thing I love about Instagram's direct messaging system is that the sender of the message will never know if I saw their message or not, unless I click accept. Just like with Twitter, I suggest that you ALWAYS allow for messages. You can check the messages and respond if you feel they warrant a message back. You also do not have to see any images sent until you accept their message. If you send me just a picture message, I will rarely open it because it is probably a dick pick. Through the sea of dick pictures though, I do get website owners, collaborators and other opportunities by checking my messages. Every opportunity that you get to get a message, take it. You never know who is seeing your content and who will want to reach out to you. I get a lot of customers as well, who send me custom requests for mp3s or set up times for a call. Many of those I speak too are often blown away I responded, because many girls will not allow them to message them.

Unlike the other social media mega platforms on here, I do not know as much about SnapChat as I should. I know that a lot of girls sell their private snap chats and allow for contact via this method. The problem with SnapChat and the phone sex industry is that you can not upload images and video onto it like you can on the other sites. Yes, Instagram is a pain in the backside accomplish this, but it is possible. You can use similar methods on Snapchat, but it will be more difficult if you are using legal content and not photos of yourself.

I believe though, where other people see a mountain. There is an opportunity! The only reason that I have not started using this myself is just due to time constraints. I want to push my other social media profiles and build them up before I add on. So how can someone not using their own photos, use SnapChat?

- You can still point the camera at a wall or some beautiful scenery and just talk from behind the camera.

- You can use wigs, makeup, and thick glasses to conceal your identity (given that the content you chose is close to how you look once you are done up in that way).

- You can show select body parts (legs, shoes, cleavage, etc.).

- Cardboard cut outs, I have not seen this yet but you could get a full length printout of your content model and then stand it up. Again, voice behind the camera type motif but this could be a new spin!

Now, if you are using your own photos, then you do not need to worry about all of these hoops to jump through. You can still use the ideas though, to mix up the content that you are producing. So on to some advice that would work with both content users and those who are the face of their brand shall we?

I have seen two separate methods of using SnapChat. There is the premium SnapChat, where you offer racier content (SnapChat is adult friendly!) and commenting back to your fans and then open/vanilla SnapChat accounts where you would just post updates. Those who I see really working the SnapChat market, have both. One is open, and the id is given out freely, but the other is only given out to those who pay.The allure of SnapChat is that once you post something, someone can see it and then it is automatically deleted. Now there are ways of saving Snaps, but for the average person, it is gone forever. You can imagine, those who are jerking off/getting naked love this feature!

On SnapChat, you can create lists of people. With those lists, you can send out 'snaps' which can be video or photos. There are also some fun filters as well too, which change your appearance and add extra stuff to your snaps. It is a great way to create a captioned photo, though other platforms are catching onto this. You can also create 'stories' which will stay up for longer than the instant view once and delete. If you do not want to maintain two different SnapChat accounts, you can create a private list to move those who pay onto it and send them exclusive snaps. Personally, I find this to be a bit better than keeping two accounts but different strokes. If it works for you, then please do it!

Those who know your SnapChat account can also send you snaps and you can begin with private 'message' them. Messages are different on SnapChat, as they are photos and videos. Again, use discretion, but I would advise applying the previous advice here. If someone takes time to send you a message, then they are showing interest in you. Take the time and respond back to each possible one you can. Do not give too much away but take it as an opportunity to convert someone who stumbled upon you into a true fan!

Tumblr

Insert praising the writer of the forward to this book – Shayna Domina. On a serious note though, Shayna is the one who turned me onto Tumblr. I can not tell you how amazing this site is and I STILL UNDERUSE IT! Tumblr is a strange cross between Facebook and Twitter when it comes to website functionality. When I first signed up for it, I HATED this site. I turned away and was resolved never to come back. I am a serious fool, no seriously a MAJOR fool! During a mastermind session with Shayna, I was shown how powerful this social media megastar can be to us phone sex operators!

First off, they are ADULT FRIENDLY. You can post just about anything on this site, and I do mean just about anything. If you have to ask, the answer probably is yes. Many fetishes that considered too taboo for the racist of phone billers to cover are still found on this site. Go make an account now! Another feature I love though is you can create multiple pages under a SINGLE account. This is AMAZING if you cater to multiple fetishes. Having a single mega-site can be an issue when you are starting out, because if you post content that your previous viewers do not resonate with… they will unfollow you. So you can easily create 2-4 profiles and have them run and promote your single website. Look at this as a funnel!

Does running 2-4 profiles sound like too much work? Well, do not worry, Tumblr is here to help you out and in a MAJOR way. So if you are a bootstrapper (or just in general cheap like Shayna and me), this is what is just jaw dropping for me! You can schedule your posts to INFINITY. By going into your account settings, you can make it where you can schedule your posts and tell Tumblr how often to publish a post. Now their system is a bit strange if you are new to it, but Tumblr will ask you how often you want to post to your page. If you set it to post every 2 hours, that means after 12 posts, you will have no more content coming out. Now you do not need to post every 2 hours (though it does help!). You can set your posts to come out 1-3 times a day and be perfectly fine!

The added bonus of Tumblr is that it will post to your Twitter accounts. Yup! You can use Tumblr to schedule multiple other sites and also gain followers from their site… FOR FREE! Before you get too excited though, I personally still use other schedulers. I like knowing the precise times that my content will come out, especially if it is strategic content. Services like Hootesuite also allow you to have a few more social media sites included in your scheduling and does include Tumblr. Starting out though? THIS IS WHAT YOU SHOULD USE!

Do not know what to post? Don't you worry my friend! Get your hashtags together and find other Tumblr blogs. You can find the others who are producing content like yours and then REBLOG what they post. This is considered totally ok and even encouraged! When you reblog, the person you are reposting from will get a notification. BOOM, another person will know how you are! Another game changer here? Tumblr keeps the tags that the post originally had. If someone posts an image with 7 tags, when you repost it, it will retain those posts and thus be at the top of those hashtag categories as new content.

Now, this brings me to another point about hashtags and being at the top. Remember again, that the adult industry is large but also small compared to other communities. Get into some of the micro fetishes, and you have large pools of viewers but very little content coming out. While reblogging can get people to find you and possible collaborations, remember to create your own content. Got an mp3 coming out? Hype it up and make a graphic for it. Tumblr does well with photos and Gif (moving image files). Creating something original and that you have the rights too and get it out there. When people look up those hashtags, they will see a bunch of posts that are reblogged and reblogged. Your fresh content will really turn eyes and thus get you, FOLLOWERS! Remember that content is always king and the better content that you can create, the more people will be interested in you.

Make sure to post content that people will want to view but also remind the viewer what you are about. Post your phone numbers and store links. Tell the viewers that if they want to see more, then to click your links. This is PIVOTAL! I know I have spoken about calls to actions, but they are the make it or break it a difference in those who have followers and those who have followers that convert to cash. Take a page from Gary Vaynerchuk and remember Jab Jab Jab Right hook! This simply means that for every three or so posts you make that are pushing content you know your customers will just love, hit that fourth post with something to remind your followers how to contact you and what they can do to support you. This is not seedy at all! If your fans do not support you, then you cannot continue to create the content that they love. Trust that your fan base will want to support you!

Thought I was done talking about private messages? Nope! Tumblr has a private message system as well. I believe you do have to follow each other, but if you find a way for fans to message you, I do suggest you respond as I have described earlier in this chapter. I find that most of the messages I get on Tumblr tends to be from people I follow and thus they are asking more for collaborations. Now responses to my posts? I am all over them and always answer as I can see them! Never leave a message unanswered, even negative ones. Find a way to spin everything in your favor and never show that your feathers are ruffled. New customers love to find ways to connect with you for free at first, and it is up to you to show that you will provide a service they will enjoy. Shoot a response or two but again not too much. I may reply about 3-4 times and maybe one to two sentences at best.

The last thing that I love about Tumblr is the mutual tag discovery and that Tumblr will suggest people to you based on your history. Yes, I know that Twitter does something similar to the side of your

Amberly Rothfield – How I Made $10,000 A Month as A Phone Sex Operator

feed but to me, Tumblr has a far better way of pushing this. On Twitter, the suggestions are based on your most recent history. On Tumblr, it seems that they pay more attention to your overall search history and interactions. The reason that this is a big deal is that once you decide to tweet to someone who is not apart of your core demographic, you start getting a lot of suggestions of people that you do not care to actually follow. This can gum up discovering new people. While on Tumblr, it seems to understand that you may look up something totally unrelated once but not continue to believe that is the type of content you want to see. I once went to look up a Jeffery Star tweet, and all of a sudden Twitter thinks I want to follow every beauty guru from Youtube. Took a week for it to begin to show me, relevant new people, again!

Discovering new people and content on Tumblr are made especially easy, as Tumblr will suggest to you hashtags based off ones you have used and looked up. If you type in Hypnosis into the hashtag search on Tumblr, you will also be suggested similar hashtags like – Mind Control, Mind Fuck, and ASMR. So when you are looking for content to reblog or just seeing what is out there, you can find ideas for future content and really see other areas to expand your brand into. Sticking with the hypnosis example, if your customers like hypnosis mp3s then they may like ASMR. Maybe try to mix your sexy hypnosis mp3s with some sexy ASMR mp3s or maybe a hypnotic ASMR mp3! See how you can mix them up? I love using Tumblr to spark some ideas when I feel that I am running low on creativity. We have all been there!

Due to Tumblr really encouraging sharing blogs with others, do take this advice if you listen to nothing else… WATERMARK YOUR STUFF. Do not put out a single stitch of original content out there and NOT watermark it with your name or website. When you place that watermark, do not make it in a place that would make it easy to crop out. Know that some girls and even some guys, will take your photo and crop out your watermark to reuse your content. If someone wants to reuse your content, then they can at least be giving you free advertising!

Amberly Rothfield – How I Made $10,000 A Month as A Phone Sex Operator

In conclusion, new social media sites will continuously crop up. I will never tell you NOT to sign up for them and test them out but know that different strokes. The sites I LOVE the best, do not work for every single girl I know. Whatever fits well with you, work it and work the living daylights out of it! Many of the tips and tricks discussed in each individual section above work on other platforms. Just try to think outside of the box and see where you can take advantage of features that others are ignoring!

Chapter 11 – Messengers

Why does this deserve a whole chapter? This is one of the biggest parts of my business outside of custom clips and my offline sales. Messengers are any program in which you use to contact your customers with on a live basis. At one point, AOL had the monopoly on this and then yahoo instant messenger until recently. The big shift has been to Skype since Yahoo's new interface is so sub-par. Even I hate it so much that I refuse to use it, despite having such a rich list of customers on Yahoo! Do not color me a fool though, as most of the contacts I had on there have also migrated over to Skype!

I want to speak first on why this is such a pivotal part of your business. Everyone thinks phone sex will/would die to cam girls and porn sites, this is simply not true. To enjoy porn or cam girls, you need usually need a larger screen, and it is hard to type on mobile devices. Whereas, guys sneak away frequently to chat with me on the phone. Before they get a chance to escape, they usually hit me up on a messenger to see if I am around. There are many times I COULD take a call, but I am just not logged in, as I like to keep regular hours. My long-term clients know though, they can hop on Skype and schedule some fun time with me. While platforms like Niteflirt do not allow it, you can have guys pay for your chat time as well. I have my clients send me Amazon E Gift Cards for text chat time (make sure you give no time though, until that email with the code is in your inbox and you check to ensure that code is real). I also will talk to my heavy spenders for free as well. This is how you cultivate a relationship with your audience, giving personal attention!

It is that personal care that sets us apart. Cam girls are beautiful but often times, they have a bunch of people in their chat room, and it isn't personalized. Even when guys get to go private with the girls, there may be other people in that cam show (as most of those girls make their bank off group shows). Porn sites are pre-recorded and thus not personal. Each call and even mp3 or video can be though. With private chat, you can send photos and actually engage at a more relaxed pace. I can also have several chats going in different windows at once, this is my version of a group show. Each person feels as if I am only talking to them and I can work multiple clients. This, of course, maximizes profits! Being on the phone is great, but you can only talk to one person at a time, whereas I can have as many chats open as I personally can handle (I max out at about 12 before people have delayed response times).

Which messenger you choose is entirely up to you. Your guys will download/follow whatever lead you put out there. I would advise against having too many different types though or using social media private messaging as your only form of private messaging. With social media private messages, you often can't have multiple windows open as they are created for mobile devices. I also do not want to be forced by their terms of service, should someone become upset and try to turn you in. Could your messenger shut down your account? It is true they could, but the chances are less likely. I have yet to have heard of Yahoo or skype deleting someone's account unless there are actual threats or illegal stuff going on.

Yahoo

Now Yahoo instant messenger is still pretty popular, but honestly, the new interface is awful. I literally used it solely for 11 years. I tried other things as they popped up but never really liked them or my clients. When they changed their interface to be more 'modern,' it actually lost a lot of its ease of functionality. I also found that it was no longer compatible with my desktop, where I do most of my work at. It was clunky at best with my devices that are newer as well. My clients complained about incoming pictures I sent not getting to them and trying to watch someone's webcam became more involved and extremely difficult. I found most of my conversations with my clients became more tech

Amberly Rothfield – How I Made $10,000 A Month as A Phone Sex Operator

troubleshooting and no, my clients were not paying for this. This was about two years ago. The more recent releases are able to be worked on my computer, but the interface is still really clunky. It may be that it took Yahoo too long to figure it out, but I get maybe one or two message a month from older clients who haven't made a move to Skype yet.

Modern-day Yahoo no longer allows you to go back years into your conversation archives. It used to be that your messages were saved onto your computer, but now with their move, it is saved onto Yahoo's cloud storage. They seem to delete it. If something is said that is important, make sure to screenshot and save it to your device. It could be that they just wiped the old files when they brought out the new interface but being safe is always better than being sorry.

For the sake of this book, I did have a trusted client of mine go to test the new interface and even redownloaded and updated Yahoo for my computer. It still takes forever to send photos via their new system. I also could no longer see who was online and who is offline. If you are familiar with Skype or even Facebook messenger, you can usually see if those on your contact list are actually available to chat too or logged out. You once could also put a link in your profile status for those on your contact list to be able to click to see your latest information. Both of these features seem to have gone the way of the Dodo bird and are extinct. Yet another reason why I do not use Yahoo.

Now I bring up Yahoo as there are plenty in the industry who still use it and love it. Like social media, I want you to use what works best for you. I totally suggest having a place to funnel all your guys too, and that makes it easy for you to contact people on the fly. Direct or private message systems on social media are still a great way for new people to contact you but those that start spending money on me, I always pull to something more private. If you are on my Skype, then you are a verified non-timewaster. All of that to say though, if you like Yahoo, ROCK IT! Knowing the pitfalls though, will allow for you to come up with a plan if one of your customers really hates it.

Skype

Now I stopped doing webcam years back and just now beginning to do it again. Those who have grown large doing webcam all love Skype for 1 on 1 as a messenger. It has an extremely clear picture and doesn't tend to freeze. I also love that Skype allows me to mute someone. If they send me a message, I do not have to delete them but can mute them and check in later. This helps for those who chat you up a ton and do pay but aren't at the moment. Or someone who is beginning to e-stalk you. They can just chat away with themselves without your notifications constantly going off.

Skype also allows for me to just pick up my phone and move around my house from my office. With Yahoo Messenger, I had to re-login if I was logged in elsewhere and it was just an extra hassle. I also could not call from my phone if I had a call on my desktop going. With Skype, I can almost seamlessly transfer my calls to another device without too much stress. If I went to take a bath, I can pop in my waterproof blue tooth and keep the fun going. Yes even with just text, as I can do text from speech with my phone. After a long night of typing, this is truly needed in life! Careful though, switching between conversations will need to be done manually.

Skype allows me to put a status update as well, that I use primarily for putting my websites as an advertisement. Those looking for when I take calls generally know when they will be able to find me, as the times in which my profile is greenlit are all super consistent. I also want those who just add me to see the sites I want to highlight. Whenever I log on, they get an alert and when they go to click on my name, they see my status just right there. PERFECT! It also serves to give my clients a way to scratch their 'Amberly itch' when I am offline. Remember that offline sales are pivotal to your business construct.

Amberly Rothfield – How I Made $10,000 A Month as A Phone Sex Operator

I want to take this time to discuss time wasters. Now time wasters can come in MANY forms and will come at you in any kind of contact you can find. The trick is to spot them early and handle them appropriately. While most time wasters will not pay you a dime, there are some who will pay you here and there to draw out as long as they can get. Even if you have 'time' because the phones aren't ringing or sales aren't coming in, they are not worth it. The more attention they receive, the more they will try. Yes, my Skype is full of non-timewasters, but there have been many who earned the right and then got a bit too comfortable!

The biggest place you will find time wasters are where your messengers are concerned. If you give away your messenger names, which I suggest you do especially at first, they will contact you and present themselves as a potential customer. These guys are SAVVY, and this is rarely their first time trying this. Hell, in some cases they are working several girls at once. They hunt for new accounts, assuming it is a new girl who will not know their ways. If someone hasn't paid for my time in any sort of way within 5 minutes, they are ignored. May not get muted or blocked, but I will put my attention on something more worth my time. Skype will allow you to add a nickname to those on your list. I like to put a big fat TW next to the name of someone who is just constantly running their mouth. When they send a new message, I instantly know that they have tried to test me before. I will send a line to politely remind them that they do need to pay for my attention, and if they do not within about five minutes, I just ignore them.

NEVER talk about anything sexual either till they do pay you. Think about it, if someone really wants your attention, that 'customer' would pay for it. It is also my way of weeding out or screening those who come before me and children. Children will not have access to a payment method, but they may have access to skype/the internet. Your time is worth something, so treat it as such. Do not fall for someone saying, what will you do to me? Or them saying, talk about what you will do to me and I will pay... NOPE! This is also why I do have some freebies available. You can quickly drop that link as a sample and move along. If they buy something, great! If not, then you're either not a match, or they have no intention of paying. Either way, no time stolen from you.

The best way to rationalize this is, time is the only resource we can NEVER get back. Why let someone be a vampire to yours? These guys are super skilled as they have practiced on thousands of girls, and I do mean thousands of girls. Another warning sign, does this guy change his id frequently? There really are only two reasons to change your id.

1. You got locked out and forgot your log in information

2. A massive amount of people have blocked you, and you want to start anew.

When I was green to the game, I knew a guy I talked to daily for a few minutes each time didn't eat up too much time in any one go, but it added up. The odd thing about him has he CONSTANTLY had a new id. I found out why after realizing that little by little, he got a few jollies from me and I was probably one of the few giving him any attention... For a good reason. Lesson learned and I have never had such a situation again. Remember, this is a business, and we absolutely pay to play.

Now that a huge mistake in vetting a potential client is to immediately say PAY ME! SOOO many girls do this and guys are actually sick of it. Instead, I like to ask them how did they find me. Regardless if they are time-wasting or not, this tells me what marketing techniques are working or which I should pursue more. If a bunch of guys are coming from someplace, someone dropped my link or mentioned me; I should probably go check that place out. This gives me instant benefit in knowing what aspects of my marketing are working and in many cases, shows me new websites or forums where I am being discussed. Apparently very few girls tak this approach too and thus the guys are a bit taken back and become more intriqued.

After asking how did they find me, I like to ask them how are they and other pleasantry type questions. NOTHING SEXUAL! Once they start getting sexual, I remind them that unfortunately, I am in massive demand and only have time for paying customers. If they just want to say hi, they are more than welcome too, but I really do not discuss such things for free. Yes, that is long winded PAY ME, but it shows that I have others who want my attention. I am not merely ignoring them waiting and praying money will come along. This destroys any, tease me, and I'll pay because why would I? I already have people paying. This is basic sales psychology. If no one is perceived to be paying you, then why would that customer want too? The instant they know that others are paying for the same thing they want out of you, they will dip out or pony up!

Frequently, those who once tried to get free time or products out of me, become paying customers. I am dead serious. Once someone becomes interested, but they see they can not get anything for free, they typically break down and pay. We all have done it. When it comes to running your business, think about how you shop. When I go makeup shopping, I will find a product that I like, but it isn't JUMPING at me for to purchase it then. I shop a lot at Sephora and will often get a sample. That sample will usually wear on me for a few days or even weeks, but eventually, if it really jelled with me I will go back and buy it. It is the same with the customers and part of the reason I have samples available. Examples mean I can direct them to my freebie spot, and if they like it, they will pay and if not move along.

How does all of this pertain Skype though? This is how I deliver a good portion of my freebies. Remember back to the chapter on sales funnels, well how do you get the customers into those funnels? When a new customer is added to my messengers, I will frequently send them a freebie on a page that will set them into a sales funnel. They sit there talking to me on messenger and buying my wares. I am getting notifications via email, each time they make a purchase. They are then paying to message back and forth with me in real time as well. Best part though? They are rarely the only person I am speaking too!

Some time wasters, do not mean to be a time waster though. They may be on a strict budget and can not afford much, BUT they truly do like you. They can be the WORST kind of vampire if you let them . Since they have paid out before, you assume they will pay out again. Instead, you get engaged in long conversations that end up nowhere and yes I mean nowhere. If someone is not paying you, you are giving your product away for free. Your time is better spent elsewhere. What is worse, you are teaching that client that you are worthless with each passing free minute they get. If they begin to cry about money, tell them kindly that you will speak to them when they are in a better spot. Their financial problems should not becomes yours.

You have to be firm, and you have to be consistent. You need to train your clients to respect your time. I, in fact, LOVE using that phrase. I always tell clients to respect my time and realize that I am not here for little fun. If someone says that you must not enjoy it if you want to be paid, tell them that you love it so much, you never want to stop! Which means you charge for it. But remember, no more than a sentence or two answers, OR they are baiting you into the conversation. Which leads me to my next topic within the time-wasting genre...

DO NOT FALL FOR BAITING! Again, these guys are PROFESSIONAL time wasters. They get a product that others have to pay for FOR FREE! They spend hours cultivating this craft, and they know what to say to get under your skin. Do not let it. If they haven't paid, their opinion doesn't matter and fighting with them ONLY MAKES THEM HAPPY. Tell them you are pay to play and roll on. Yes, they will have a retort, they will continue to try to get you back into the conversation, but they do eventually give up... they will move on. I see girls talk about being frequently baited and showing proof of how they fell

Amberly Rothfield – How I Made $10,000 A Month as A Phone Sex Operator

for it. I will never understand why someone will take to social media to sound off about a time-waster to 'out' them when you are giving them free attention. They brag about telling a guy off. Chances are, he was into humiliation, and you just gave him free attention. You never know what someone is into so do not attempt to try to 'turn them around' and no you did not win by 'telling them off.'

Those same guys who tried to bait them, often end up calling me for almost double the amount per minute then the other girls are priced at. Many time wasters are not poor or losers, far from it. Many of them actually have significant money, but they just do not want to spend it, or they want to see if you will fall for their tactics. Regardless the size of their bank though, it is your time and your time is best spent on those actively paying you. A good thing to look into is that of toping from the bottom. Guys will try this a lot and do so more on private messengers than on social media. They do not want to do it out in the open, where other girls will see they are doing it. Rather they do it privately and in hopes that you will fall for it and they can get something from you.

Whats App

Ok, so the Skype portion of this chapter covered a ton about timewasters... so I will not go into that here, but even if you do not wish to use Skype, it is worth reading through that so that you can avoid those pitfalls when it comes to What's App. What is WhatsApp? Well, it is a pretty awesome service that allows you to get a phone number to give out to others that will work as a mask for your real number. People can call, text and send media files to you like a normal phone but they do not get your real phone number. Better yet, you can turn the app off and not receive notifications from it when you are not logged in.

Some people really like this as you will not have to pay for extra minutes on your phone if you are not on an unlimited plan and calls can be routed via wifi rather than your data plan. Whether or not this benefits you will depend on what type of cell phone and internet plan you have. I do not personally use this app but have had it from time to time. Due to a new service called SextPanther (I may write about this on my industry blog at AmberlyRothfield.com but I have not really played on this site yet, and it is considered 'new'), I do not see the need for the App. SextPanther allows for the same thing, but I can get paid for messages back and forth. Some girls use the app to call other girls without having to get out their information, in case of collaboration as an example. I just give out my cell phone number in that case or my Skype if I am concerned about privacy.

Nevertheless, though, this is considered a method of messenger and most that I see using it, do so as a premium service. With SextPanther, every message you receive will be being paid for where WhatsApp would be free. Similar to Snapchat, but not considered a social media platform, those who use this in the sex industry do so if fans have paid. It makes a great upsell, but I would limit who gets access. You do not want someone paying you $10 for a short phone call and then having access to chat with you endlessly for free. A slight warning, if you have friends or family who have the app on their phones, this app can detect it and then notify them. While I am totally out of the adult industry closet, I originally steered clear of this app for that reason. I do not openly talk about where my online profiles are with my friends or family. If they find it cool, but I never would push it in any of their faces. Most who choose phone sex vs stripping or being a cam girl is because they do not want others to know what they look like. Use caustion if you decide to use this app.

Chapter 12 – Taxes, LLC, and Retirement

The most unfun chapter in this book right? I know, I am NOT a tax professional, but I do have some advice that is pretty universal. I also wanted to take a chapter, even if it is short, to explain how important this is and the best way to set yourself up to pay your taxes. No matter the route you go, you will be responsible for paying your tax liability. Your check will not automatically come with your taxes already out of them. Trust me, it is TEMPTING to just spend every dime that comes in. DON'T!

I spent 5 years of my life not paying taxes as I was ignorant to needing to pay them. When I did file, I owed more than I ever physically seen. Luckily, the IRS has worked with me and educated me on how to stay on the straight and narrow. The cost? I had to pay so much in penalties and fees. Miseducation and ignorance truly have a pretty high price, and I want to spare you from it.

I do not care how much you are making, put 25% away. What you do not end up owing, goes into a retirement fund. Oh even more depressing? Thinking about your old age care. Well, this is the reality for us all! We will get old and at the very least, fall on hard times. I literally had a house burn down and lost everything. Yes, I had insurance, but there is a lot that insurance is unable to cover or cover quickly! I was so glad to have a nest egg to fall back on. I did not have to wait for my insurance to put money in my account, I just went to a hotel. When my car was totaled by someone running a red light, I did not have to wait to get my rental car. When my bags went to the wrong airport, I was able to go grab clothes I liked on the spot to tie me over. If I didn't put my pennies aside properly, I would have been up you know what creek!

That money can also be saved for future marketing or opportunities that come your way. Some of the best websites to market you on are super expensive but how can you get on there if you do not have the dough? As Robert Kiyosaki from Rich Dad Poor Dad says, pay yourself first! Trust me you will

thank me. Plus if you put this money aside, it can earn you interest. Yes, you will have to pay money on

the interest, but that is another form of income for you. I absolutely count that as a part of my $10,000 a

month. The money generated from my phone sex work that gets set aside makes me more money. It is

almost like it goes to find other friends to bring home with it. Unless your last name is Rothchild, then

the amount set aside will not be making crazy money, but it will indeed begin to gain for you

Back to taxes though eh? My favorite adult accountant is the Tax Domme, Lori St Kitts of

http://www.taxdomme.com/. Be sure to tell her I sent you! She not only prepares adult industry taxes

but non-adult as well. She is super understanding, and you do not have to hide what you are doing for a

living, she has literally seen it all. She can tell you what you can and can not write off. She was the first

person I told about not having filed for years when I learned I had to pay taxes. She did not shy away but

instead help point me to where I can find aid and relief. Her rates are fantastic too. Seriously, other

preparers I have gone to for quotes charge almost double and when I told them what I did, their eyes

bugged out of their heads. One even told me to take a hike and believed that I was doing something

illegal. Another reason you want an industry tax professional is that they know ALL the ends and outs of

your business. Lori St Kitts even gave me advice on what other things I can write off that may increase

my revenue and quality of the clips I created in the future.

You would be amazed at what all you can write off. Not only your phone and internet but also

fuel if you take packages to the mail (if your customers buy panties for example). You can write off

portions of your mortgage or rent, utility bills, makeup (cam girls or if you use your phone photos),

content you buy legally, computers, office equipment, microphones, paper, pens and just about

anything office related. There are so many things you can write off! When I go on trips to visit other cam girls or adult conventions, I can put the tickets and other travel expenses on my taxes. Of course, Lori would be a better person to discuss this with, and I am just giving you a basic idea.

Being responsible for your own taxes, it is best to do your taxes quarterly. Yes, tax season is one point out of the year but for us business owners (even company workers), we do them quarterly. This means you assess yourself every 4 months to see where you are, this allows for the best prediction of how much you will owe. Being as you will have so much you can write off, it helps to keep your paperwork in order as well. I also highly suggest you make quarterly payments. It makes that April 15th payment look smaller as 3/4th will be paid already, but it also helps you stay on track.

Keep the 2nd savings account that you can not access and ship the money twice a month off into that account. If you are putting 1/4th of the money you make in there, eventually there will be more money on that account than you will owe for your taxes. KEEP IT THIS WAY. Even if something awful happens, you want to ensure your taxes get paid because Uncle Sam does not care that your car broke down or that you needed to fly to your cousin Sally's funeral. Come April 15th, you should have extra money in this account. These funds now roll into a Roth IRA. Now without knowing your living situation or marital status, I can not say how much you can contribute a year but as a rule of thumb, being single you should be able to contribute 5,000 a year. I have heard that this could be upped for those of us who are self-employed. This is another thing you want to talk about with your tax professional.

I would suggest that you MAX THIS OUT! Put in every DIME you can because it is not only another write-off, BUT this is for your retirement. You can not phone bone forever and no matter the job you have, everyone should have an exit plan. This world is very feast or feminine, and even if you are slinging a 9-5 job, there are layoffs/downsizing. Having something to fall back on is critical to keep you afloat for the next gig. What makes this even more (potentially) problematic is when there is no

Amberly Rothfield – How I Made $10,000 A Month as A Phone Sex Operator

guaranteed paycheck based on how many hours you have worked. Put money aside and do not make excuses why you can't. Your future self will be thankful for you doing this. If you are doing phone sex but can not afford to set money aside, you may not be at the point where you can be independent yet. Consider getting a more vanilla job while you build your business up or supplement by working for a phone sex company. Your retirement and emergency fund are not optional.

Research your banks as well. I say this because when my father died, I had to dip into my IRA a bit to help pay for his final expenses. My bank allowed me to take the bit out as a loan and pay it back quickly as to avoid penalties for going into it too soon. See IRA's are individual retirement accounts and meant for you to keep your money there long term. If you take money out early, you will have to pay CRAZY penalties because it goes against the purpose of the account. Banks are growing more and more understanding though, and that feature meant a lot to me. I was able to pay it all back within a few months and was given no penalties at all. Do not use this as an excuse to upgrade your car or move to a bigger house or live outside of your means. That money should ONLY be dipped into for extreme emergencies. In my case, I knew that my dad's life insurance would pay me back for the expenses. Being inconvenienced is not a reason to take this money out. This is your lifeline should anything happened. Treat it as such!

Another place that allows you to save and do so cheaply is Lending Club. This is a legit website, I have used it myself for years. It is crowdfunding loans. You get the same financial information that lenders get (a person's income which is often verified and their credit scores) and can put in as little as 25 dollars towards their loan. Once their loan is funded, they pay for it, and you get your money back *slowly* with interest. If you do not know about other types of investments, this is an excellent way to start but do know that if someone doesn't pay, then you do not get paid. Choose people wisely, and this won't be too much of a problem. I have yet to have had someone default, but it could happen. You can also sell the loans you have invested in, but you will have to take a loss on most chances. It is a decent way to save, but the money is still accessible (if someone decides to take the loan up for you) if you absolutely need it! If you have limited funds, you can buy loans from other people at discounts, though you need a special account to do so. Contact Lending Club by calling them to set up your account and save a headache I had to go through.

I want to touch back on taxes though. Not only do you want to pay on time, but you also want to keep all your documentation. You run a higher risk of being audited when you work for yourself. It is also harder to get all your documents/keep them in order than someone getting just a W2. You also will need your tax documents to obtain loans or apply for mortgages/rent a place to live. These documents prove your income and show that you do in fact pay your taxes. How do I know? I have lived in many apartments, purchased multiple cars, obtained business loans and had to prove income for credit cards; and while my bank statements show how much I am making now, they still wanted to see my taxes sheets to prove I am going legit.

Another option is to form an LLC or your own company. The independent contractor is what you automatically are, but if you go the business route, you may get more deductions. Again, speak to a tax professional to see if this is the best option for you. Forming an LLC also allows you to 'pay' yourself. This method allows for you to take taxes out of your paycheck and not 'owe' when tax season comes around (unless you owe more than was taken out). I know quite a few girls who have gone this route once the decided this was their choose industry to stay in. Just to ensure that no one is getting the wrong idea though, you are PAYING taxes but the money that hits your personal bank account has taxes taken out.

Amberly Rothfield – How I Made $10,000 A Month as A Phone Sex Operator

You will also have to file taxes for your business as well. It can be a bit more complicated of a process, but if you have a decent accountant, then you should be just fine!

Many places take you more seriously when you have a 'company' you work for. Now it is a legitimate business, so the air quotes are not indicating it isn't BUT it is a corporation ran by you. What I also like about this option is that it is a lot easier to separate your finances. With a registered business, you can have a separate account to which to put all your business expenses through. If you were ever audited, it makes life easier for you and the auditor. Easy life for auditor equals more comfortable life for YOU! It also makes your accountant happier as they do not have to slush through as much guff. For me, it also allows me to monitor my spending more. It is a lot easier to justify if an expense is worth it when I do not have my personal stuff muddled up in it.

Though it has a lot of benefits, I would not suggest an LLC until you have been making enough money in this business to carry you month to month. If you are just going to give up on the industry, which is ok, then you may not want to spend the money on forming the LLC. It all depends on where you live and how you build it, but it can be a few hundred dollars to do so. Make sure you are serious before you do so. There are some benefits, but that will not mean much if you decide this business is not for you. Again, consult a tax professional.

Retirement, yes I am going back to this subject because an IRA is simply not enough. No matter how much we all love this industry, there will come a day that we hang up our golden phones. Be it for more time with our family or moving on to another career, you will want an exit strategy, and phone sex is a great vehicle to get you where you desire to go. With all things though, you do have to be smart about it and think early what you want to do. I am not saying you have to have concrete plans but know which way your shoes are headed.

Amberly Rothfield – How I Made $10,000 A Month as A Phone Sex Operator

If you wish to retire, figure out how much you will need to get by and add about 10% to keep up with inflation. Decide what age you would like to retire by and how much you may have already saved up. Now if you have little to no savings and you want to retire in five years, I will applaud your ambition but will most likely be too soon. If you want to retire after your career in phone sex, I would say set your bar at about 10 years from the day you start treating this like a serious business. That will give you enough time to perfect your method, put money back and build investments to make your money grow. This will, of course, mean that you will have to set weekly minimums and stick to them.

If you just want phone sex to get you through a shorter period and perhaps fund your next project, I would start thinking what is that project now. Also consider, that if your past were to come out, will it hurt your next career/project? There are many paths out there that have been in the adult industry could ruin. Unfair? Absolutely, given that so many partake in porn only to create legislation against it. That is life as we know it currently though. If your path is hampered by this little secret, I can tell you that in the age of the internet, it may become a hard secret to keep. If you tell anyone about what you do for a living currently, it could/can come out later. It is not a death sentence though. The longer I have been in the industry, the more people I see exiting to do things I never thought possible. One girl, I know just graduated from law school, and another has gone on to start an all-girl school. Yes, they are very open about their adult history, and no one actually cares. I have seen people get backlash when they came out but it was usually people who acted like they were better than strippers or made comments about prostitutes in the past. If you have not been hypocritical about sex positivity in the past, chances are those in your life will not be too worried if they were to find out about you having been in the adult industry.

What types of ventures won't be affected by your adult industry path? Actually, most things won't be harmed by it. Especially if you are not dealing yourself with the direct public. Teachers, police officers and political figures may have an issue, but if you just own a local business, most people will not care. How many women start their college career as a stripper? In fact, many police departments purposefully recruit sex workers to help them work in vice. People are also VERY understanding. I was thoroughly frightened of telling people what I did for a living for some years. It wasn't till someone threatened to tell everyone around me, some online competition had discovered who I really was, that I just came out with it. Now at that time, I only told those who were close to me, but I came completely out of the closet just recently. Not a single person had anything disparaging to say to me. In fact, I found out many I knew had been strippers or escorts. I found my tribe surrounded me and in fact were more relieved to have someone they could then confide in.

While considered taboo, when confronted with someone that they know, most people will not care. Even strangers who find out, such as many of my Lyft drivers who ask and I am not shy to tell, are more curious than disgusted. It is an honest living, and most people respect that. Will some people be upset? Indeed. The worst stories I have heard are family members who think that it will reflect back on them. Even then, those who this has happened to said the person usually came back around after thinking about it. We all believe it is a bigger deal in our heads than it truly is. Look at all of those social media stars and even some reality TV stars who have adult industry pasts.

Back to topic though, if you are going to use your lessons gained from this industry and money for something you actually want to do, I would advise a similar structure as those who go into phone sex for retirement. The difference being, the last 4 -5 years you want to start your new project. Basically,

Amberly Rothfield – How I Made $10,000 A Month as A Phone Sex Operator

you will have two jobs, and as the new project takes off, you can back off the phone sex. Continue to sock money away for your full retirement though. That money is NOT to fund your new project.

If you choose this, make sure you focus HEAVILY on building your library. This will be flat out integral because as you take time for your new project, you can continue to push your library. In fact, when you are first starting out in phone sex, I would try to make double the amount I have suggested before. I would honestly create no less than 40 different products a week. Many in the industry will read that and shake their heads, but I am DEAD serious. This will allow you a back stock that you can release later. I suggest that regardless because if you go on vacation, you still have stuff you can release. In this case, though, it will be more than needed.

Once you have a stable business, begin to cut down on your expenses and take that extra money and set it aside, around year 3.5. Continue doing this for about a year as you form a concrete business plan. This will be your starting capital for the project. Once your new project begins to bring in money, reinvest into your business but only set a certain number of hours to work in this business a week. Your phone sex business should not be cut back on until at least year 4. Doing so prematurely could mean that you get behind on your bills. During this time you should also be investing still, money which is not for your startup. By year 5, your investment money should be bringing you in a decent side income (if were to need it). I would still not touch it unless it was for a dire reason.

Around year 7, you can begin scaling back if your new project is bringing income. By this point, you should have started this new venture and have some income coming in due to it. If it has been more than 2 years and no income is coming from it, I would reconsider this venture. Seek out professional advice at least. IF it is producing income though, continue to shift focus over the next 3 years. To do so, scale back first on phone calls and increase your per minute rate. I would continue to make mp3s/videos as that is further building your library, which will continue to give you residual income. You also need to keep marketing and blogging. You can start to step off more and have others guest blog for you. By year 10, you can keep your websites up or sell them. I would not suggest just not renewing them though. They will have an age at this point, and someone will be willing to pay for them. In 10 years, you would have paid at least 250 in renewal fees alone. With the age and traffic, it wouldn't be a hard ask to get at least double that.

Truth be told though, you can continue to sell your library and promote it and rather than just taking phone calls, you can just sell items from your library. This will become passive income. Yes, as new stuff comes out slower or not at all, you will find that you do not sell as many as you once did but that is still money coming in. I would never turn that facet off completely but rather just let the sales go straight into a savings account. Since it is not money you are banking on to pay bills, just use it to line your pockets!

Now if your goal is just to straight retire forever and never work again, make sure you do the calculations that I suggested before and create your cut off date. I have known many women who were older who began in phone sex to pad their retirement accounts. Funnily enough, they tend to outperform the 20-year-olds I would see joining the game. They came in creating tons of products, taking tons of calls and giving the best customer experiences. They did not get caught up in drama but kept their eyes on the dollar. It was from them that I learned the most from. So let me impart the lessons they taught me about squirreling away money if you want to use phone sex to ensure a happy retirement.

You will need to not only build your library as fast as you can, get on every platform that is possible but also be logged in to take calls every second that you can. You want to keep your expenses as low as possible and really strap yourself in for at least four years of hardcore work! No traveling, no real vacations, and no excuses! You want to network with others in the business and really focus on building your client base more so than someone who has 20+ years. This means taking calls for a minimum 8 hours a day or more if you can. You will want to put aside at least 30% of your income just for savings, and then 20% for your taxes and the rest is what you live off of. Sound harsh? It is far better to struggle now when you can afford to then when your body will not allow you too. Our bodies only go downhill, so preparing now will mean that when we can't, we won't have too!

As you are maxing out your IRA's every year, you also want to squirrel money away in money market accounts or an account that is deemed to be more of a safe investment. Volatile or high-risk investments are no longer an option as you will soon be depending on this money. Talk to an investment professional who is licensed and bonded with the state and get their professional opinion. You also want to ensure you have HEALTH INSURANCE! Being self-employed, you will have to get independent health care plans, and when you are getting ready to retire, you want the best one you can possibly afford! Health care costs only go up as we get older, so you want to make sure that you are covered while you are working and try to get the cheaper premiums while you are healthier.

Most of those I know who started at an older age also started their call rates FAR lower than I would consider but within two to five months were almost double the price of those who have been around for a while. By taking more calls, their demand went up, and they were able to raise their prices. Now if your goal is to retire off phone sex, I would raise your rate, but I would stop at a more median rate for the fetishes you cater too. Look at your competition and determine what that may be. Early on, you will want to take every call you can, and as long as your phone is not ringing off the hook, then you can maintain the rate that you are at. Remember, you want the calls so that you can sell more from your library!

The last thing that I do believe everyone should worry about but especially those who are looking to retire from the workforce completely... life insurance. Life is a terminal illness and is 100% fatal. For this reason, life insurance is needed for every member of your family no matter the age. Someone will be left behind when you pass away, and you will not want to leave them without the funds to take care of your final requests. You can also put extra money into your life insurance policies. This money will gain interest, and you can also pull it back out as you need it. Now, this is all very technical, and I AM NOT a professional on this. I would talk to a life insurance professional if I were you but trust me, this can be a great investment as well as just the right thing to do for your loved ones.

Not only your insurance but a will is very important. Let people know what you will want them to do with your belongings! You can rest peacefully knowing that those left behind will not be able to fight over your stuff and that you will not be leaving them with a large burden. This is something many girls in the industry struggle with. They constantly ask me about what will happen to their family if they died. You do not have to live this way. Even if you get a cheap policy that covers just your burial, know that even basic cremations can be $1-2000 and that is with no fancy urn, viewing or memorial service. My father was a Vietnam veteran, so his burial was paid for, but his cremation was $800. The city did not want to wait for his life insurance policy to come in or even for me to get into town, they wanted payment for storing the body! A simple Google search shows you can get $250,000 in life insurance for about $25 a month as a 35 year old female. That is enough to pay off most people's houses, car and give a decent burial. If you ask me, it is more than worth it!

Closing —

Does that all seem complicated? Does it seem overwhelming? Do not let paralysis of analysis set in. Just start. If it is just creating an account or calling up a company, it gets easier once you make one step in the right direction.

Yes, it is a lot of work, but this is a business. No business is easy to run, or everyone would. If this still sounds like something you wish to do, I totally suggest you get on board and ride this roller coaster. It is cliché, but it is true; there are ups and downs followed by massive turnarounds. You will go through dark tunnels, only to see beautiful horizons in front of you. You have to go into this knowing it will be tough and will seem harder before it gets easier.

Know that you are also not alone! Few of us in the industry are so jaded that we will turn away helping someone who is newer. In fact, one of my favorite flirts on Niteflirt is named Robin Wildheart. She is super knowledgeable in coding for Niteflirt but also in how to market and help flirts get started. Make sure to tell her I sent you if you ever need help. I also want to offer my own personal help. Send me a message, and I will respond! I will also be keeping my resource page on www.amberlyrothfield.com as up to date as possible and put relevant articles to help anyone who comes along. My goal is to help others as I was helped. There is great money to be made in this industry and plenty to go around.

What I can also tell you is that I wouldn't change a single experience for the world. I have learned so much from owning my own business. I have the highest levels of customer service, I can build websites and market the living dickens out of them, I can create impressive graphics and make audiences from scratch. That last part is the best part, from scratch. I literally started from less than nothing, and now it seems that the world is open for me. The lessons I have learned here will ensure that I can make it in any industry, as many of the principals taught here are just basic business practices but set to the adult industry. If you learn how to market, you can do so for any business. If you learn how to code websites, you can do that for others (look at Robin, she is making money by coding and doing graphical work). If you learn how to sell your products to customers, you can sell other people's products. Even if phone sex were to die tomorrow as an industry, all of us in the industry could easily roll into any other company and be equally as successful. That gives me confidence and it gives me security. You can have this too with dedication and work.

If you have the dedication and grit, you can go far in this industry. Harden that outer shell and but that head down but know you don't have to go it alone. Just reach out, and I will help you the best I can!

Printed in Great Britain
by Amazon

41677243R00149